LAND BEYOND THE RIVER

LAND BEYOND THE RIVER

The Untold Story of Central Asia

Monica Whitlock

THOMAS DUNNE BOOKS
ST. MARTIN'S PRESS ⚬ NEW YORK

THOMAS DUNNE BOOKS.
An imprint of St. Martin's Press.

www.stmartins.com

ISBN 0-312-27727-X

First published in Great Britain under the title *Beyond the Oxus* by John Murray (Publishers) Ltd

First U.S. Edition: October 2003

10 9 8 7 6 5 4 3 2 1

In memory of my mother

Contents

Illustrations

The author and publishers would like to thank the following for their kind permission to reproduce illustrations: Plates 1, 2, 3, 4, 23, 26, 28, 29, 30, 31, 34, 36 and 37, Richard Wayman; 7 and 9, the Shakuri family; 8, the Muhammadov family; 10, 14, 15, 17, 19, 20, 21, 24 and 25, Gennady Ratushenko; 11, 12 and 13, Nabijan Baqi; 16, Vali Qayum Khan; 18, Douglas R. Powell; 22, UNHCR/H. Hudson; 27, UNHCR/P. Labreveux; 33, Topham Picturepoint; 35, © Fatih Saribas/Reuters/Popperfoto.

Plate 5 was taken by V. Yasvoin. Plate 6 was taken by the author. The photographer of Plate 32 is unknown.

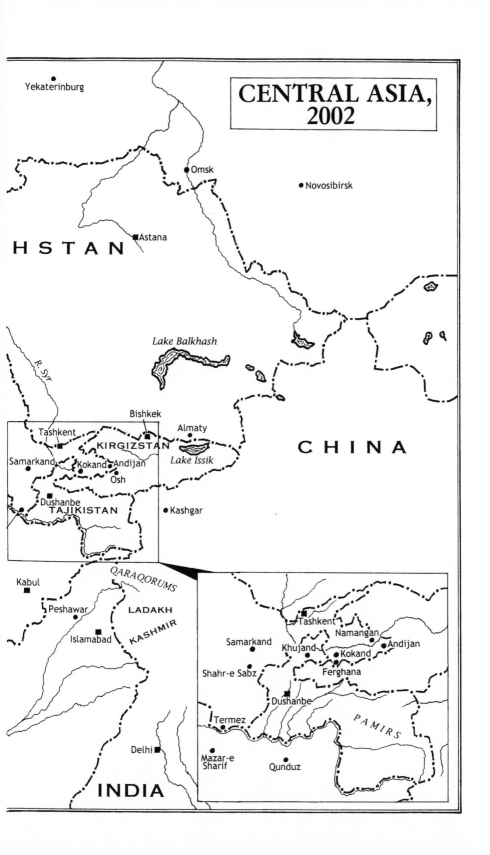

CENTRAL ASIA, 2002

Yekaterinburg

Omsk

Novosibirsk

Astana

H S T A N

Lake Balkhash

R. Syr

Bishkek

Tashkent

Almaty

KIRGIZSTAN

C H I N A

Samarkand

Kokand

Andijan

Osh

Lake Issik

Dushanbe

TAJIKISTAN

Kashgar

QARAQORUMS

Kabul

LADAKH

Peshawar

KASHMIR

Islamabad

Tashkent

Namangan

Samarkand

Khujand

Andijan

Shahr-e Sabz

Kokand

Ferghana

Dushanbe

PAMIRS

Delhi

Termez

Mazar-e Sharif

Qunduz

INDIA

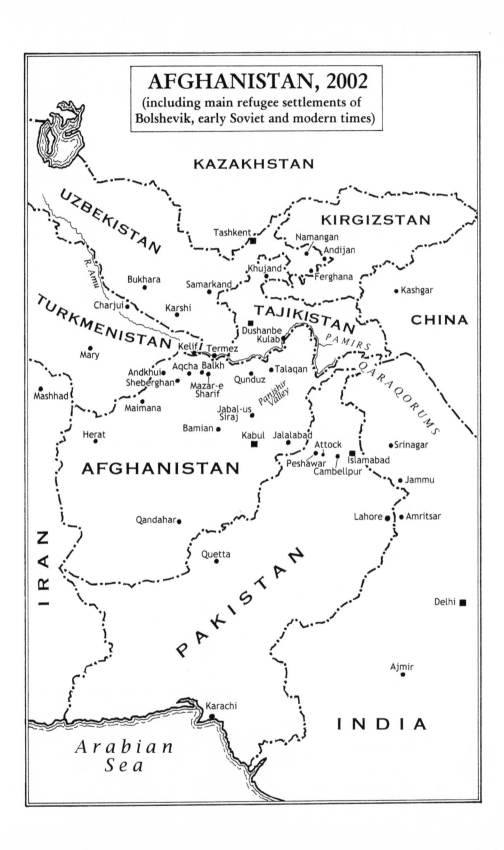

AFGHANISTAN, 2002
(including main refugee settlements of
Bolshevik, early Soviet and modern times)

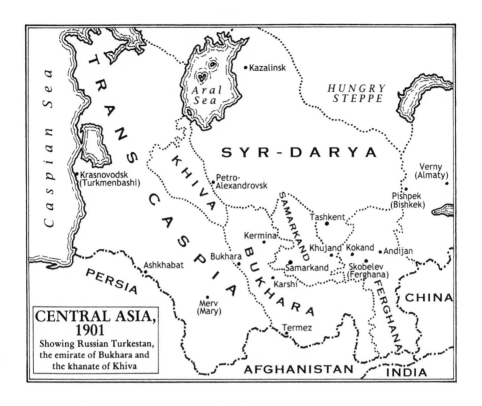

CENTRAL ASIA, 1901

Showing Russian Turkestan, the emirate of Bukhara and the khanate of Khiva

Caspian Sea

Aral Sea

• Kazalinsk

HUNGRY STEPPE

TRANS

CASPIA

KHIVA

SYR-DARYA

• Krasnovodsk (Turkmenbashi)

Petro-Alexandrovsk

• Verny (Almaty)

Pishpek (Bishkek)

Tashkent

SAMARKAND

Kermina

Khujand Kokand

• Andijan

Ashkhabat

Bukhara

BUKHARA

Samarkand

Skobelev (Ferghana)

PERSIA

Karshi

FERGHANA

CHINA

Merv (Mary)

Termez

AFGHANISTAN

INDIA

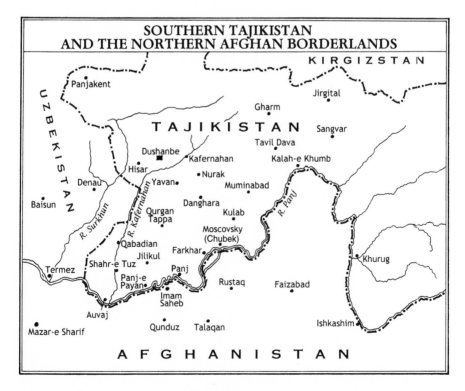

SOUTHERN TAJIKISTAN AND THE NORTHERN AFGHAN BORDERLANDS

KIRGIZSTAN

• Panjakent

• Jirgital

UZBEKISTAN

TAJIKISTAN

Gharm

Sangvar

Tavil Dava

• Dushanbe

Kafernahan

Kalah-e Khumb

Hisar

• Denau

Yavan

• Nurak

Muminabad

R. Kafernahan

R. Panj

• Baisun

R. Surkhun

Danghara

Qurgan Tappa

Kulab

Moscovsky (Chubek)

Qabadian

Farkhar

• Khurug

Jilikul

Shahr-e Tuz

Panj

Termez

Panj-e Payan

Rustaq

Faizabad

Imam Saheb

Auvaj

Ishkashim

• Mazar-e Sharif

Qunduz

Talaqan

AFGHANISTAN

The setting: The shrine of al-Hakim of Termez

'Transoxiana comprises many countries, regions, districts and townships . . . The history thereof may be ascertained from the records of ruins and midden-heaps declaring how Fate has painted her deeds . . .'

ON THE SOUTHERN frontier of Uzbekistan, a small building of pale bricks stands like a guard-house in a fiercely hot, dun-coloured plain. It is the shrine of Abu Abdullah Muhammad ibn Ali, called al-Hakim Termezi, a sage of renown and authority who lived and taught near this spot in the third century of the hijra, the ninth Christian century. An unglazed opening in one wall sends an oblong of light to fall on a white tombstone carved with a chronicle of his life, and of his travels across the Muslim world on pilgrimage to Mecca and to Baghdad, then the seat of the Caliphate, before his return to his birthplace.

The shrine of al-Hakim stands at a focal point in Central Asia. It is the only spot at which Uzbekistan and Tajikistan, the countries at the centre of this book, and Afghanistan, which also concerns it, meet. This place has an important role in the fortunes of all three, one that can tell us something of their history and their setting, and of the condition of the land and the people around it.

Just outside the window-opening of the shrine run the milky-green waters of the river Amu, midway on their course from their source in the Pamir mountains to their delta at the Aral sea, a journey of 1,578 miles. This river has been a defining line on the world map since very early times. The Greeks knew it as Oxus; the Arabs and

I

Persians called it Jaihun, which may derive from words for 'world' or 'river'. Jaihun is the name the authors of the Old Testament used in the Book of Genesis for the second river created by God to flow from Paradise. Some dusty humps poke out of the raised riverbank a few yards from the shrine. They are the remains of the wharf and warehouses of Termez, a busy dock and ship-building centre in al-Hakim's day. Modern Termez, set among lemon and tangerine orchards a few miles inland, is the main port and only city of the Amu.

Al-Hakim was a Muslim when Islam was still a relatively new religion, newer still in this part of the world. It arrived with the Arab armies who came east as raiders in the middle of the seventh century, after the founding of their faith in 622. They attacked Termez many times from a large, shallow island in the Amu, and in about 682 wintered for the first time on what they called *mawara-an-nahr*, the land 'beyond the river', or the right bank: what we now call Uzbekistan and Tajikistan. Very slowly, town by town, the Arabs conquered *mawara-an-nahr*. Islam began to replace the old religions, Manichaeism, Zoroastrianism, Buddhism, Christianity and Judaism (there are still remains of the lamaseries that once housed more than a thousand monks within the walls of old Termez). Most cities had mosques within about two hundred years. Today, virtually all Uzbeks and Tajiks, as well as the Afghans, the Turkmens, Kirgiz and Kazakhs and other peoples of Central Asia, count themselves as Sunni Muslims of the tradition of Abu Hanafa (699–767), one of the authorities who sifted and codified Muslim law and practice in the early period and so gave his name to one of the four legal schools (Shafi, Maliki, Hanafi, Hanbali). A small minority, living in the Pamir mountains, are Ismaili Shi'as – followers of the Aga Khan – but this is not a distinction that troubles Central Asians in the main, and Shi'a-style names (like Husain, and Nurali, 'Light of Ali') appear all over Central Asia, especially in Tajik areas.

Islam drew *mawara-an-nahr* into a world with not only a shared God but a shared alphabet, currency and, to some degree, legal and social codes, a world that at its greatest extent stretched from the Chinese and Indian borders all the way to Spain. People who wanted to travel or to send letters throughout these territories, such as clerics, intellectuals and people in administrative jobs, learnt the language of the empire: Arabic. The mathematician Ferghani, an early Arabic speaker of *mawara-an-nahr*, went to Egypt to build the improved Nilometre at Fustat that was in use from 861 to the twentieth century. Al-Hakim of Termez spoke Persian, his cradle tongue, at home, but corresponded with other scholars and thinkers of his time in Arabic.

As the empire expanded, and its capital Baghdad became one of the biggest and richest cities on earth, it generated tremendous opportunities for trade. Termez sold soap and asafoetida to the west. Other parts of *mawara-an-nahr* exported leather, carpets, various kinds of cloth and different foods, most famously watermelons. The paper for the ever-growing volume of written works required by the Muslim world was produced in Samarkand, one of the main cities of *mawara-an-nahr*, after paper-making arrived from China in the 750s. The shipwrights of the Amu built small square-sailed craft from hollowed tree trunks and heavy wooden barques designed to transport goods in bulk while navigating the shifting sands of the river.

When al-Hakim was in middle age the Muslims began to do business with Viking fur-trappers, whose sable, fox and beaver pelts fetched good prices in Baghdad. These Vikings had made their way to Finland and sailed their longboats down the Dnieper to settle in Kiev, where they converted to Christianity. The Vikings, called 'Rus', did business all around the Caspian coast. In 862 they founded their own state and began to expand, much as the Muslims spread north and east. More than a thousand years after the death of al-Hakim, the armies of Russia reached the Amu. In the nineteenth and twentieth centuries they conquered *mawara-an-nahr*, initially in the name of their Tsar and finally in the name of the revolution that overthrew him. Al-Hakim's shrine became the most southerly point in the USSR, and the lands to either side of it became Union republics.

East and upstream of the shrine, the desert continues for fifty miles or so before a finger of highland appears, a peripheral spur of the mountains massed to the north and east. This is the gateway into Tajikistan, a country that came into being for the first time when the Soviet Union collapsed in 1991. The plain remains arid in the borderlands, and the summer sun pushes temperatures up beyond 50 centigrade. The land is so empty that one can hear the wings of bright turquoise roller birds as they swoop out of holes in the road. At the confluence of the Amu and its feeder rivers – the Kafernahan and, further upstream, the Vakhsh – farmers coax water along irrigation canals only a few inches wide to feed cotton fields and kitchen gardens in ground as soft as flour. Wild mallow appears, and a few fruit trees. There are villages, built of the dust of the plain mixed with water and baked by the sun. Around the village of Chubek – where the Amu takes the name of Panj – the land rises into beehive hills, each with a path dug into it so that people can get to the pistachio thickets that cling to the sides. These are the first signs of the highlands: above Chubek, the heat drops, the ochre turns to green, and the ground rushes up to become the mountains that form about ninety-five per cent of Tajikistan.

The Pamir mountains, also called Badakhshan, where the headwaters of the Amu gather, constitute the entire eastern half of the country. They are among the highest in the world, peaking at 7,495 metres, above the Andes or any African or European range. The Pamirs are the western edge of the Himalayan plateau, and the core of a great wheel of mountain chains descending into Asia. The Hindu Kush fall away to the south; to the north, the thin spine of the Tien Shan is at the extreme edge of China. In the south-east stand the Qaraqorums, gateway to Pakistan and the plains that run all the way to the Indian Ocean. In climate and appearance much of Tajikistan resembles its better-known neighbour Kashmir, with which Tajiks had a long-standing trading relationship until links were suspended during the Soviet period.

Tajikistan is a fairly small country, the size of Syria or Greece, with a rapidly growing population of about six million. It is poor. The Tajik Soviet Socialist Republic was by almost all standards the least developed of the Soviet Union. Independent Tajikistan is in many ways much poorer, partly because it is isolated in a way that has become unusual in the twenty-first century: its topography, politically sensitive position and weak infrastructure make cheap communication with the world difficult, and there are few flights in and out. Tajikistan was the only Soviet Central Asian republic, and among the first of all the Union republics, in which the Communist-era leadership lost its grip on power when independence dropped 'like a meteorite', as the then President of Tajikistan put it. The cost of this half-accidental overthrow of the old order was high. On the way

Tajikistan, alone of the Soviet Central Asian republics, fell into civil war, from which it emerged with a new – and very close – relationship with the old colonial power, Russia.

Tajiks, partly because of their disasters, were the first ex-Soviet Central Asians to talk, at home and in the streets, about the important questions of statehood – who should be in charge, what their obligations might be, what part religion should play in political life. They were the first to challenge the given, to analyse, to think about where their country stood in relation to the wider world. When Tajiks heard about the attacks in New York and Washington on 11 September 2001 – which city people did at once, and country people over the next week or two – most were quick to voice opinions about what should happen next.

The Tajiks are Persians. Their language is the same as that spoken by most people in Afghanistan, where it is called Dari, and by nearly everybody in Iran, where it is known as Farsi. In this they share a common tongue with perhaps seventy-five million people. This does not mean that there is necessarily much social or political understanding between the three countries: very many Iranians could not pick out Tajikistan on a map. But it does mean that Tajiks are heirs to a shared and famous literature, since Persian has been a written language for at least three thousand years. The poets and scholars through whom this literature has passed from generation to generation came from all over the Persian-speaking world. One of the earliest writers of modern literary Persian was the poet Rudaki of Samarkand (880-954). The poet Jalaluddin, called 'Rumi' (1207–73), was born in Balkh, a short journey from the shrine of al-Hakim. Al-Hakim's Persian would be readily understood by modern Tajiks, who have retained many features of classical Persian in their everyday speech. Historically, Tajiks were often the scholars, men of letters and scribes in the towns of Central Asia on both banks of the Amu. In the twentieth century, their language alone made them unusual citizens of the USSR: Tajikistan was the only one of the fifteen republics to share a language with a whole country outside the Union. Only the Moldovans, who speak the same language as Romanians, and the Azeris, who share a language with the large (perhaps 25 per cent) Azeri minority in Iran, were at all comparable.

About a quarter of the people of Tajikistan are Uzbek, their language Turkic rather than Persian, sharing a common stem (but not mutual comprehensibility) with Istanbul Turkish. Most Tajikistani Uzbeks live in the north around the city of Khujand, on the plains near the Amu, and in the west around the border town of Hisar. There are sizeable populations too in the hills to the east and south of the capital, Dushanbe, and in some hill regions such as Kulab. In predominantly Tajik areas many Uzbeks also speak Persian, especially the men, who are the bridge between the family and the outside world. Very many Tajiks speak Uzbek, and many more understand enough to communicate if need be. There have been only modest levels of intermarriage between Uzbeks and Tajiks in modern times, but the two populations live side by side, generally in harmony, often praying at the same mosques and attending one another's wedding parties. Traditionally, their roles are complementary. Uzbeks are often shepherds and stockmen, whose settlements lie in urban outskirts beyond city walls. In times of friction this has often given them a great advantage over the townsmen: however strong the walls, it is the Uzbeks who control the supply roads.

The capital of Tajikistan, Dushanbe, is a modern city, but most towns in Tajikistan are of great age, as are those of Uzbekistan and Afghanistan. The ancestors of the people we now call 'Tajik' were settled: they cultivated land, and built towns upon it. Archaeologists have found sealed flasks of fossilised grain and traces of rice four thousand years old close to the Amu. The fired-brick underground water pipes, many of them hundreds of years old, that thread beneath the plains in some places suggest a steady history of sophisticated irrigation. There are stumps of citadels that far pre-date the coming of the Arabs. At Khutal, in Kulab, there are what may have been brick-built living rooms and a bath-house, to judge by the chess pieces and the phial of scent picked out of the foundations.

The main towns on the plains of southern Tajikistan are Qurgan Tappa, Qabadian and Shahr-e Tuz, all of which grew up along tributaries running from the mountains to the Amu. They are set among wheat and cotton fields and patches of watermelons and pumpkins, which feed people through summer and winter and bring in revenue. Traditionally these were also market towns whose economies were supplemented by foreign and local goods traded down the Amu, including soap and resin from Termez and Indian dyes and tea.

Tajiks also live all the year round at great altitudes. The poplars that grow around the tree-line, at about 3,500 metres, provide both shade and roof-beams for small mud-built villages. The alpine valleys of the Pamirs are very fertile, despite bitter winters that can leave them cut off from October to May. Wheat, walnuts, almonds, cherries, pistachios, apricots, peaches, quinces, figs, apples, pears and pomegranates all grow well, and bread, nuts and fruit are important staples, augmented by mutton or beef when guests come or at holidays, when families slaughter an animal. The highland meadows are filled with small red wild tulips in spring, poppies and, on the lower slopes, tiny spring irises called *siah-gush*, or black-ears. Tajiks are fond of flowers. They create arbours over the raised wooden verandas that are their living rooms in the summer, and often set aside part of the kitchen garden to grow roses. A Danish ethnographer, Lieutenant Olufsen, travelling through the Pamirs and down part of the Amu in 1896, described the grounds of the bek's residence in Qalah-e Khumb as being as lush as a greenhouse, cared for by an elderly Uzbek gardener who was an expert in growing from grafts and cuttings.

Life begins for a country baby – that is, most babies – swaddled and tied firmly into a carved and painted wooden cradle, the *gahvara* (*beshik* in Uzbek). Children play about freely, safe in the quiet lanes of the villages and in the courtyards of their own and the neighbours' homes. When a girl is little, her mother will probably cut her hair very short or shave it off, against the summer heat and to make it grow more thickly. At the age of eight or nine, or when her parents think it proper, she will grow and plait her hair and may start to wear a small headscarf, at least in public, to go with her bright dress and trousers of artificial silk, adult clothes in miniature. She begins to help with the baking and milking (looking after cows is women's work), and serving tea to her grandparents, father and any guests, who are encouraged to visit as much as possible, for hospitality is the cornerstone of Tajik life.

A boy learns early to help on the smallholding. He is circumcised, probably before he is ten, when a tremendous party is held in his honour and he wears a bright cardboard crown for the day. Often a family will circumcise two or more boys together, or go in with neighbours, to defray the costs of this expensive welcome to the adult Muslim world.

When a boy reaches his majority (in Soviet times, this generally meant on his return from service in the army), his parents or other senior relatives will start to choose him a wife, unless a cradle-match has been made. They pay formal visits to a family with a daughter of suitable age, usually between seventeen and twenty, whose parents may also have been making discreet enquiries. Each side checks that the other is of good character and circumstances and they fix the *kalim*, that is, the boy's family's gift to their new daughter-in-law (a cow, for example, for a well-off village family in 2002) and the wedding date. The girl's side reassures itself that the boy's family will treat their daughter kindly and accommodate her properly. In the case of a love match, negotiations can be over quickly; when the families are strangers, there may be much groundwork to be done.

At dusk on the wedding day, the boy and his friends come to the girl's house and take her to his – her new home. In the lane, at the threshold, the couple circle several times around a little fire, accompanied by drummers and trumpeters. They then take their place at the top of the tables laid in the garden, and receive their guests. If the couple have not met before, or only very briefly, these hours spent standing together against the backdrop of a carpet for all to see can be miserably stressful. All their relatives who can, and most of the village, turn out dressed in their best to eat, drink and dance to the music of a hired band, if the family can afford one. The wedding sometimes lasts for several days, with both families acting as hosts and some guests shuttling between the households.

The young couple may not live with the boy's parents for long. If he is an elder son, the families will probably help find them a place of their own, perhaps in a nearby town. If he is a younger son he may well not leave the family house; instead, his parents will perhaps build on extra rooms as his family grows. The youngest son is supposed to remain at home all his life, and one of his wife's primary duties is to take care of her mother- and father-in-law as they grow older, though she will also stay in close touch with her own family. It is this youngest couple who may eventually take the place of the boy's parents when they are gone. They are the central pillar of the household even far-flung family members call home and, though much advised by their elders, it is they who are the conduit through which tradition marches on.

There are many variations on these themes. Customs vary from place to place. A betrothal might necessitate gifts of sugar-candy or decorated bread. In some villages the boy must give seven new dresses for his bride's bottom drawer, in others the number is twenty. Sometimes a new bride must wear a gold cap to show her status. There may be detailed rules governing which family pays for the rice, the firewood, the matches, all the paraphernalia of the wedding. Some people hate tradition and suffer its requirements with gritted teeth. Some city people block it out as best they can. They have girlfriends or (less openly) boyfriends before marriage, then hold the wedding party in a restaurant and circulate, chatting to their guests and joining in the dancing. But the lines along which life runs are far more deeply grounded than any interpretation of them.

A village family will bring up perhaps eight or nine children, more if the husband takes a second wife later on. They may also take in orphans and often give a home to needy nephews and nieces as a matter of course. The daily round is so communal and filled with other people that it is possible to go through life without ever sleeping in a room alone, or spending even a few daylight hours without company. Many people find the prospect of solitude frightening. One important reason why the birth of boys is so welcome is because they will bring more children to strengthen the household, whereas girls bring them to another.

In late middle age a man becomes a *mu-e safid*, or white-hair, and probably takes to wearing a turban and a long coat called a *juma*, if he does not already do so. The *mu-e safid* is much loved and respected in almost every family and has ultimate authority over all the younger generations; the *mu-e safids* of the village can be a very powerful body. When death comes, the women stay at home, cooking and getting ready for the prescribed days of mourning. The men carry the body to the graveyard before sundown; they bury it in nothing but a shroud, and leave the mound unmarked but for a lath from the bier driven into the ground.

Many Tajiks who have left their homes for the wider world have been impelled to do so by wars, famines or other misfortunes; Tajik graves near Karachi in Pakistan show where one community lived and died after fleeing from the armies of Chingis ('Ghengis') Khan in the thirteenth century. Others have set out intentionally, generally travelling west on hajj to visit the holy places of Islam, as al-Hakim did. Such journeys could take many years and become odysseys, sometimes described in journals filled with observations on the ways of the world, such as those of the eleventh-century Persian poet Naser Khusrau. He was born in Qabadian, near the Amu on land called Ja-e Kadu, the Pumpkin Ground. Today, the smallholders of Ja-e Kadu are proud to live on his ancestral land. It is a crumb of solace in a daily round close to destitution. Sitting in their courtyard beside a double armful of wheat, a few pots of mint and the hollowed pumpkins they use to carry oil and water, they pray for a better harvest next year. Life in Qabadian as Naser Khusrau knew it was similarly poor and insecure. When he was nine an early frost left the wheat black in the fields, heralding a terrible famine. An educated man, he found a post in the local administration, possibly as a clerk. On a December day in 1045, aged forty-one, he set out for the west, accompanied by his brother and a servant. They crossed the Alborz mountains north of modern Teheran and skirted the Caspian coast before bearing north almost to the foot of the Caucasus. The small party then moved south to the Mediterranean port of Beirut and on to the holy sites at Jerusalem. Once in the Arabian peninsula they made their way to Mecca, then crossed the Red Sea into Nubia and took ship down the Nile to Cairo. Naser Khusrau was transfixed by its cosmopolitan grandeur. He admired in particular the roof-gardens and the extraordinary diversity of merchandise, and was impressed to find paper so plentiful that shopkeepers gave it away as bags.

When he returned home, seven years after his departure, he was considered a dangerous free-thinker and was exiled to the Pamir mountains. There he wrote his razor-edged poetry, much of it timeless satire on bad political and religious leadership:

> Your minds are dirty, even though you wash
> Your fine turban with soap and bleach your skin with potash.
> If only your ignorance could hurt you,
> Then your screams would rise to the heavens.

Naser died in the Pamir, where he has been appropriated as a local poet and is much revered.

The country downstream from al-Hakim's shrine is different from most of Tajikistan. After the arrival of one more tributary into the

Amu, the river Surkhun (Red, or Red Blood), flat, ochre desert stretches away for more than a thousand kilometres. The teenaged border guards catching a few minutes' respite from the feverish sun by paddling beneath the bluffs of the Amu have blue, white and green flashes on their shoulders. This territory is the southern rim of Uzbekistan, until 1991 the Uzbek SSR. Ten years after independence, the old ex-communist leadership was still in charge, hanging on to power by arresting potential dissidents and forbidding any open discussion through the newspapers or on the streets. Most of those detained were young men, brought to the edge of despair by poverty and powerlessness, who saw Islam not only as offering solace in the midst of a corrupt and repressive system, but also as some sort of political alternative. At the start of the 1990s, President Karimov backed up his policies with the argument that if such people had their way, Uzbekistan would follow Tajikistan into war. After September 2001, his hand appeared very much strengthened. The 'fundamentalists' demonised by Washington included a group of anti-government Uzbeks living in Afghanistan as guests of the Taleban – like Usama bin Laden, the man President Bush blamed for the attacks on his country. Small wonder that Karimov became the first Central Asian president to offer air and ground space to US troops for operations in Afghanistan.

Despite this turn of events in Karimov's favour, however, the political situation in Uzbekistan may well change soon – probably in the next few years, perhaps much sooner. And when change does come, it may well come very fast.

Most of Uzbekistan is too dry to support any sort of life other than that led by a small population of nomads who survive on the meat and milk of their flocks, desert plants, and underground water sources invisible to settled people. It is, however, the most populous country in what was Soviet Central Asia, its twenty-four million people living where life is possible – that is, in clusters of towns and villages close to water. These settlements, necessarily limited by physical geography, are often over-crowded. The villages of Tajik highlanders are separated by mountain ranges; those of the plainsmen of Uzbekistan by great tracts of uninhabitable land.

The capital of Uzbekistan is Tashkent. With a population of about two million, it is by far the largest city in Central Asia. It was the biggest Soviet city east of the Urals, and at times ranked fourth in the entire Union. It was the first city of significance in *mawara-an-nahr* to fall to the Russian army, in 1865, and it grew rich and strong as the cradle of Russian power in Asia.

South-central Tashkent still has a nineteenth-century Russian feel. '*Moloko, moloko*' calls the milk lady as she trundles a churn along tree-lined lanes off Shota Rustaveli Avenue, where a grandmother, her thick socks stuffed into slippers, sells a pyramid of plum jam beneath the faded silvery green balconies of the imperial town. A stone stag guards the palace built for a member of the Romanov family exiled to the deep south. The Christian faithful come to the Russian Orthodox cathedral with its china-white and blue bell-tower, though these days they are more likely to be beggars than officers' families. A young woman in a pink dress picks her high-heeled way across the tramlines that ran from the Russian cantonment to the edge of the medieval Muslim city and still serve their purpose – new and old Tashkent have never integrated much. The statue of General Konstantin Kaufmann, the founder of Russian Tashkent, was long ago replaced by one of Lenin, then of Stalin, who in turn gave way to Marx. The most recent occupant of the podium in what is again a park for the evening prom-enade is the fourteenth-century emperor Timur ('Tamerlane'), con-queror of lands from Delhi to Moscow to Anatolia, who was born and raised his capital on what is now Uzbek territory and who has been taken up as the hero of independent Uzbekistan.

Uzbekistan means 'land of the Uzbeks', but the idea of who counts as an Uzbek is fairly loose. Broadly speaking, an Uzbek is a Muslim who calls himself Uzbek and (probably) speaks the language. Three-quarters of all Uzbeks live in the countryside, following a rhythm of life much the same as that of Tajiks. They have the same inordinate respect for their elders or white-beards (called in Uzbek *aq-sakal*) and only slightly smaller families. There is also a narrow sense of 'Uzbek'. Tradition has it that each family is descended origi-nally from one of ninety-two nomadic tribes said to have taken their collective name from Uzbek Khan, the fourteenth-century ruler of the Mongol Golden Horde. These tribes fought their way to power in around 1500 under the warrior-lord Abdul Fath Muhammad Shaibani Khan, who descended on *mawara-an-nahr* from the Qipchaq plains above the Aral sea. These days, only a few Uzbeks are conscious of their tribe outside *aq-sakal* circles. Tribal names live on, however, in place-names like Katta-Ming, Kunghrat and Manghit.

These diverse peoples, often living very far apart, naturally see the world differently, and the defining details on the general canvas of life – wedding customs, recipes and so on – vary considerably. A fairly senior officer of the secret police (formerly the KGB) sent from the town of Shahr-e Sabz in 1998 to take notes in Namangan described the people he was watching as 'foreigners'. The classic 'Uzbek' look – long eyes, wide face, straight black hair – is by no means universal: Uzbeks can have ginger hair, round grey eyes and translucent white skin. Many people in eastern Uzbekistan, until very recently, called themselves 'Turk'. The idea that Uzbeks are a 'national' group is a modern one, brought in with the creation of the Uzbek SSR in 1924; philologists have been working ever since to compile a standard written Uzbek. Large numbers of people in Uzbekistan belong to non-Uzbek minorities. The biggest of these are Russians (5–8 per cent), Tajiks (about 5 per cent) and Kazakhs (3–4 per cent), according to official figures.

One of the most important populated strips of Uzbekistan lies along the banks of the last quarter of the Amu in the western region of Khorezm. The river there becomes wide and slow, stable enough to be dammed and released into dozens and then hundreds of small, raised dykes. Were one to take a bird's-eye view, one would see the steady ribbon of river split into hundreds of blue fingers, pushing outwards into the desert and onwards towards the Aral delta, now only about 250 miles downstream. The change is startling: the air becomes cool and damp, while wheat fields, kitchen gardens and even small rice paddies flooded with water replace the dunes. Houses appear. Pink hollyhocks and roses, pansies and sweet Williams fill the verges.

Khorezm is littered with the stumps of old towns that have waxed and waned in importance over the centuries. Plainsmen, unlike mountain people, need fortifications, the bigger and more visible the better. Desert towns often had high protective battlements (similarly, the modern Uzbek army has tanks – strong and conspicuous on the flat, useless in mountains). Often these towns were beached or flooded as the Amu shifted course with unusual frequency. Sometimes they fell to invaders.

Mongol-led armies were particularly active in this rich section of the plains. Medieval ribcages and skulls still stick out of the ground in one ruined town, Kuna Urgench in Turkmenistan, where they have been preserved by the extreme dryness of the sand around them. The city rulers of Khorezm used the river as a defensive weapon, opening sluices and flooding the suburban plains to fend off attackers. In cases of extreme necessity they moved their gold, abandoned their forts, and built new towns upstream. In this way the capital of Khorezm has shifted many times over the past thousand years and taken many names.

Khorezm produced some of the most remarkable luminaries of the Muslim world in its heyday between the ninth and thirteenth centuries. A column of herring-bone brickwork still marks the castle of Kath, built at the beginning of this period to be the biggest and finest of the Amu delta. Kath was the birthplace of perhaps the greatest Muslim scholar of all, Abu Rayhan Muhammad ibn Ahmad, called Biruni, born in 973, when Europe was in the Dark Ages. His study of the rotation of the earth was revolutionary. He calculated longitude and latitude, observed solar and lunar eclipses in detail, and was an early cartographer, mathematician, physicist, geographer and anthropologist. He spoke Aramaic, Greek and Sanskrit as well as Arabic and Persian. Biruni is also famous for his expedition to India, about which he wrote the first detailed Muslim study of a foreign country. He wrote many of his books at Garganj, which replaced Kath as the capital of Khorezm and became a vibrant university town.

On of the most important figures in the history of mathematics also came from the Amu delta. Abu Abdullah Muhammad ibn Musa of Khorezm disseminated, though his treatise written in Baghdad in about 825, the Indian counting system that included decimal places and the concept of zero. Knowledge of this system, far superior to Greek or Roman add-on numbering, spread throughout the Arabic-speaking world. It reached Muslim Spain about a hundred and fifty years later, and Khorezmi's treatise was translated into Latin in 1120 by an Englishman, Robert of Chester, who visited Spain to study mathematics. The system caught on very slowly in Europe. There was general misunderstanding of the conceptual leap involved, and opposition from Florentine bankers who thought the new figures more easily falsified than Roman ones. But the thirteenth-century

Italian, Leonardo of Pisa, known as Fibonacci, championed the 'Arabic' figures and they began to make inroads. Seven hundred years after Khorezmi wrote his treatise, these numerals became widely used in Europe. Khorezmi's name lives on in the broad term given to his system, *algorithmus*, or *algorithm* (a corruption of al-Khorezm) and his book on equations, *Hisab al-jabr wa al-muqabela*, brought the word 'algebra' to English, while the Arabic *sefr* gave us 'cipher' and 'zero'.

Garganj was succeeded by Khiva as the capital of the delta region. By the late nineteenth century Khiva was a busy commercial centre, exporting cotton, wheat, tobacco, green tea, clothes and carpets to Iran and Russia, and importing rice, hides and manufactured goods. An Armenian businessman noted that, in 1875, a thousand large grain boats put out from Khiva docks every week. Khiva was the seat of the khans or rulers of Khorezm until the proclamation of Bolshevik power there in 1920. Under the Soviet administration Khiva was replaced as the regional capital by the new town of Urgench.

The easternmost arm of Uzbekistan is another thickly populated area, a string of towns set in the floor of a long valley beyond Tashkent. This, the Ferghana valley, is watered in part by snow-melt from the Tien Shan mountains that form the westernmost Chinese border, and the rulers of some of its cities paid taxes to Beijing as late as the nineteenth century. As in Khorezm, different towns in Ferghana held regional power at different times, but the most consistently significant were, as they remain, Andijan, Namangan and Kokand. On the eve of the Russian conquest Kokand was ascendant, and the valley formed the khanate of Kokand. Many Ferghana people are proud of the self-contained nature of their valley. There are plenty who have never set eyes on Tashkent and elders who are hazy about where it is. They have a reputation for piety and have produced most of the influential religious leaders of modern times. It takes half a morning to travel from one end to the other of the Ferghana valley by car; it takes eight days on foot, the way the shepherds do it when they move their flocks between winter and summer pastures twice a year.

The most famous son of Ferghana became ruler of his birthplace, Andijan, when he was only eleven years old. Zahiruddin Muhammad Babur, born in 1483, was gradually driven out of *mawara-an-nahr* by his rivals. Once across the Amu he captured much of Afghanistan and India, where he founded the Moghul empire. ('Moghul' means 'Mongol': Babur was descended from both Timur and Chingis Khan and described himself as a Turk. He loathed the Uzbeks, to whom he lost his homeland.) Babur left a vivid account of Andijan and the valley of Ferghana in his diary, the *Baburnama*. He describes iron and turquoise mines, and the excellent apricots, almonds and melons, tulips, roses and violets produced by the hot, dry summers and snowy winters. All his life Babur was homesick. He sent from Delhi to Andijan for melon plants and vine cuttings, and was cheered by the small but acceptable crops produced by the palace gardeners. Even the wall-paintings that decorate the shrine of his great-grandson Jahangir at Lahore depict plates of long Ferghana melons.

In the middle section of Uzbekistan are the cities best known to the outside world – Samarkand and Bukhara. Samarkand is very much an earthly city. It owes its grand façades to Timur, who made it his imperial capital and imported craftsmen from across half the world to build it. Bukhara, on the other hand, holds a special place in Central Asia as the seat of Muslim scholarship second to none in *mawara-an-nahr*. The great flowering of Bukhara was around the tenth century, when its scholars dazzled academies from Baghdad to Shiraz with their radical work in literature, astronomy, physics, philosophy, chemistry and music.

Of the many renowned Bukharans perhaps the most famous is the polymath Abu Ali ibn Sina, called Avicenna, whose *Qanun* or Canon, a medical encyclopaedia, explored (among other things) the nature of tuberculosis and meningitis and the anatomy of the heart and the eye. Translated into Latin, the *Qanun* became the standard textbook for the medical students of Europe for five hundred years. The international pharmacists' symbol of a serpent coiled around a glass – so local legend has it – stems from Avicenna's use of snake venom as medicine.

The reputation of Bukhara as a seat of education long survived that of Khorezm, and remained supreme and unchallenged even at the start of the Soviet period. The city has spent the twentieth century as a poor and unremarkable town, more famous for its monuments than the scholars inside them. There is still a special dignity attached to being a Bukharan, however, especially among Tajiks, and

Persian remains the language of the city centre, decreasing in use towards the Uzbek-speaking outskirts. Many Bukharans are bilingual.

Returning to our reference point at the shrine of al-Hakim at Termez, we can easily see the third country that concerns this book. Standing in the rose garden outside the shrine, with one's back to the window-opening, one looks straight across the Amu – very narrow at this point – to an identical sandy plain spattered with the same scarlet camel-thorn. This plain is in Afghanistan. The Amu became a state border for the first time in 1895 when Abdu Rahman, the amir of Afghanistan, conceded the right bank to the amir of Bukhara. The Amu later became the southern boundary of the USSR, and marked the limit of Russian territorial power.

Were the guardians of the shrine to wade across the river, they would have no difficulty talking to the Afghan shepherds who graze their flocks on the midstream islands; they might even find they were related. Northern Afghanistan is populated largely by Tajiks and Uzbeks (some of whom still use the tribal names that have been put away on the right bank). The Tajiks – though many Persian-speakers would not use the term – at about 5.5 million are the biggest group in Afghanistan after the Pashtuns of the south (approximately 8.5 million). There are about 1.5 million Uzbeks in the borderlands. There are also about 300,000 Turkmens in areas contiguous to modern Turkmenistan.

Migration to and fro across the river has been going on for centuries, mainly from the more invasion-prone right bank to the left. When al-Hakim fell out of favour with the authorities in Termez, he caught the ferry to Balkh and stayed there until things quietened down. Countless less fortunate people have waited in vain for their times to return to normal. At the start of the Soviet period between a quarter and half a million people from the right bank sought sanctuary in Afghanistan; they never went home, and their children and grandchildren are Afghans.

The city of Afghanistan that mainly concerns this book is Mazar-e Sharif, which stands on a desert plain about fifty miles south of the border. Mazar-e Sharif has enjoyed shifting fortunes over the years.

The *mazar*, or shrine, is a large and beautiful mosque complex in the centre of town, built to honour Caliph Ali in 1136 and elaborated many times since. It is an important place of pilgrimage, and for hundreds of years the pious travelled between it and the shrine of al-Hakim at Termez. The city around the shrine was developed in the nineteenth century to replace the ancient city of Balkh, ten miles or so to the west. At the time when the action in this book concerns Mazar-e Sharif, it was a busy place with a population of about a quarter of a million.

The fortunes of Uzbekistan and Tajikistan cannot be separated from those of Afghanistan. Nowhere is that more evident than at Termez. A few miles upstream from the shrine stands the Friendship Bridge, built by Soviet engineers as the only iron bridge over the Amu. It was across the Friendship Bridge that the bulk of the Red Army ground troops invaded Afghanistan in 1979 on what was to prove their final campaign, and the last defeated Soviet soldiers re-crossed the bridge ten years later. The Soviet Union collapsed two years afterwards, and with it the Russian empire. The Afghans won the war but fared immeasurably worse than the losers. Apart from the million or so killed, the millions more made homeless and a country largely destroyed, the conflict left the state too weak, too full of guns and too vulnerable to foreign meddling to prevent further strife. For the Afghans, the war went on. In October 2001 yet more military aircraft bombed Mazar-e Sharif. This time they were those of the United States.

This book opens in the year 1909, a time of the utmost political delicacy in *mawara-an-nahr*. Half a century had passed since the night of 27 June 1865 when Major-General Mikhail Chernayev led his soldiers across the narrow river Anhar into Tashkent and claimed the city for Tsar Alexander II of Russia. The residents of Tashkent had been declared Russian subjects, and internal passports had been introduced. Tashkent had become the headquarters of the Governorate-General of Turkestan, to which territories captured subsequently would be added. The foundations of Russian power in Central Asia had thus been laid.

The Russian cantonment of Tashkent had grown fast. In 1909 there were about 12,000 Russians in a city of about 180,000. Traders, hotel-keepers, railway-workers, singers and entrepreneurs of all kinds made their way to Tashkent to service the military and take advantage of all the other prospects offered by a brand new colony. Ground prices rocketed upwards and soon reached five dollars a square yard in the commercial quarter.

Great quantities of goods were being imported from Russia, from wires for the telegraph (they wore through quickly, because of the sandstorms) to the paint for the sets of the new opera house and the six million oak, elm and lime saplings the city planners hoped would turn the desert to shady forest. The budget for the Turkestan region was always low, however, while transport costs were huge and journeys long and difficult, even after the Transcaspian railway was extended to Tashkent in 1898. Yet several schools were built, some academies, and more than one art school. There were also cheap cinemas for the troops, with films sent down fairly frequently from Russia. Russian Tashkent had tarred roads, electric light, running water, telephones, and trams – the first three seats on which were reserved for Slavs, who paid twice the price. We know from advertisements in the *Turkestan Gazette* that Minakov's shop on Moskovskaya Street sold British Humber bicycles, and that Darazhnov's ('Always a big choice! Tel: 110') stocked table linen, paper goods, men's and ladies' wear and eiderdowns.

Asians in Europe, in Asia the Russians were Europeans. 'The women wore low-cut evening gowns with sparkling jewels and flowers in their hair,' wrote Count K. K. Pahlen, a Latvian sent from St Petersburg to assess conditions in Tashkent in 1908. Invited to dinner at the Governor's residence, Pahlen found the garden hung with coloured lanterns. 'One would have found the same setting anywhere in St Petersburg, Berlin, Vienna, or Paris . . . The menus, printed in French, informed us that we were to be served with a dinner of six or seven courses . . .'

With Tashkent as a springboard, the military offensive proceeded apace. When the khanate of Kokand was dissolved in 1876, the whole valley of Ferghana passed under direct Russian control. By 1909 there was a discrete Russian town at Kokand with a large Orthodox church, a gambling club, a theatre, and a branch of the Russo-Chinese bank used by the exporters of hide, wool and cotton.

It was through cotton that most people felt the impact of these changes. Russia had customarily bought its cotton from the southern states of America, but when Unionists blockaded the Confederate ports of the south in the early days of the civil war there, the supply-chain was broken. In urgent need of raw cotton, the Russians had laid down plantations throughout the fertile, sunny valley of Ferghana. Between the conquest of Kokand and 1909 the area of land under cotton there increased from a hundred acres to about six hundred: almost half of all arable land. Central Asia was established as a much cheaper source, and the proportion of Russian cotton produced there shot from perhaps 20 per cent to roughly 90 per cent, with the centre of the industry at Ferghana.

Conditions for plantation workers were poor. They were paid in kind, and encouraged to give over their mixed-crop land to grow more. Food shortages were frequent, and unemployment high. The large Russian standing garrisons in the Ferghana valley put down several insurrections. In 1898, an Andijani called Ishan Madali led a raiding party into the Russian barracks and killed twenty-two soldiers. Eighteen of the raiders were hanged on a public gallows, more than three hundred others were sent to labour camps in Siberia. Ishan Madali's village was burnt down and a Russian village built on the site.

Meanwhile, the khanate of Khiva had been annexed in 1873. General Kaufmann, founder of imperial Tashkent, led an invasion which was supposed to involve ground forces marching across the desert connecting with a convoy of troop-steamers made in Liverpool and London and brought overland in pieces by pack-animal. In the event, the Amu flotilla was too slow and heavy to be useful, but Kaufmann's men shot their way into Khiva none the less. Kaufmann sent the silver and wooden throne of the Khivan khans to Russia and imposed terms which included a measure of internal autonomy, much like those imposed by the British on some nawabs in India. One can still see the smart green and black carriage sent from Russia for Abdullah, the last khan, and trace the deep grooves its steel wheels have left in the stone streets around the palace. Abdullah Khan ended his days in a Soviet prison, having written letter after unanswered letter to Stalin.

The situation in Bukhara was both similar to that in Khiva and also quite different. One essential difference was that of scale. Bukhara in the early twentieth century was a city of about a quarter of a million people and the capital of a country that encompassed land at least as far south as modern Karshi and east into what is now Tajikistan. Besides the capital, Bukhara the country included several important provincial towns and had an overall population of perhaps two and a half million, with considerable natural resources such as gold and some silver, and substantial revenues from trade. In 1868 Russian armies had defeated Amir Muzaffar of Bukhara, and annexed his second city, Samarkand, and the important province of Khujand. The emirate retained some autonomy, however, and Bukhara city remained a capital – partly because, from the Russian point of view, this was the cheapest option. Amir Muzaffar turned defeat into victory as best he could: with the Russians behind him his throne was more secure than before, and he took the opportunity to consolidate his powers. Russian forces put down an attempted palace coup and even assisted Bukharan troops to penetrate into some inaccessible pockets of the Pamirs such as Ishkashim.

Bukhara minted its own coins, flew its own flag and raised its own army. The law was the shari'a, the holy law of Islam – the teachings of the Quran and the sayings ascribed to Muhammad – in conjunction with decrees issued by the amir after consultation with his cabinet. The most powerful men in the land after the amir were the Khush Beki or Prime Minister, followed by the Qazi Kalan, the Chief Judge or Minister of Justice, who was head of all legal matters and often the bridge between the amir's court and the powerful clerics of the madrasas. In the regions, the amir ruled through local governors, called beks. Under subsequent treaties signed in 1873 and 1885 none of this structure was altered, although Bukhara gave up its rights over the river Amu and to direct relations with foreign powers. A Russian agent was installed in a tiny office at the heart of the citadel called the Ark, from which successive amirs had ruled Bukhara for the last thousand years, and with him came a telephone – the first in Bukhara – connected to the Russian garrison in Tashkent.

Bukhara's main link with the outside world bound it even more firmly to Russia, for it was agreed that each station of the Transcaspian railway and the ground on which the sleepers lay belonged to the Russian empire. The railway workers were all Russians, and they formed their own Slavic settlements. One such,

Kagan, was only nine miles outside Bukhara. 'There are peasants in linen shirts and caps, long blond beards and round hair-cuts,' noted the American William Eleroy Curtis, in Bukhara in 1908 as a reporter for the Chicago *Record-Herald*. 'Their women sell raspberry shrub, cider and jars of milk at the station.' Curtis reckoned that there were about 250 Russians, Germans and Poles living inside the city walls, whereas ten years before there had been only a handful, all of whom, including a well-known pharmacist, had worn Bukharan dress.

Trade had doubled and redoubled since the coming of the railway in 1888. Russian chintz, sugar, matches, ironmongery and medicines passed through Bukhara to Afghanistan. Indian traders brought animal skins, dyes and tea for the markets of the north. The big fur-houses of Geneva, Moscow and London each kept an agent in Bukhara to buy the qaraqul fleeces sold in Europe as 'Persian lamb' or 'Astrakhan'. Curtis recorded a trade turnover of twenty-two million dollars a year. He noted American goods (sewing machines, phonographs, revolvers), and Brazilian indigo, shipped through Marseilles, on sale in the bazaar beside indigo from India.

The amir in 1909, Abdulahad, whose ill-equipped army numbered only five thousand, tied his fortunes to the Tsars as firmly as his father Muzaffar had. He was the first Bukharan ruler to travel extensively in Russia – attending, in an official capacity, the glittering coronation of Nicholas II in Moscow in 1896. But as the century turned, it became increasingly difficult to find virtue in the necessity of the Russian relationship. Amir Abdulahad's pragmatism raised angry protests among certain establishment figures, many of them clerics, who saw Bukhara as being but a step away from complete subjugation to foreign rule, and in danger of losing its very identity. Curtis observed that the amir had lost so much prestige that his person was no longer considered sacred. At the same time, Amir Abdulahad was under pressure from political and social reformists anxious to find a new way forward for Bukhara. 'As fast as he [the Khush Beki] discovers and disbands one political society a dozen others spring up in its place, and matters are rapidly approaching a crisis . . .,' observed Curtis. As political tensions grew, parts of the administration disintegrated. Salaries went unpaid, while policemen and other officials grew ever more corrupt. The great public buildings of Bukhara became increasingly dilapidated. 'There is only one hospital . . .,' Curtis noted, 'and that is in very poor condition. It is supposed to be sustained by the emir, but he gives very little money to it, and that grudgingly . . . A man who was employed as cook at the hospital for three months is now a prominent practitioner . . .'

This book begins in the troubled atmosphere of that time, when political debate was intense and people's lives were filled with uncertainty about what might come next. It starts with the recollections of two men who survived their turbulent times long enough to write down their stories, though the life of one was cut short soon afterwards. The two men had little in common but their courage and honesty. They never met.

Muhammadjan Rustamov, called 'Hindustani', was a farmer's son, an Uzbek from Kokand, and a religious scholar. He worked towards the exquisite exposition of already known fields of study, many of which would have been familiar to al-Hakim in the ninth century. To Hindustani, what mattered was the word of God: the works of men were important only in so far as they illuminated it.

Sadr-e Zia was a Bukharan and an intellectual. His mind constantly questioned and analysed the new. He enjoyed reading foreign newspapers and discussing the affairs of the day in stimulating company. He was an anthologist of modern Bukharan poetry, and a writer of it. A Persian-speaker, he also knew Uzbek, and carried a small Russian dictionary though he never spoke the language well. When the Russian revolution came, Sadr-e Zia was one of the few who understood what was happening, and that Bukhara as he knew it was about to be swept away for ever. Sadr-e Zia's diaries have been translated into English by his son Muhammadjan and grandson Rustam, who very kindly made some entries available to me.

The works of these two men have been kept safe through famine, war, exile, book-burnings, and endless official revisions of the past. The sons of both grew up as Soviet citizens, but at opposite ends of the social scale – one a gardener, the other a university professor – and were alive to all the suffering and all the advantages that came of being a part of that colossal political and human experiment that so dominated the twentieth century. To most people inside it and out, the USSR felt everlasting. Few predicted its downfall until the very last years, and not many even then.

Yet the duration of the USSR was less than that of a lucky human life. Throughout this book I have drawn as much as possible on the memories of people – housewives, farmers, soldiers, children – who witnessed and were part of the immense events of the last century, some of which have been smudged out by received versions so falsely interpreted as to be unrecognisable. The stories of these people are remarkable in their own right as well as being testimony to what happened. At the time of writing, the children and grandchildren of those same families have been caught up yet again in a sudden and extraordinary turn of world history, in which they play a critical part.

MJW

Tashkent, November 2001

I

Witnesses and actors

'And today no town in the countries of Islam will bear
comparison with Bokhara in the thronging of its creatures, the
multitude of movable and immovable wealth, the concourse of
savants, the flourishing of science and the students thereof and
the establishment of pious endowments.'

ONE EVENING in 1909 a boy passed through the gates of Bukhara
for the first time, walked into the courtyard of the Mir-e Arab
madrasa, one of the largest and most famous colleges in the city, and
so realised the ambitions of his short life. His name was
Muhammadjan, but later generations knew him only by the name
Hindustani. His remarkable story survives in the terse account he
wrote in old age and through his stepson Ubaidullah, who is the
keeper of family memories and custodian of the past. It endures too,
at least in fragments, in the recollections of friends and students who,
after a great period of silence, are now free to talk.

Hindustani was born in about 1892 in the village of Chahar Bagh
(Four Gardens), three hundred miles or so to the east of Bukhara in
the dry, stony outskirts of the city of Kokand, in what was then
Russian Turkestan. The family could hardly have been more ordinary. His father, Rustam, was a poor smallholder but a literate man, a
village mulla, and anxious that his eldest son should value scholarship
and make something of his life. Hindustani could read and knew the
alphabet by the age of eight, and was soon pleading to be sent to
Kokand to study further.

'When I was twelve my father agreed,' wrote Hindustani later, 'so
we set out for the city on his little horse, a bit bigger than a donkey.

We had only gone a short way when the horse balked at a ford. We dismounted, and I heard shouts behind us. I realised I had forgotten my Quran! My mother was rushing after us with it. My father said how merciful God was that the horse had stopped!' Rustam left his son in the care of a Kokand mulla, under whom Hindustani worked hard. He was declared Qari – a reader of the scriptures – two years later. To mark his achievement Rustam slaughtered an expensive sheep and held prayers of thanksgiving, as was proper.

Hindustani, the only poor man's son in the class, continued to excel. He followed the common curriculum of his time, reciting and memorising verses from the Quran and the *Chahar Ketab*, a famous anthology of writings on Islam that included lessons on *adab* – that is, good manners and correct behaviour. As a keen student, he went further than many boys and girls by learning how to write, using the Arabic script universal in Central Asia. He studied elementary Arabic grammar and poetics, as his father had, and also Uzbek, his mother-tongue – a new subject, lately introduced to the classrooms.

The copy-books of the day reveal something of the children who used them. A primer and a reader in Uzbek, printed not handwritten and kept safely over almost a century by an elder in the Ferghana town of Osh, show rows of small drawings from everyday life – a boy, a tree, a pomegranate – with naming and writing exercises beneath. 'These are the clothes we wear', reads one heading: '*Shalvar* [trousers], *Chapan* [quilted robe], *Pustun* [sheepskin topcoat], *Kamar* [sash], *Charoq* [long, soft leather boots].' 'These are the Muslim cities', reads another: 'Mecca, Medina, Istanbul, Baghdad, Fez, Isfahan, Kabul, Balkh, Baku, Bukhara, Tashkent, Samarkand, Khujand, Kokand, Kashgar . . .' The books contain moral lessons for the encouragement of respectful conduct, and a few simple tales.

Once Hindustani had the minimum qualifications, he supported himself by offering ritual prayers in exchange for bread and money at local sites of pilgrimage, to which he sometimes walked with his shoes stuffed in his sash to save the leather. 'Our people sit idle in the dust and fill empty minds with *bangi* [hashish],' he wrote, depressed by the poverty of the countryside. 'Our people ask for china bowls and find rough pottery – our bread is not wheat but chaff.'

Hindustani made the five-mile trip from Kokand back to Chahar Bagh each summer to help on the farm, as was usual for a schoolboy, but he knew that this was not the life he wanted. Though he had learnt much in Kokand, he was eager for a wider horizon: he became determined to reach the university city known to every student from Herat to Kashgar to Mashhad and beyond, the Oxford and Heidelberg of its time – Bukhara. When he was seventeen Hindustani sold his watch to pay for a railway ticket and said goodbye to his family. He boarded the train, one of those that had steamed into Kokand for the first time a decade before, and set off. Once beyond the border fort at Makhram and the old city of Khujand the train skirted the hills, cut through the plain, and passed from Russian-held territory into the kingdom of Bukhara. A kindly elder on board tutted over Hindustani's rashness. 'I told him that I knew nothing and nobody. He said, "Bukhara is an enormous city. Didn't anyone tell you that if you don't know anything you'll end up on the streets?"' When they arrived, the elder introduced Hindustani to a famous teacher connected with the Mir-e Arab.

Hindustani passed his entrance exams and was admitted to the madrasa, lodging at the house of his master and devoting himself to study and prayer. As a raw student he had no income from teaching. Often, he wrote, he lived on a couple of rounds of bread a day, with no money for rice or fruit, let alone meat. He was able to pay his fees only because he stumbled upon a gold ring in the street and sold it in the Caucasian jewellers' bazaar after some keen bargaining. He worked as he had never worked before. His memoirs record the fields of study he mastered, step by step: Arabic, of course, as the language in which God revealed himself to the Prophet, and Persian, as the literary language of Bukhara. He also studied poetics and calligraphy.

Outside the Mir-e Arab lay the most sophisticated and cosmopolitan Central Asian city north of the Amu. From five in the morning, Hindustani noted, the square outside was filled with crowds of different peoples. Tajiks, Afghans, Turks, Arabs, Kashmiris and Jews lived inside the eleven gates alongside Uzbeks like himself. Outside the city wall Tajik and Uzbek villages were set among wheat fields and orchards of apricots, persimmons and pomegranates, watermelon patches and mulberry groves. Herders and Kazakh nomads lived in the steppe beyond.

In 1909 Bukhara was thick with talk – not only of university matters, business and the harvest, but also of politics – world politics and Bukharan politics, the politics of appeasement, the possibilities of invasion and war. They talked in the tea houses, in the painted wooden courtyards of the well-to-do, and in the streets. They also talked in the mosques, and Hindustani records that his master's house was tryingly full of guests from morning to night. Already he loathed politics: what he loved was books. 'I had', he wrote, 'a passion for knowledge.' He gave up blocking his ears and moved to other lodgings, close to one of the cemeteries, in search of quiet.

At the heart of the political debate was a schism between different groups of intellectuals about what sort of place Bukhara should be, and how it should respond to the changing times. One lively group advocated opening new avenues in Bukharan cultural life – such as the establishment of printing presses – and political reform at the palace.

> In the name of God, Wise and Knowing
> I, an indigent slave of God, Mirza Muhammad Sharif-e Sadr, al-Zia by pen-name, in the year 1306 of the hijra, at the end of his excellency my father's life, committed myself to inscribe and record the internal and external events and affairs of my life, which are of importance, describing them day after day, some in detail, some in brief . . .

So began, in 1888/89, the diary of the eminent Bukharan scholar Sadr-e Zia. In the first decade of the twentieth century Sadr-e Zia was in his prime, a high-ranking judge in the Bukharan judiciary. Man of letters, poet and anthologist, he was also a keen horseman and a genial host, and a champion of the young, father of many children and sponsor of numerous young scholars.

Sadr-e Zia represented the spirit of intellectual openness for which Bukhara was once famous. The five hundred pages of his diary – a later re-creation of the original – are full of news of the outer world as well as of Bukharan matters. He records the Boxer uprising in China in 1898–1900, the Russo-Japanese Wars of

1904–5, and the crumbling of the Ottoman empire. In 1910 Sadr-e Zia gazed into the night sky and saw a star 'like a huge minaret, with its head directed eastward and its tail stretching westward, it pervaded the entire sky.' It is typical of Sadr-e Zia that he knew the European name for the comet – Halley – and could also cite references to tailed stars by poets of medieval Persia, who thought them heralds of misfortune.

Twice a week Sadr-e Zia, a tall man in his forties, dressed generally in a grey robe and wearing a silver ring, opened his house to people he called *ravshangaran*, or bringers of light – 'poets, wits, tellers of entertaining tales and devotees of literature,' recalled the celebrated poet Sadriddin Aini, who was taken into Sadr-e Zia's household at the age of eleven, having been spotted by the scholar as a promising boy. These young intellectuals were grounded in the Persian poets, in Hafez, Sadi, Ferdausi and Rumi, and were often poets themselves. They read their own works aloud, and spoke too of social and political matters. They, and other young Bukharans, were not all of one voice. Some advocated an independent parliamentary monarchy; others saw annexation by Russia as the only feasible way forward. The *ravshangaran* discussed tax reform, ways to reduce the corruption that rotted the Bukharan system, and the possibility of starting a newspaper.

A few months before Hindustani began work on his texts at the Mir-e Arab, the *ravshangaran* had launched a bold project: they had opened a school of a kind never seen in Bukhara, though there were several in Afghanistan and in Russian Turkestan. Gone were rows of boys crouched on the ground reciting scripture in a tongue they did not understand. In came modern mathematics and geography, local languages, and cotton mats on the earth floor. Amir Abdulahad had given his consent to the New School, but the Qaziat, the religious judiciary, indicated its displeasure; the amir withdrew his consent. The New School, and many others like it that had sprung up, went underground.

The Qaziat opposed the *ravshangaran* not just over education but in many regards. The Qazi Kalan, Mulla Burhanuddin, argued that Bukhara would be severed from its roots, even lost altogether, by such radical alterations. Many of his followers were adamantly opposed to the Russian presence and felt it was only a matter of time before St

Petersburg drew in the net and made Bukhara part of Russian Turkestan. In parish mosques, some mullas preached against the train, calling it the *aruba-e shaitan* – the devil's cart – and against the telephone, the bicycle, the potato and tomato – foods new to Bukhara that had arrived from the farms of the Russian pioneers on the steppe. When Russian advisers promoted a means of killing the swarms of locusts that stripped the fields each spring, there were mullas who forbade the murder of God's insects.

Abdulahad's uncomfortable relations with both clergy and intellectuals went from bad to worse. When pro-reform demonstrators took to the streets on 24 February 1910, he called out the troops. A few weeks later, however, protestors brought to the palace a new petition, more strongly worded than ever. According to the American reporter William Eleroy Curtis, 'They demanded a constitution, a legislature, a free press, freedom of speech, and the privilege of electing by ballot municipal and provincial officials. They . . . gave the emir six months more to answer and act. When the time was up, nothing was done; but the spirit of freedom is growing.'

It was on one of Amir Abdulahad's frequent sojourns out of his claustrophobic capital, in late December 1910, that he died, apparently of kidney disease. His son was hustled to the Ark and there, borne aloft on a carpet into the coronation room, he was crowned Amir of Bukhara. His name was Alim Khan, he was thirty years old and an experienced politician, having served as the governor of Kermina (modern Navai), north-west of Bukhara. In the streets below, a crowd waited expectantly. The future of the businessmen and the mullas, of intellectuals like Sadr-e Zia, of the quiet student Hindustani of Kokand – the future of Bukhara itself – all depended upon what sort of ruler Alim Khan would turn out to be.

A photograph of Crown Prince Alim Khan taken in 1893 survives. He stands up taut and straight for the photographer, a small boy, his hands almost buried in his robes, his round face expressionless beneath his turban. It might be the image of a Bukharan prince of a century earlier, or of five centuries before that. Yet the photograph was taken far away from Bukhara, in St Petersburg, where the young Alim Khan had been sent to receive the schooling his father hoped would fit him for the modern world.

A second photograph shows Alim Khan as a cadet at the Emperor Nikolai military academy. His chubby face peers out under a smart peaked cap above a brass-buttoned suit: dressed as a Russian, he stands between an upholstered chair and an ormolu clock. Alim Khan, groomed for compromise, learned Russian well, and some French. He is said to have read Dostoyevsky as well as the Bukharan poets. He also acquired a taste for women and cars – he drove a Mercedes – and for champagne, called tactfully *kand-su* or sugar-water. Alim Khan spent three winters in St Petersburg. Each summer he made the journey home across the steppe, over the Caspian Sea and through the desert to Bukhara.

The accession of this relatively worldly man gave the intellectual *ravshangaran* hopes. He promised an end to corruption, some freedom of expression, and limited controls on the power of the clergy. It was not long before his authority was put to the test. In 1912, the reformists realised one of their ambitions and brought out the first newspaper Bukhara had ever seen. *Bukhara-e Sharif* (Bukhara the Noble), published daily in Persian, brought literate Bukharans news not just of their own country but of the outside world. Alim Khan had approved: 'I myself have read newspapers in Russia,' he had said. Soon a supplement in Turkic was added. The Qaziat was enraged – 'Do you want to make *kafers* [infidels] of Bukharans?' one demanded – and pressed Alim Khan to revoke his consent. The battle was long, but by the end of the year *Bukhara-e Sharif* had been banned.

It was a sour moment for the *ravshangaran*. They continued to meet, but their discussions became more private. Some left the country in disappointment, others printed pamphlets for underground circulation. Copies of the Afghan newspaper *Seraj ul-Akhbar* (The Light of the News), launched in Kabul in 1911, passed from hand to hand; it was renowned for its wide international coverage, and for its editorials attacking both European imperialism and reactionary mullas. Many felt that if Alim Khan would not or could not reform his state, Bukhara was headed for an internal collision from which no one would benefit.

The chubby prince of the photographs, meanwhile, ran to fat. Wadded in his robe, feet apart, he looked gigantic. A rare reel of film survives, showing the stout amir climbing from the royal train in Crimea – where he kept a summer palace adjoining that of the Romanovs – and greeting the Russian princesses on the terrace. When the Romanovs held celebrations for the three hundredth year of their rule, in 1913, Alim Khan and the Bukharan court attended. Alim Khan was obviously aware that, in the event of insurrection, the Russian soldiers just outside the walls of Bukhara could slaughter his army – which was armed and trained by the Russian military just enough to give it the appearance of being a fighting force. Yet he seemed powerless to bridge the differences among the political classes, caught between the old order and the new, between the state and the mosque, progress and tradition, foreigners and Bukharans, ever more dependent on the Russian military – the very people who could so easily bring about his fall. Weighed down by these insoluble affairs of state, Alim Khan began to spend less time in the oppressive Ark and more in a new palace built for him by the Russians outside the city walls. The move left his capital more vulnerable than ever.

The Setara-e Mah-e Khassa, the Star of the Magnificent Moon, stands just outside Bukhara. Its red majolica gates still open on a striking confection of east and west. The main doors reveal a banqueting hall panelled with mirror. The solid bronze chandelier weighing half a ton hanging overhead (carried all the way from Poland as a gift from Tsar Nicholas) gave out the first electric light ever seen in Bukhara. There is a Russian refrigerator made of glass, a wheeled dessert trolley and a Venetian looking-glass.

At every turn, in every corridor, Alim Khan must have seen his image winking back at him, from glass, from mirror, from glossy lacquer. Even his clothes shone: every gold thread of his embroidered trousers and fur-trimmed cloaks was solid metal, brought from India and Iran. Some of his sets of clothes must have weighed tens of kilos.

Beyond the french windows, at the end of an avenue of quince trees and roses, is the bathing pond. Above it is a raised wooden throne, from which Alim Khan is said to have enjoyed the play of the water while casting an eye over his private zoo. Yet even outdoors, as much as in its glittering rooms, the Star of the Magnificent Moon is an airless place. As he admired his imported elephants, Alim Khan must have known that the political quarrels of the city were reaching boiling-point.

'I found the summer very hot in Bukhara,' Hindustani recalled of 1916. It was freakishly hot even in Europe that year. When term ended at the Mir-e Arab Hindustani left for his family village near Kokand. It was to prove a short stay. To his alarm, Hindustani heard that soldiers were rounding up local men and sending them to a war in which the Russians were fighting against the Austrians and Germans. A man was to be taken from every fifth family, and Hindustani's name was on the list. Rustam implored his son to go back to Bukhara, and Hindustani left just in time. Fuelled by grievances that had smouldered for the past fifty years, anger at the conscription of Muslims sparked an anti-Russian riot in a neighbouring town, and throughout this intolerably hot July and August city after city rose up. In the countryside, farmers and herdsmen set upon Slav peasant settlers. No official reports survive of what turned into the most serious anti-imperial uprising ever seen in Cental Asia. One officer reckoned that about 2,500 Russians were killed. The number of Muslim dead was not recorded, except in a few surviving documents from local courts. Of the 184 men arrested in Khujand after the uprising, 22 were executed, 130 sentenced to hard labour (probably to work on the new railway at Murmansk, on the Barents Sea) and the remainder imprisoned. There were public hangings at Samarkand, recorded by Tsarist photographers for police dossiers.

In Bukhara, the madrasas were still shut for the holidays. With three or four friends, Hindustani decided to go on pilgrimage to the famous shrine of the Caliph Ali at Mazar-e Sharif, across the river Amu in Afghanistan. They collected some presents – books and embroidered hats – to smooth their way on the other side, took a ferry over the river, and hired a pack-donkey. The pilgrimage went well until the morning Hindustani woke to find that his fellow students from Bukhara had gone their own way in the night. He never found out why. He had no money, few provisions, and nothing to sell. He was utterly alone in a foreign country, but he did know the names of a couple of people in Afghanistan to whom he might go for help. Having crossed the river, he thought it was probably wiser to go on than to try to return.

Hindustani set off to find a mosque, and soon came upon a big house from which he could hear the familiar sound of boys repeating *suras* of the Quran. After his years in Bukhara, his Persian was reasonably good. He explained his predicament to the teacher, who offered him lodging in return for help with the class. He also suggested a well-known scholar under whom Hindustani might, if he proved worthy, continue his studies.

Hindustani's first interview with Mir Muhammad Ghaus reduced him almost to despair. Ghaus was an expert in jurisprudence, well known in Mazar-e Sharif and beyond. He asked Hindustani a few questions, pronounced the young man's years of study to have been a waste of time, and recommended that he start all over again. 'All my studies in Kokand and in Bukhara had been worthless,' Hindustani wrote. 'I realised how, in my homeland, we simply recited everything by heart, whereas here things were very different. I realised how complex was Islam, how many schools and traditions there were to learn.' None the less, Ghaus agreed to take him on.

Hindustani spent the next few years labouring doggedly through an intensely demanding syllabus which included, he recalled, *Sarf u Nahv* (grammar and syntax); *Harakat* (the study of vowels); Ibn Hajib's *Qafiya* (the theory of rhyme); the *Sharh* of Abdulrahman Jami (a commentary on the *Qafiya*); '*Elal* (irregularities in certain prosody types) and the work of the early thirteenth-century grammarian Izzuddin Abdul Wahhab Zanjani. He studied formal logic, using *Sharh e Badi'e Mizan* (elementary logic); *Mizan e Mantiq* (logic); the *Tahzib ul-Mantiq wa'l kalam* by Sa'duddin Taftazani (logic and dogma); the *Shamsiya* of Najmuddin Qazvini (a Sufi jurist who died in 1276) and the *Hashiya e Qutbi* (a commentary on the *Shamsiya*). He paid particular attention to the *Sharh* or Quranic commentary of Bidel, the seventeenth-century poet whose works are part of the canon of Central Asian literature.

Ghaus was satisfied enough with his pupil to take Hindustani with him when he was offered the prestigious post of Qazi Kalan of the city of Jalalabad, between the capital, Kabul, and the Khyber Pass, near the border with India. He taught Hindustani every morning before he set off to work at the court, and his student gradually became proficient. When Ghaus grew frail, he counselled Hindustani to continue his studies in one of the great Indian madrasas. In about 1920, therefore, Hindustani journeyed eastwards across the Khyber Pass, through what is now Pakistan, to the city of Ajmir in Rajasthan, where he entered the madrasa of Usmania. (Most of Hindustani's students – and others – maintain that he studied at Deoband, in Uttar Pradesh. It is possible that this was so – Deoband was popular with students from Central Asia – but Hindustani makes no mention of Deoband and repeatedly specifies Ajmir.)

The journal of Sadr-e Zia is one of the very few first-hand, personal accounts of what really happened north of the Amu in the years while Hindustani was away. A few months after the riots in the Ferghana valley the crisis in Bukhara came to a head, and Sadr-e Zia logged it step by step. It was February 1917, and far away in St Petersburg rioting workers and army mutineers forced the abdication of Tsar Nicholas II. Amir Alim Khan lost his protector, and Bukhara was left exposed. The reformist *ravshangaran* considered it imperative that the amir appoint a new cabinet without delay, and at the end of March he agreed. Sadr-e Zia was appointed Qazi Kalan, the third most powerful position in the country.

On 8 April a hundred or so young enthusiasts gathered to welcome the Amir's proclamation of his proposed reforms. 'Long live the Amir!' they shouted, 'Long live the reforms!' and made their way singing through the streets. As they arrived in the square in front of the Ark crowds of counter-demonstrators poured in from the opposite corner. The followers of the outgoing Qazi, Burhanuddin, had played their trump card, and called out their madrasas. Between them they could count on the allegiance of several thousand students, many of them charity boys from remote villages whose futures depended on the mullas who had taken them in. 'God is Great!' they shouted. 'Shari'a! Shari'a!'

'At that moment, there came a message from the Vazir's Residence by telephone, according to which I had to intercept them [the madrasa students] and find a way to calm them down,' Sadr-e Zia records. He rushed to the square, where he found a mob beyond calming. He struggled through the crowds towards the Ark to seek an audience with Alim Khan. He reached the ramparts, but there students blocked his way to the gate. Seated in his window high above, Amir Alim Khan looked on motionless as the crowd surged around his new Qazi Kalan. As he watched, a student – 'a bandog of the sacked Burhanuddin' – grabbed Sadr-e Zia's robe, pulled him from his horse, and beat and kicked him to the ground.

'For a short time I retained consciousness, but then lost the awareness of what they did and how I got free from their clutches,' wrote Sadr-e Zia. 'Extreme weakness seized me. I did not know what sort of condition I was in, I had no feeling in my limbs. I knew only that I lay in a small, dark room, and that the doors of the room were closed. I had no doubt that I was under arrest. When I had reached that point in my guesswork the door opened, and someone came quietly into the room and very carefully moved towards me. The darkness prevented me from recognising him. From what had gone before, I supposed that he meant to kill me.'

But the unseen figure turned out to be a loyal friend, who helped carry Sadr-e Zia home. By the time he came to his senses two days later, events had moved on. Amir Alim Khan, seeing the mullas' strength in the square, took what seemed to offer the best chance for his personal survival, and threw in his lot with them. The reforms were immediately repealed. All over Bukhara, educated men were taken in by the police. Sadr-e Zia was especially grieved to hear that the young poet Sadriddin Aini, whom he had fostered and educated in his own house, had been thrown into prison, where he received seventy-five lashes. Aini's brother was killed, as were unrecorded numbers of other intellectuals. Their colleagues, friends and relatives fled the country, many into Russian Turkestan. Officials of the Russian Consulate in Bukhara did nothing to stop the purge that threatened to tear the state apart, and nothing to discourage the exodus; on the contrary, they removed some of the wounded from prison for treatment in Russian hospitals.

Sadr-e Zia left for the southern provincial town of Karshi, halfway to the river Amu. When the amir's soldiers eventually caught up with him they built a bonfire, and made him watch as they burnt all his books and all his writings, including his journal. When they had finished, they took him and his family to prison. Four hundred and fifty people were killed that day, Sadr-e Zia records, and another fifteen were taken away for execution in the night. The dead included a young cousin of his, lately come from Bukhara and still dressed in his wedding robes. An order of execution arrived for Sadr-e Zia – but the governor of Karshi, an admirer of his, refused to carry it out.

Throughout the summer of 1917 the Bukhara police hunted down anyone suspected of the least connection with the modernist movement. Libraries were sacked. Houses were pillaged. Intellectuals watched despairingly from their exile. Then, two thousand miles away, during the night of 6/7 November (25/26 October by the old Russian calendar) the Red Guard seized the Winter Palace in St Petersburg. By the morning of 7 November, Lenin and the Bolsheviks were in control. Early in December their Soviet of People's Commissars proclaimed the right of 'all toiling Muslims in Russia and in the east' to build their national life 'freely and unhindered'.

A radical group of Bukhara reformers – the Young Bukharans – seized the moment. Led by Faizullah Khujayev, the son of a city wool merchant so rich that he reportedly lent money to the royal exchequer, they approached the Bolsheviks. The man they went to was General Kolesov, the commander of the Russian garrison outside Bukhara. A few months before, Kolesov had been an oil-man on the railway – now the revolution had catapulted him to power.

At the end of February 1918 a detachment of Bolshevik troops set up camp about six miles outside the city, and the Young Bukharans delivered an ultimatum. The amir must, they said, include reformists in his government, or risk the consequences. Alim Khan refused. On 1 March the Reds, armed with artillery, marched up the road towards the walls of Bukhara.

It should have been a rout, but even Faizullah Khujayev was impressed by what happened next. The 'adherents of the old, the mullas,' he wrote later, 'though poorly armed – with knives, axes, rusty swords – fought desperately. I myself saw how one of them, holding a cudgel in his hand and a long knife in his mouth, advanced unflinchingly against our machine-guns and hurled himself against and killed one of our gunners.'

The Russians were forced back. Slav settlers living around the railway station fled as local people – in some cases even people they knew – turned on them. Amir Alim Khan ordered the track to be torn up, to prevent new troops being brought in, and sent word to the provinces for local beks to do the same.

One woman, Ikrama, remembers seeing the men of her town, Shahr-e Sabz, set upon the railway camps. 'We liked the Russians,' she said. 'They used to come and buy milk from us, and they gave us the first oblong bread I had ever seen. Then one day we Muslims rose up and killed them all, even the children. Some of them were crucified.' Ikrama was then about ten, an educated, quick-witted girl. Her father was the bek's scribe, and the family lived on the main square. When the Russians came up from the garrison to put down the insurrection, she saw everything. 'The elders welcomed the Russian troops at the city gate with pans of *pilau*, but the soldiers were not appeased,' she recalled in old age. 'They sacked the bek's palace and took everything, even his wives' trousers. Then, again the townsmen rose up and attacked the Russians with axes and sticks. The women took the children and ran away to the mountains. When we returned, we found the streets full of Muslim corpses and all the houses looted. There were too many people to bury, so we piled them up on the hill and pushed a wall over them. My elder brother is under that wall.'

Ikrama remembered that one young woman, a scripture teacher, stayed in town during the battle for fear of losing her gold. 'When we found her body, we saw she had been horribly raped. At that time, even we little girls blacked our faces with ashes and wore veils, to keep the soldiers off. They used to show themselves in the street to frighten us. I remember those soldiers so well. They used to stick frogs and tortoises on their bayonets and roast them in their bonfires.'

Alim Khan sent gifts to Afghanistan and Persia, hoping for arms in return, and declared Holy War.

Two years later the Bukhara countryside was filled with rumours that the government had finally fallen to the Bolsheviks. Sadr-e Zia found it impossible to know from the wild, frightened stories reaching the provinces what had really happened, and who was now in power. Profoundly alarmed, and troubled by nightmares filled with foreboding, Sadr-e Zia, now freed from prison, left his goods, gathered some companions, and set out from Karshi for Bukhara.

'Entering a dangerous desert, sometimes on roads, sometimes without roads, we marched ahead.' It was the summer of 1920, and 'the ground was as hot as a smith's furnace,' according to Sadr-e Zia's diary. The party set out, sticking closely together for fear of Bukharan army deserters who roamed the plains in gangs. 'Those who were stronger robbed the weaker ones. Those who fell injured or murdered in this way were too many to be counted. We saw many times how a victim, carried off from the main road, was robbed or killed.' Red Army soldiers, meanwhile, looted their way through desert settlements, helping themselves especially to horses, and shooting people who resisted. Sadr-e Zia and his party rode into one village, hoping someone would put them up, only to find that all the inhabitants had run away.

'In that manner, we travelled two nights and days, apart from stops. We encountered no inn on our way; at night, thorns were our beds, stones our pillows. Children and adults were *in extremis* from thirst; young and old were at death's door. At that time, unexpectedly, we reached a well. Having neither cord nor bucket, we bound our horses' reins and girths together and, using a nose-bag as a bucket, took up some water. The nose-bag was full of insects the like of which we had never seen. The little water we managed to draw was discoloured by animal excrement. All our companions were in the most dire plight.'

When Sadr-e Zia at last passed through the gates of Bukhara, he found the heart of the city 'turned into a wilderness so awful that the sight struck one with horror and inspired terror'. All the taller buildings had been damaged by 'the crash of mighty cannon', the Ark was in flames, a shell had burst through the golden crow's-nest of the Minar-e Kalan, the great minaret opposite the Mir-e Arab that had stood as the beacon of Bukhara for five hundred years.

Sadr-e Zia's own house had been holed by a shell, and all his possessions looted. Nevertheless, he gave thanks, rested, and rejoiced when several old friends appeared at the door, safe and well, having heard of his return. They told Sadr-e Zia how much of the city had been wrecked, as well as the countryside around. Thieves had stripped carpets, gold and books from fine houses, pots from the poor, orchards and kitchen gardens.

A clue to the speed and thoroughness with which old Bukhara had been brought down lay in the damage to the taller buildings, as noted by Sadr-e Zia. Before they heard the noise of propellers overhead and went out to look, many Bukharans had never seen an aeroplane. Bombs fell for three days and the city of dried mud and wood went up like kindling after the long desert summer. At the same time, at 4 a.m. on 31 August, the ground offensive had begun. G. Omeliusty, a Red Army officer who took part, later recorded his surprise that the walls of the old city stayed solid in the face of modern artillery fire. 'It was only on the third day that we broke through,' he wrote, 'to find everything prepared for defence: the houses, streets, and even the graveyards.' Clutching Qurans, the mullas incited the defenders. People threw boiling water and stones from the roofs. 'We had to fight for each house, for each square,' Omeliusty recalled; but in the end, the Amir's holy warriors did not stand a chance.

On 2 September 1920, the revolutionaries hoisted a red flag from the broken top of the Minar-e Kalan, led by Faizullah Khujayev. They proclaimed the People's Republic of Bukhara shortly afterwards, and signed a treaty of friendship with revolutionary Russia.

As for Amir Alim Khan, he had already vanished by the time Sadr-e Zia rode through the Karshi gate. He gave the order to evacuate when the first shells hit the Ark, and fled with his retinue towards the foothills of the Pamir. The party moved quickly over the pass to Hisar, the gateway between Bukhara and its outlying mountainous provinces in the east, and on to the village of Dushanbe. The revolution was at his heels and fighting was breaking out even in the smallest mountain towns as new leaders took power. The amir held makeshift court at Dushanbe for several months. He had every intention of reclaiming his throne, and he put out a call to arms. Some beks rallied to his side, and he sent presents to groups of fighters from Ferghana who after the sacking of Kokand in 1917 had taken to the hills, from where they had been harassing the Soviet authorities ever since. An effective army, however, would need outside support. 'I hope that in this hour of need Your Majesty will extend to me your kindness and favour and send me from your high Government by way of friendly assistance £100,000 English as a State Loan, also 20,000 rifles with ammunition and 30 guns with ammunition and 10 aeroplanes with necessary equipment,' wrote Alim Khan to King

George V through the British Consul-General in Kashgar. He did not broadcast the fact that his request was turned down.

For the most part the district beks melted away. As many elderly people recall it, they generally slipped into the highlands before the troops arrived. In the plains along the river Amu, especially in southern Tajikistan, one can see the remains of the beks' abandoned forts. That at Qabadian – large enough to house a madrasa and a bazaar within its wall – had a watch-tower and a wide, shallow moat around it so that the guard would hear the oncoming hooves of enemy horses. The nephew of a sentry and the cook's son, who still live in the shadow of the fort, tell family tales of the paranoid state possessing the bek towards the end. 'No one was allowed in and he refused to come out,' they recall. 'He shut himself into a tiny room in the watch-tower. When the Red soldiers came from Termez, they burst the gates and rode in to arrest him. But they found an empty room. No one ever found out where he went and they never caught him.' The soldiers looted the fort and burnt it, but the foundations and much of the perimeter wall remain.

Some beks joined Alim Khan when in the spring of 1921 his court finally fled Dushanbe. The royal party made for the village of Chubek on the bank of the river Amu. His retainers built a raft of wood and inflated sheep-gut, and floated the last Amir of Bukhara over to Afghanistan.

'A year and a half has passed,' wrote Sadr-e Zia in his journal. 'The amir has been in Afghanistan all this time, while his family, his children and his mother have been under the guardianship of the Soviet authorities. Some of the amir's attendants remain in Bukhara, serving in the administration. Another faction is in Afghanistan, with the amir; still others wander in the wasteland and desert, and others are shopkeepers in the streets and bazaars.'

Those mullas who had led the bloody demonstrations of 1917 – the 'leaven of the dough of tumult' Sadr-e Zia called them – were sorely punished. 'After spending a few days in disposing of sewage and cleaning the streets, and thus becoming an exemplary warning for people and disgraced before God, they were put to death by the Soviet government. Every one of them dug his grave with his own

hands, and afterwards was killed and buried.' Sadr-e Zia added a pro-
phetic line from the Quran:

Take warning, then, o ye with eyes to see.

The People's Republic proclaimed in September 1920 was the last
attempt Bukharans made to hold their country together. Its laws
spoke of their fractured times. Private property was allowed, and the
fundamentals of Islamic law remained sacrosanct. A banner reading
'Proletarians of the world unite!' hung in the Mir-e Arab madrasa;
beneath it, the mullas read and recited as before. Shari'a courts still
functioned, and the clergy continued to manage the *waqf*, the lands
and properties they had held for many centuries. Sadr-e Zia had a job
in the legal administration, and worked in the library. Despite his
'abundance of duties', he also set about rewriting the enormous
volume of papers burnt by the amir's soldiers on the bonfire at
Karshi. Painstakingly he re-drafted his master-work, an anthology of
modern Bukharan poetry. 'After the revolution I lived in poverty and
hardship, till the time when the Government of the Soviet Republic
gave me back my estates, which at one time had been confiscated
from me by the amir,' he wrote. 'Because of this, I felt some ease;
selling some of these estates, I had money for my everyday needs.'

In 1924 Moscow dissolved the international states of Bukhara (and
with it the short-lived Bukharan People's Republic), Russian
Turkestan, and the Khivan People's Republic of the south. In their
place came an entirely new idea: *national* republics that would be part
of a group of many such republics – the Soviet Union, first proclaimed in 1922.

   'Uzbekistan' was by far the larger of the two national republics that
ran along the Amu. Its territories stretched west to east from the Aral
Sea to the mountain ranges bordering China, and north to the edge
of Kazakhstan, an expanse of steppe the size of western Europe. It
took its name from 'Uzbek', the common name for the numerous
Turkic-speaking peoples of the plains, and Tajiks, Turks, Persians,
Armenians, Jews, Turkmen, Kazakhs and a myriad of other minor-
ities living in this territory were also absorbed into the Uzbek SSR.

With a population of about four million, Uzbekistan was one of the largest republics in the Union, taking its place after Russia itself, Ukraine, Belorussia and – just – Kazakhstan. The city of Tashkent, foothold of Russian power in Asia ever since its capture by Tsarist troops in 1865, became the capital of the new 'nation'.

The Uzbek Republic was a hub around which the smaller Asian republics – Tajikistan, Turkmenistan and (to a lesser extent) Kirgizstan – spread out almost as satellites, each with a Russian-built administrative capital. Roads, railways, power-lines and money all reached the periphery through Uzbekistan, giving Tashkent tremendous local power and every interest in staying loyal to the Soviet Union. The old centres of power like Bukhara, Samarkand and Kokand became provincial Uzbek cities – Khiva was later turned into an open-air museum.

The vertiginous mountain territories along the Amu that Bukhara had conquered in the nineteenth century ('Eastern Bukhara') became 'Tajikistan', with its western limit at the old Bukharan town of Hisar, which means 'gate' or 'barricade'. Its capital was made the village of Dushanbe where Alim Khan had kept his last court as the Amir of Bukhara. Tajikistan was intended as a national home for the Persian-speakers or Tajiks, but included a great many Uzbek-speakers, some Turkmens, Kirgiz, and local 'Arabs'. It was initially an autonomous part of the Uzbek Republic, but Tajik territory was so inaccessible from Tashkent that the assortment of young men who made up the Tajik Revolutionary Committee had to be flown in from Uzbekistan, landing their Junker Yul 13s in a field by the river Dushanbe. In the winter of 1926 the Tajik Communist Party held its first congress in a plywood pavilion built specially for the purpose in a public garden, painted cheerfully with communist slogans in Arabic calligraphy and decorated with an ornamental hammer and sickle.

Demarcation made a profound difference, not just to the map, but to one's sense of self. Several people relate parents' stories of how, before demarcation, ordinary people of Bukhara and Ferghana rarely used the words 'Uzbek' or 'Tajik', except, perhaps, when tempers were up in a bazaar row. During the late 1920s, however, race became important, from village to requisitioned palace. Politicians and others easily manipulated the soft-centred idea. Whispers about 'mixed' blood, as founded, say, on talk of a grandmother from Samarkand, were enough to suggest that a rival was not 'really' the nationality stamped on his papers. Faizullah Khujayev went down in history as the revolutionary leader of the Uzbek SSR; he is remembered variously, however, as an Uzbek hero and as a Tajik 'pretending' to be Uzbek – even as a Tajik who 'sold his own people' to the Uzbeks. Some bilingual families stopped using one language in public so as to be seen as 'pure'. In this way a peculiar brand of knowingness crept in and created layers of identity in Soviet Central Asia impenetrable to the outsider's eye.

The boundaries so drawn were far from arbitrary. Local party leaders, scrambling for what they could get, bickered venomously over them for five years or more. They counted heads in disputed areas and claimed people as one nationality or another. As the modern map reveals, the Uzbeks won hands down. The prima-facie reason for this is that there were more Uzbeks than Tajiks. But that, as so much else, is a matter of interpretation, and there were surely other factors in play. For all the local rows, the nationality question was decided in Moscow not in Central Asia. It is possible that the Russians needed a political bridge to Turkey after the end of the First World War and the collapse of the Ottoman empire, more than one to Persia. The young Macedonian officer newly elected president in 1924, Mustafa Kemal, who became Atatürk, the father of the modern Turkish state, had good relations with Russia at this time. It is also the case that, because Tashkent, a largely Uzbek city, had been colonised a full seventy years before, declared Uzbeks had the ear of Moscow in a way that declared Tajiks had not. Yet the borders were also calibrated so as to keep a check on excessive local power-building. Each republic had at least one secondary border to another – Tajikistan, while almost completely reliant on Uzbekistan, also had passes to Kirgizstan through the mountains of the east.

'The proletarian knows no country' wrote Marx in *The German Ideology*, yet it was the Soviets of the 1920s who laid the ground for nation-states where none had been, in very much the same way that the British laid lines over the Middle East. 'Nationalism' quickly became ideologically unacceptable, and then a crime. Uzbekistan and Tajikistan flew their own flags, yet their loyalty was supposed to belong to the Union. They took their place alongside the Armenians, Latvians, Georgians and all the other minorities, as colours in the Soviet spectrum.

Sadr-e Zia's wife gave birth to a baby boy just after demarcation. The family had already lost twelve children (not an unusual number for the time), including a son for whom Sadr-e Zia had written a heart-wrenching elegy, and a two-year-old daughter, Khursanda, 'as dear as my soul'. They gave the new baby the name Muhammadjan.

'My father knew very early on that Bukhara was finished,' says Muhammadjan Shukurov seventy-five years later. It is 2001, and Sadr-e Zia's only surviving child is sitting in his cosy flat, surrounded by books. His grey suit and blue tie belong to his times; his cheerful independent-mindedness is that of his father. It is Muhammadjan who keeps safe the short stories, prayers and other writings of Sadr-e Zia, preserved through a world war, two civil wars, repression and countless book-burnings, and a long migration.

'He understood what was happening before others realised. You can feel his pain in the last entries of the diary. Because it wasn't just the end of a city, you know. It was the end of a long, long tradition, a culture . . . a civilisation, even.'

Some people, he thinks, were glad the amir had gone. 'He was a weak man, a rotten man. And for some ordinary people, it was only a fight between soldiers. In fact, in the bazaar near the Karshi gate, the tea-house never closed: they just went on serving tea and watermelons as before.'

Khujayev he recalls as being a magnificent orator. 'I remember hearing him speak as a boy. And some people thought he really believed in communism. But there are still older people who cannot bear to speak of him. Perhaps he just wanted to be the Amir of Bukhara himself. Khujayev! He took away our freedom and sold us. A thousand years were rubbed out in those days.'

All this time Hindustani had been away, first in Afghanistan, then in India. But by the mid 1920s he was nearing the end of his courses at Ajmir. He had saturated himself in learning there. The food, the languages and the climate had been strange to him at first. Many of the subjects, too, were new, but he had grown to love zoology, astronomy and mathematics. He learnt to play chess with exceptional acumen, and became a skilled amateur apothecary, learning the properties of many plants unknown in Bukhara. In 1927 he began his final year at the madrasa. It was ten years since he had seen his family. In that time, he records, he neither sent nor received a letter from home. To all appearances, he had given up his Central Asian past. He had long since learnt Hindi, and he dressed, ate and conducted himself as an Indian.

Feeling jaded one morning after a particularly strenuous period of study, Hindustani took his doctor's advice, put away his books, and walked into town for a change of air. His stroll took him to the railway station, where a train had just arrived. The Ajmir train was part of the elaborate transport network, including carts, pack animals and boats, that led from Central Asia to Mecca. Hindustani scanned its pilgrims, hoping by some happy chance to see someone who might be able to give him news from home. To his delight, he spotted three Uzbeks – easily distinguishable by their faces and dress – and climbed into their carriage to talk. The elderly men were puzzled to meet an Indian asking questions in their own language. But then, as his memoir records, 'one of them shouted: "It's my son! I have found my son!" How we hugged and kissed.'

Distressed by Hindustani's long silence, Rustam had set out four years earlier to look for his son, trailing him first to Bukhara and then to Mazar-e Sharif. The search depressed and wearied him and at last he gave up. Rustam was an elder now, and decided instead to fulfill his Muslim duty to go on hajj before he died. The money he had made as a journeyman mulla after leaving Chahar Bagh – 110 gold 'Nikolai' roubles – was enough for his travelling expenses, and he arrived at Ajmir with the money safely in his sash. Hindustani resolved at once to accompany him.

Returning to the madrasa with his father to prepare for the journey, Hindustani was given a book as a leaving present. 'The Travel Guide to the Pilgrimage to Mecca' advised that the pilgrim should take with him 'six or seven lengths of rope, a big pot, some jars of salted lemons, and some black tea.' One must also, it said, at all costs book one's passage on the upper deck. Having rested, father and son set off on the long journey across India to the port of Bombay, where because of Rustam's poor health they had to tip a medical clerk to let them sail. Neither had seen the sea before, and it was with trepidation that they paid their five rupees for upper-deck tickets and climbed aboard.

As the ship put out of Bombay docks into the Indian Ocean, the Travel Guide came into its own. All the lower-deck passengers were dreadfully seasick, and only salted lemons seemed to help: Hindustani sold his for a rupee each. As there was little washing water, he helped the other pilgrims perform their ablutions by drawing up sea-water in his pot, let down on the lengths of rope. In this way, his memoir notes, they made 'good money' during the two-week voyage. When they arrived at Jeddah they rested and had proper baths, then rented camels for the journey on to the holy city of Mecca.

Rustam struggled his way through the pilgrimage and, supported by his son, managed to stumble around the sacred Ka'ba. But he grew ever weaker, and died soon afterwards. Having buried his father, Hindustani returned to India alone. He was by now thirty-five ('How come you are still a student?' his father had asked) – close to middle age – and without a proper job or a family of his own. For all his Indian dress, he was still a foreigner, and after his final year of study there was nothing to keep him in Ajmir. It was time to go home.

Pausing only to wind up his affairs at the madrasa, Hindustani began the return journey over the Khyber Pass. In Jalalabad he stopped to pray at the tomb of his old teacher Ghaus before going on to Kabul. There were many Uzbeks and Tajiks in town, quite apart from the exiled Bukharan amir and his court, now established there. Among the incomers was an old friend from near Kokand who told Hindustani of the extraordinary events that had occurred on the north side of the Amu since his departure, and advised him not to take his religious diplomas home with him, for safety's sake.

From Kabul, Hindustani retraced his steps northwards to Mazar-e Sharif – also full of émigrés from Bukhara and elsewhere – and north again to the river. More than ten years after first crossing the Amu he took the ferry back to Termez. Border guards with stars tacked to their caps met him at the quay. A red flag hung over the official building where the new authorities checked his papers and gave him permission to travel on towards the place he still thought of as home.

Hindustani went to the railway station, found a seat on a train, and began his journey through the long, dry sweep of plains leading to the north and Kokand. Here he found the royal palace still sparkling with blue, green and yellow tiles, and much of the imperial Russian town as he remembered it; but the palace was empty, and in the old city he had known as a boy half the houses seemed to be abandoned, boarded up or looted. In the surrounding villages, whole families had simply disappeared.

2

Journeys in the dark – the migration across the Amu

'. . . and the people of Bokhara, because of the desolation, were
scattered like the constellation of the Bear and departed into the
villages.'

HAJJI PARMAN does not appear different from many other elders
living in the poor village outside Peshawar in western Pakistan
in 2001. He wears an unremarkable white turban, a long, pale grey
shirt and white trousers. His concerns are local and immediate: the
drought that has left the small, mud-walled fields bone-dry and
cracked, the price of flour, the cost of the wool and dyes from Lahore
that keep his sons' carpet-making business going, the rent he pays his
Pakistani landlord.

Yet Hajji Parman calls himself an outsider. He does not speak
Urdu, and is a little halting even in the Persian spoken by his children
and most of his neighbours. Hajji Parman was born on the right bank
of the Amu – what he refers to as *par darya*, 'over the river'. He is one
of up to half a million people (to judge from Soviet records) who
scrambled to leave Central Asia between the revolution and the mid
1930s. Most of them crossed the Amu into Afghanistan, a minority
went over the mountains to China.

The great majority of people in Central Asia can have had little idea
what the revolution and the coming of Soviet power were supposed
to be for. What was essentially a convulsion in political circles rever-

49

berated throughout Russian-held territories, however. As the old order fell, power struggles and muddled battles broke out all over the north side of the river. Very many families left for fear of losing their property through confiscation or theft, others were afraid of being attacked as 'anti-revolutionary' in some way. The Amu is narrow in parts and even fordable in winter, and for countless centuries people have migrated to and fro across it in times of famine, war or persecution. It was natural, therefore, that in this time of emergency, frightened people in their hundreds of thousands should do as their forefathers had done. Only one side – the Soviet authorities – kept records of the exodus, and at their fullest these were patchy tallies of abandoned houses. The only other account lies in the stories of those who were there.

'Our house was just like this one,' Hajji Parman said, nodding at the bare, white-washed room spread with thin red quilts in which he sat with his sons and grandsons. 'I remember playing outside in the square, and the water running down the canals of our street, Kucha Ishan.' Like many survivors, he says his father made a hurried decision to leave when he heard that Red Army soldiers were on their way to his village, near Kerki, to take away the elders. Parman was seven when his parents got him and his six brothers and sisters up in the night. 'We left the house silently, one by one. It was so black we could see nothing. We knew not to cry or make a sound. My mother lit the lamps so that the neighbours would think we were still inside. Then she closed the door behind us.'

The family walked for half an hour through the dark, until they reached the Amu. Smugglers waiting on the bank rented out rafts of inflated cows' skin, three per family, and, for a fee, arranged for them to be met on the Afghan side. Parman and his family got across safely and made their way into north-west Afghanistan on a hired camel. They stopped at the village of Aqcha, just south of the river, where they settled. They had little to start their new life but the clothes they wore, having of necessity left behind their four hundred head of sheep. They had been luckier than many: some families, Parman said, had left their youngest children by the road when their crying put at risk the safety of the rest.

Turkmen families like Parman's, primarily stock-breeders and shepherds, were better able to fold and reassemble their lives elsewhere than those tied to arable land. Almost a quarter of a million Turkmens decamped into the plains of northern Afghanistan between 1917 and the middle 1920s alone, turning Aqcha and the settlement of Ankhui from trading posts to full-sized towns. A smaller but still considerable number drove their flocks through the plains into Iran, where they settled on the windswept eastern corner of the Caspian coast. These Turkmens remained at the margins of Iranian society. Very few married out, or even visited Teheran or other big cities. Their children gradually learnt Persian as a second language, but they did not convert to Shi'a Islam, as the scatter of Sunni shrines near the Caspian testifies. The close-knit Turkmen communities around the port of Bandar-e Turkmen, three generations later, resemble the villages of Turkmenistan, even down to the style of the *piala* or tea-bowls – used throughout Central Asia and China but not in Iran.

Many of the Turkmens who lost their flocks belonged to families specialising in the qaraqul sheep whose fleece had been the most lucrative export of Bukhara. They gradually acquired new stock which they raised on land many already knew well as winter grazing grounds, and did business with traders from Herat and Mashhad as before, selling skins, and the deep red carpets made by their wives and known on the world market as Bukharan rugs. The border was still loose in the early days of the Soviet Union, and some Turkmens crossed back and forth from time to time when the grass grew thin. The great majority of families, however, including Hajji Parman's, never saw the *par darya* again.

By the time Hindustani returned home, hundreds of thousands of other peoples from towns and villages throughout Central Asia had joined the exodus. They came from every corner of society. Farmers and factory-owners left, goldsmiths and paper-makers, saddlers and carpenters, weavers, dyers, tanners, and tailors. Very many had never set eyes on any kind of Soviet official, but left when they heard 'the Russians' were coming. They feared for their businesses, and many were also frightened by tales of what the soldiers did in the villages. There were many – well-substantiated – stories of elders being imprisoned and shot, and rumours of Muslim girls, once orphaned, being made to 'dance for the communists'. When religious persecution began in the late 1920s many mullas – often, in effect, the literate men of a village – left. Doctors, teachers, and madrasa-educated lawyers and calligraphers left, for fear of being thought mullas. 'We were big people,' one survivor remembered with pride. 'We had four cows, and my father could write. We had to leave.'

Richer families in the later waves of migration sometimes managed to send goods such as seeds and looms and small libraries on ahead before shutting their houses. Women who had them sent the embroidered cloth and dresses that made up their dowries. A very few grand people had their photograph taken before they left. In the meagre boxes of family mementoes that survive are solemn pictures of émigrés and their children, taken on the point of departure and given to relatives in case they never met again. Those who enjoyed the luxury of thinking ahead were in the minority, however; in the rush to get out, most took nothing but what money or goods they had and could carry.

The people of Ferghana left in particularly large numbers, especially from Kokand, which by the 1920s had seen several cycles of violence. The uprising sparked by the conscription of Muslims into the Tsarist army in 1916, weeks after Hindustani's last visit to his family, had been followed by another, then another. In late 1917 anti-imperialist Kokandis heeded the clarion call of Bolshevism, took up the slogan of freedom, and declared independence. The Turkestan Autonomous Government, led by Mustafa Chaqai Bek, ran up its own flag – a star and crescent moon on a red and blue ground – on 10/11 December, but did not last long. Bolshevik troops despatched by the Tashkent Soviet the following February threw out the government and stripped Kokand for three days before setting fire to the old city. A census taken before the revolution indicated a population of 120,000, that of 1926 a population of 69,300: a loss of more than one family in two.

The natural escape route for Ferghana migrants lay eastwards through the mountains into China, a way familiar to the traders in tea, wool and opium who travelled between Kashmir, Kashgar and Ferghana for a living. Mir Bahadir Khan, a rich Ferghana businessman, lived uneasily under Soviet rule in Khujand until a relative was arrested and killed (electrocuted, according to Mir Bahadir Khan) in prison. Relatives tried to retrieve the body for a Muslim funeral; soldiers caught them, shot them and threw the bodies into the burial pit. Only Mir Bahadir Khan got away. He assembled his household and left without taking the time even to dig up all the gold he had hidden in the garden. He, his wife Khumri Bibi, their three children and thirty-five other family members set out with their remaining coins and jewellery sewn into the seams of their coats. Travelling by night through Soviet artillery positions, held up frequently by blizzards and moonlit nights, they crossed the border into China and settled temporarily in Kashgar before descending southwards through the Qaraqorums. The journey took more than two years altogether, and in the course of it they lost everything to looters. They arrived in Ladakh snowblind and broke.

The obvious crossing-point for southern families, many of them Tajiks from Kulab, Shurabad and Qurghan Tappa, was opposite the little Afghan port of Imam Saheb on the Amu. It was relatively exposed, and Soviet troops kept up a ragged watch. The men of an escaping party were frequently arrested. Some women, left without their husbands in this way or widowed on the journey, took their children and pressed on alone. Gul Muhammad of Kafernahan was seven when his family set out. His father had been stopped twice before, and took great risks by making a third attempt. 'It was very late at night,' he remembers. 'We tied the cowskins together and the women sat in the middle. Some men held on to the edges and some rode horses alongside. The water ran fast and wide – it was spring – and once we were in we had to keep going, whether the horses rolled or not. Sometimes they rolled. I don't know how long it took, but when the morning star came up we were in Afghanistan. We had to give the horses back then, and we began to walk.'

In Afghanistan the émigrés found a mixed reception. Some recall being stripped by thieves of everything they had brought with them, others being jeered at as runaways who had 'drunk water with *kafers*'. Yet there are more who remember how the Afghans shared what food they had, even during a three-year famine in the 1920s. Refugees were put up in local mosques. Some Afghans lent horses to sit weary migrant children on as they took the road to the nearby town of Qunduz. 'At home we had suffered,' one survivor said. 'Here we were comfortable, in a free and Muslim country.'

In Qunduz, Mazar-e Sharif and other towns and villages along the northern rim of Afghanistan the migrants picked up their lives. They declined Afghan citizenship, organised their own schools, and lived by their own laws. Very many clung to the hope of returning home once the trouble had died down, saying prayers each night for peace in the home country.

The announcement of Soviet power and the often bloody suppression of local leaders did not bring calm to Central Asia. From the fall of Bukhara until the 1930s armed partisans whom the Russians called *basmachi* – meaning bandits – waged an often vigorous resistance campaign wherever, broadly speaking, there were mountains to hide them. They naturally concentrated in Tajikistan, because of its terrain and its long secluded river border with Afghanistan, home to the exiled Amir Alim Khan, the figurehead of the *basmachi*.

Elders in the villages between Dushanbe and the surrounding highlands still remember the edgy calm and the bouts of violence that dominated their lives in the early 1920s. 'The robbers [the *basmachi*] used to come from up there,' an elderly farmer said seventy-five years later, pointing with his stick at a gap in the hills above his house. 'And the soldiers used to come up from the town. One lot would bash us, and then the other lot.'

By far the best-known *basmachi* commander in this region was Ibrahim Bek, a long-eyed, black-haired man half a head taller even than most Russians. He was born, an Uzbek of the tribe of Lakai, in the village of Koktash, near Dushanbe, in 1889, twelfth and only surviving child of a smallholder named Chaqabai, a reservist in the Bukharan army who is said to have left his son nothing but debts. When Ibrahim Bek took the title of Commander-in-Chief of the Armies of Islam in 1920/21 he rallied large numbers of Lakais around this part of the river Kafernahan and cemented the tribe by taking the daughter of another Lakai leader and *basmachi* as his third wife.

Ibrahim Bek made the most of the gorges and river bluffs of his native territory. Kafernahan has been famous for its bolt-holes since at least the Arab invasion of the eighth century (*nahan* is the hiding-place of *kafer*, non-Muslims), and he moved his Lakais through the mountains to the Afghan border, mounting ambushes and sabotage raids. The Red Army was stretched to the limit by wars and uprisings from Siberia to Ukraine, and the troops garrisoned at Dushanbe could do little against him. Most Slavs had never seen mountains: still less did they know how to fight in them. The majority – 90 per cent in some detachments – came down with malaria. Russian-speaking soldiers were unable to communicate with local people, whom they felt to be both hostile and incomprehensible. The reprisals they took against civilians did little to help their cause.

Each valley of Tajikistan soon had its own commander. Davlat Manbai led the *basmachi* in Kulab on the Afghan border, Fazel Maqsum those of the Gharm valley, further to the north. Under each commander was a ladder of lesser leaders, down to farmers who took up arms when needed. All in all, according to Russian estimates, the *basmachi* could count on about twenty thousand men. Even if there were in reality possibly less than half that number, they constituted a very large fighting force, given the terrain.

Some officials of the short-lived Bukharan Republic fell in with the *basmachi*, feeling betrayed both by Moscow and, in many cases, by one another. The president of the republic, Usman Khuja, did what he could to organise the *basmachi* and, by his own account, led a prolonged attack on the Red Army garrison at Dushanbe in early 1922. In this he was joined by the adventurer Enver Pasha, who spent an uneasy few months with the *basmachi* after his fall from grace in Turkey. On 14 February 1922 the *basmachi* overpowered the weak city garrison and captured Dushanbe. A few weeks later, a separate group laid siege to Bukhara itself.

The *basmachi* did not build on their success, however. Proliferating commanders were divided among themselves: some for the amir, some against; some Tajik, some Uzbek; even some so hostile to the others that they fought beside the Bolsheviks against their fellow Muslims. Ibrahim Bek never trusted Enver Pasha; many Persian-speakers trusted neither. Communication between the commanders was anyway erratic – the passing of messages between valleys several days' ride apart was difficult in summer and almost impossible between October and April. Competition for scarce horses, money and ammunition was fierce.

'Some *basmachi* came to our village and sat down in the house of our own commander. They demanded three things: a woman, a boy and a horse,' remembers an elder from the Tajik–Afghan border village of Shurabad. 'Our commander, Mulla Qader, said "I have none, but you must stay and drink tea and eat with me." In reality he had five horses, and when he sent out for a sheep to slaughter for his guests, he used the time to summon our people. The *basmachi* did not wait to eat. The leader drew his gun and shot Mulla Qader. They escaped, and as they passed through the villages, whatever they saw, they stole.'

The Red Army reclaimed Dushanbe in July, and the *basmachi* fell back to the hills. Soldiers cordoned off the provincial market towns, imported wheat for the townspeople, and cut supplies to the villages, many of which had been ruined twice, first by the *basmachi*, then by the army. The *basmachi* extorted food from peasants with nothing to spare. 'When the *basmachi* were strong we bowed before them and said they were right,' recalls one man, a bargee on the Amu at the time. 'When the Soviets were strong we bowed before them. All of them stole the grain of the poor for their fighters. What could we do?' Once the Red Army had the upper hand, soldiers brought gifts to the villages – a little sugar, some oil, a few yards of bright satin – with the promise of more to come.

As popular support ebbed away, many *basmachi* commanders switched sides. They went where the jobs were, and became low-level government functionaries, a state of affairs that did not tend to increase Russian trust in local Communist Party cadres. ('*Regional apparatus?* They are the apparatus of the *basmachi*,' one officer is said to have told a Moscow greenhorn.) Yet the compromise began to hold firm enough. Hundreds of fighters came out of the highlands and returned to their villages in the plains north of the Amu.

Leaflets said to emanate from Amir Alim Khan continued to circulate around Tajikistan, urging the populace to rise. This one supposedly dates from 1924:

> . . . There is no reason to doubt our final victory. I have had conversations with the Europeans who live in Kabul and who have taken an interest in our affairs. They have promised to sell me rifles at the price of one sheep per old rifle and two sheep per new one. They also promised to aid our armies by sending five hundred aeroplanes that are due to arrive here any moment. Also inform my people that the Soviet Government is at present in very bad straits. It has been attacked by the English, French and Chinese armies, which are already near Moscow. Just hold out a little longer. The end of the Bolsheviks is near. Let every-

one join the armies of Islam, always bearing in mind that the field of a holy battle lies on the road to Paradise. Believe that everything I say is the holy truth.

> [signed] Amir of Bukhara Said Mir Alim Khan
> Kabul 1343, Shoval 26

Ibrahim Bek and other commanders carried on their raids against Soviet enterprises, but the tide had turned. The Luddite nature of the *basmachi* campaign enabled the Soviet authorities to vilify them not just as religious fanatics and hucksters in the pay of foreign powers, but as simpletons. One handy story that did the rounds for years was that Ibrahim Bek had conned peasants into believing the imported tractors to be greased with pig fat, and this was why Muslim farmers stuck to their ox-ploughs (the first tractors arrived with neither fuel nor spare parts). Another revealing tale involved a car found on the north bank of the Amu with smashed headlights. The *basmachi*, it was said, had captured it but were so ignorant that they 'believed it to be a creature, and blinded it'.

'It was senseless to remain on Soviet territory,' Ibrahim Bek later dictated to his scribe. 'I had run out of money, men and ammunition. My problems were insurmountable. The only way out was to cross the border into Afghanistan.' On the night of 21 June 1926 Ibrahim Bek and fifty fighters crossed the Amu at Chubek, just as Amir Alim Khan had five years earlier.

He and his *basmachi* at once became caught up by the wider play of ideas and politics unfolding in Asia. The king of Afghanistan, Amanullah, was at that time in a delicate position. He had throughout the 1920s staked his leadership on numerous social reforms – much along the lines of those forced through by Atatürk and, later, Reza Shah of Iran – some at least as ambitious as those beginning on the north side of the Amu. The first modern élite girls' school in Afghanistan had opened as early as 1921, under the patronage of Queen Soraya and the sponsorship of the French – a surviving photograph shows lines of girls in tam-o'-shanters and pleated skirts on a trip to Turkey. As part of his policy of balancing political influences in his country, Amanullah also kept up good relations with Soviet Russia. He accepted a delivery of Russian aeroplanes and had Russian engineers lay telephone lines between Afghanistan's major cities.

In December 1927 Amanullah set about expanding his relations with foreign powers still further and embarked on a world tour. As the first royal progress of its kind since the First World War, it received much attention in the world press. His queen at his side, Amanullah visited India, Egypt, Turkey and Persia. They were fêted in Rome, Paris, Brussels, Bern, Berlin, London and Warsaw. The couple walked through the Grand Hotel in Moscow on a carpet of flowers: a re-creation of an honour once paid to Tsar Nicholas II, organised and paid for by rich Afghan businessmen.

Amanullah returned to Kabul in 1928 to face insurrection on several fronts from long-standing rivals and those who disapproved of his policies – photographs of the unveiled Queen Soraya, snapped in Europe, were already circulating around Kabul. In November, with armed opponents at the gates of the capital, Amanullah escaped Kabul in his Rolls-Royce.

Early in 1929 a Tajik named Habibullah, from the Shamali plain north of Kabul, took the city, and in May Amanullah fled the country. When Pashtun forces reclaimed the throne in October, led by Amanullah's cousin, they hanged Habibullah and began a purge against the Tajiks and Uzbeks of northern Afghanistan, including the émigré community.

The Kabul government could not ask the deposed Alim Khan, its guest of necessity, to leave, but it had no place for Ibrahim Bek or his men. Many émigrés decided that life in Afghanistan was no longer safe. Large numbers of Turkmens decamped quietly across the border into Iran, following their leader, Ishan Khalifa. Some Uzbeks and Tajiks decided to chance it in the old country, despite the Soviet presence there. Village by village the émigré households made their way back towards the Amu. On the morning of 30 March 1931 about three thousand families began the crossing under fire from the Afghan side. Only about a thousand made it to the north bank. Soviet troops interned them at Chubek.

Ibrahim Bek and his men followed the civilians. They lasted two months at home before they were captured by local police, who found only two rifles and two pistols on them. Ibrahim Bek was sent to Tashkent, where he was charged with 'armed rebellion and invasion with counter-revolutionary purpose', an article of the Uzbek and Russian criminal codes that sent millions of Soviet citizens to their deaths a few years later. Ibrahim Bek was found guilty. His fifteen friends and companions were shot on 10 August 1932 and their leader three weeks later.

Ibrahim Bek was the last senior *basmachi* commander to be executed. Fazel Maqsum's group had fought its last significant battle at Gharm in April 1929, when the Red Army dropped forty parachutists into the little mountain town. The drop – the first ever in Russian military history – founded the Red Army paratroopers. It must also have been an astonishing sight for the Gharmis. Fazel Maqsum was neither captured nor killed, and was thought to have slipped across the border to Afghanistan.

In the years that followed, people whose fathers and brothers had been *basmachi* – or who had fought themselves – said that the *basmachi* had been nothing but thieves and liars all along, with never an honest patriot among them. To say or even think otherwise would have been dangerous. People taught their children to fear the very word *basmachi*, and to believe the article of Soviet faith that all those who had crossed the river to Afghanistan were rich feudal lords who had oppressed the workers. Some parents, hoping to protect the new generation still further, never told their younger children that they had relatives on the south side of the Amu.

Alim Khan, the last amir of Bukhara, remained in Kabul for the rest of his life. He was never able to provide much help to the *basmachi*; in practice, most field commanders seem to have made their own local deals for weapons, food and men. His appeals to the British for arms merely handed the Soviets a useful stick – 'spies' – with which to beat their opponents. An honoured and protected guest, Alim Khan was also effectively a captive. His repeated requests for permission to cross India for the Hajj were turned down by the British, who saw him as a potential rallying-point for disaffected Muslims in a part of the world where their own colonial authority was now being challenged repeatedly, and with rising conviction.

Amir Alim Khan lived out his days, surrounded by his retinue, in the Qalah-e Fathullah quarter of Kabul. In later years he railed often against Russians, British and Afghans alike. 'In his last hours, he yelled at us to fight for Bukhara, to stand firm,' recalls a member of his household, then a young girl, who saw and heard the frame of his mind collapse at the end. Alim Khan died in 1946 and was buried in Kabul, leaving fifteen daughters and thirteen sons who are now scattered throughout the world.

The treasures of the Bukharan emirate had long since been broken up. The exchequer was plundered of its gold and silver, part of which probably ended up in Moscow. According to the British agent, Colonel Bailey, as early as 1917 the amir had borrowed the equivalent of fifteen million pounds sterling, which he sent to banks in London and Paris; the Bolsheviks, Bailey assumed, took the securities. The world price of qaraqul dropped in the early 1920s as bales of fleeces appeared suddenly on the market. Some household treasures ended up in private hands. One sealed basket came to England, passed by the princesses' English governess, Ethelberta Coles, to a Lieutenant Stephen Fox of the Royal Naval Reserve during the evacuation of the Russian nobility from Yalta in April 1919. We know what was inside because Fox left the basket in the strongroom of his local Lloyds bank at Devonport docks, and the manager tried to track down the Amir through the British India Office. The inventory lists silver bowls, cake plates and champagne glasses. The service, for which the Amir never sent, was almost certainly a present from Russia.

The border with Afghanistan was closed abruptly, without warning, one day in 1936, turning Afghan guests at a right-bank wedding party into instant Soviet citizens. One draper and tailor from Balkh happened to be on a business trip on the north bank, fortunately with his wife and baby son. The family never returned to Balkh, and the boy grew up a Soviet Tajik – still living in Dushanbe in 2001. Some Tajiks who had gone on a shopping trip in the south became Afghans. Some families still managed to cross to Afghanistan in the 1940s – to avoid their sons being called up in the Second World War – and even later, but the exodus proper was finished. Much of the right bank became a military zone, guarded by watchtowers and fenced by barbed wire. Fishing boats were forbidden. Kerki boatyard closed down and miles of towpaths disappeared into the desert.

Many of those who fled Central Asia moved on from their first place of sanctuary. Those with money did so straight away. Some got leave from the British authorities to pass into India and founded businesses in Peshawar, Lahore and Karachi, cities of retreat for Central Asians since Mongol times. When what some call the 'Second Partition' took place in 1947, most chose to become citizens of the new country intended for all Muslims: Pakistan. The grandsons of Mir Bahadir Khan, who had travelled from Khujand by way of Kashgar and Ladakh to become the founder of the Rahat Woollen Mill in Rawalpindi, are proud of their roots in Ferghana. Like many of their fellow émigrés they still call themselves Ferghanachi and still marry within the migrant community – a custom that appears stronger among those from Ferghana than elsewhere.

Those who did not want Pakistani nationality moved on again. Some became Indians rather than Pakistanis, by choice, or because they happened to be in Amritsar rather than Lahore at the time. The proprietors of the Samarkand Café on Marine Drive in Bombay are Uzbek to this day.

Very many Turkic-speakers went on to Istanbul, which had early become a centre for émigré intellectuals. The first President of the Bukharan People's Republic, Usman Khuja, settled there, and in 1927 brought out the first émigré newspaper, *Yeni Türkestan* (New Turkestan), in Turkish. Many became citizens and married Turks. Some joined Atatürk's expanding army.

Great numbers of migrants, especially Ferghanachi, took ship for Jeddah. They settled in the cradle of Islam, where British power was disintegrating and Abdul Aziz ibn Saud was reviving the state of his ancestors around the sacred cities of Mecca and Medina. Ferghanachi who settled in what became Saudi Arabia maintained strong links with their scattered fellow-countrymen. As second and third generations took their places in Arab society – at least two became senior army officers – they sent money back to poorer members of the diaspora and so, gradually, brought more and more Ferghanachi to settle on the Arab peninsula along the Red Sea coast.

The majority of migrants – that is, the poor – who went to Afghanistan stayed on where they first landed. Their presence altered the human geography of the country by greatly increasing the

Turkmen, Uzbek and Tajik population of the north. As well as making carpets they found work as silk weavers, coppersmiths and growers of sugar beet. Qunduz in particular was growing fast in the early twentieth century and many Ferghanachi remained there, eventually controlling four trades – tinsmithing, sack-making, ironmongery and *chapan*-sewing.

The migrants replaced the reed shacks that first sheltered them with lasting mud-built houses. They planted farms and gardens. Their children were born Afghans, and two generations later, when times grew unbearably hard in Afghanistan, it was as Afghans that these families eventually again moved on to the nearest places of greater safety, Iran and Pakistan.

Thousands of poor émigré families have stuck together through multiple migrations, making the best of straitened circumstances and building the vigorous, unsentimental lives of survivors who have no leisure to dwell upon the past. Often they have gravitated towards specific cities and city-quarters in their new countries. Rough hanks of red and blue wool hanging from the balconies show where the carpet-making Turkmans live in Campbellpur, near Attock. Tens of thousands of Afghan Tajiks live in the tattered settlement of Suhrab Godh in Karachi, where the port brings in trade and remittances from relatives who have made it to Europe and the United States, where they work as taxi drivers or in pizza parlours and kebab houses.

'I am Abdul Khalil. I am Tajik,' says a confident young man in a sports jacket, coasting in on his red Honda 125 to distribute posters for a *buzkashi* match outside Peshawar. Fluent in Urdu, Persian and Pashtu, with some Uzbek and a little English, Abdul Khalil is unquestionably one who moves with his times, and does business with the world as he finds it. Part of his sense of self, however, is rooted in the litany his father taught him: 'I am the son of Hajji Rais Abdul Bari, son of Maqsum Vali Huja, son of Damulla Zahel. I am from Afghanistan, but our family is from the *par darya*.' He can give directions to the village his great-grandfather left, and the names of people to ask for there.

Abdul Khalil's neighbour Muhammad Sharif is the son of a book-keeper and draper who, arrested 'on suspicion' by the Soviet police, whisked his family across the border when let out for a home visit. 'I am Afghan, and my country is Afghanistan, though my father was Bukharan,' he says. Outside Muhammad Sharif's mud-built house, fourth-generation Afghan–Turkmen and Afghan–Uzbek girls play in the dust, their frocks tied with silver amulets against bad luck. Like very many families, his chose to maximise their chances of survival by dividing. 'My father was one of six brothers. Five of them crossed together. One stayed behind. I heard his sons joined the Russians,' Muhammad Sharif said. 'I have no idea what became of them.'

3

The world turned upside-down

'Every market lounger in the garb of iniquity has become an
emir; every hireling has become a minister, every knave a vizier
and every unfortunate a secretary . . . every rogue a deputy
treasurer and every boor a minister of state; every stable-boy the
lord of dignity and honour and every carpet-spreader a person
of consequence; every cruel man a competent man, every
nobody a somebody, every churl a chief, every traitor a mighty
lord and every valet a learned scholar . . .'

HINDUSTANI HAD HIS photograph taken in the late 1920s. It shows
an austere face beneath a plain white turban. There are no
props, no comfortable setting, no braid on his robe. After twenty-five
years spent gaining the kind of qualifications few of his contemporaries could hope to dream of, travelling to countries many had barely
heard of, he had returned to his home village of Chahar Bagh to find
that his achievements were not just useless but a liability. Piece by
piece, the Soviet authorities were dismantling the powers of the religious establishment – the *waqf*, or mosque-held land, the courts based
on the shari'a, the pious foundations and the schools.

Some mullas, adapting quickly to the new rules of survival,
became scribes to local communists who could neither read nor
write. There was a familiar religious ring to some of the communist
proclamations – incomprehensible to Russian-speaking authorities –
issued by some of these men. There were still some jobs for old-
fashioned mullas, however, and Hindustani's former teacher got him
a position at a mosque in a district called Qizil Mehnad, meaning
'Red Labour', in Kokand. It is a sign of how parlous Hindustani's
situation was that the wife he took – very late – was a widow with
two young children. His own family was not in a position to help

much. His two younger brothers, living at the old house with their families, were both peasant farmers. His mother had died the year before.

In 1928/9 the first all-Union Five-Year Plan was set in motion: the blueprint for the 'Second Revolution' that Stalin said would wrench Russia out of the past – 'a hundred years of progress in ten years' – pulling its dominions with it. Under Lenin's New Economic Policy, large institutions like banks had been controlled by the state, but small businesses were allowed to operate privately. In the late 1920s, however, the NEP was wound down, and, the command economy began.

The reverberations of the 'Second Revolution' were quickly felt throughout the Central Asian republics. Countless traders and manufacturers went out of business. The silk-looms and paper-making shops for which Kokand had been famous were closed down and small factories were built. In Bukhara, joiners and carpenters, goldsmiths and leather workers found themselves out of work, as did ferrymen, ostlers and shipwrights the length of the Amu. 'The main difference between now and the old days,' recalls an elderly Bukharan, 'is that before the Soviets came we *made* things. A man was a smith, or a jeweller, and his son would follow him. Or we sold things. After the Soviets came, everyone had to be a factory worker or a *kolkhozchi*. We became peasants.'

Teams of agronomists were despatched to the new republics to create *kolkhozes* and *sovkhozes*, collective farms that were to be the agricultural spine of the Soviet Union. Those sent to the south largely left alone the dangerous and inaccessible mountains of Tajikistan, where they could offer no advance on the tough little oxen, black or the colour of set honey, that dragged wooden ploughs around tiny terraced fields. Instead, they concentrated on expanding the cotton plantations already established on the flatlands. The Tsars had sown the cotton plantations: Stalin made them vast.

To Qader Baba, the 'Nikolai' Russians and the Bolsheviks were much of a muchness. He remembers that his village on the bank of the Amu at Khorezm in southern Uzbekistan received the agronomists equably enough. The old khan (the word for lord in this region) had chiselled more than six gold pieces a year in tax from poor men like his father, and few mourned when Turkmens assassinated him in the bloody chaos of 1918. Each family in the village farmed three to five small plots, mainly of the desert staples, melons and barley. The smallholding fed the family, and the men also had a variety of other jobs. Qader Baba's father was both a tailor and a professional wrestler who performed at festivals and big weddings; Qader grew up to be a bargee, transporting cotton, tobacco, tea and carpets from Khiva to the railhead at Charjui. Houses were scattered far apart, as is usual in artificially irrigated places. Wells were held in common, either within an extended family or between several.

The agronomists sent to this and other villages mainly came because they were made to, but others came in a spirit of passionate altruism, determined to help the poor build a better life. Some were Russian, from Tashkent and even from Moscow, some were Ukrainians, some were Tatars, who as Muslims were thought culturally appropriate to Central Asia. They laboured under great difficulties. Most were reliant on interpreters, nearly all were hastily trained or not at all. Some had learnt what little they knew on the dark, damp farmland of the north and had absolutely no idea how to conjure wheat and melons out of a desert. Nor was it easy to find advice. Many successful local farmers and *mirabs* – the water officers who looked after the delicate irrigation systems – had decamped to Afghanistan or had been sent to Siberia as *bais* – in Russian, *kulaks* – that is, 'rich' peasants, now castigated as enemies of the state.

Despite these problems, the agronomists brought some important changes to village life. Unable to improve local methods through a process of understanding, they remodelled villages along Russian lines, some genuinely believing themselves to be bearers of progress and enlightenment to a 'backward' people, just as the Tsarists had. They pulled down the protective walls of high lanes to 'let in the light' – despite temperatures of 50 centigrade on the plains – and built themselves party headquarters with unscreened windows.

'The Soviets came and took our land and our horses and cows by force,' recalls Qader Baba. 'They knocked down our village, including our seven mosques. They made "streets" and built new houses close together along these streets. This was the *kolkhoz*. They told us to go to the *kolkhoz* and to unite our lands. We did not know what they meant. Those who refused were arrested, so after about a year everyone agreed to move.'

Most villagers tolerated the changes until the final modernising touch was introduced. The poorest men were made to strip the heavy horsehair veils from their wives, who traditionally had stayed inside their family compounds, weaving cotton, making tallow candles and bringing up their large families. Put to work in the fields, they became the first generation of Central Asian women to shoulder two jobs, labourers both at home and on the farm. This unveiling so shocked villagers that some gathered together and attacked the Soviet officials with sticks. The flutter of protest did not last long.

Qader Baba – born in around 1900 – was a grown man at this time and well able to compare the new order with the old. His earliest memory is of the khan processing through his village to check the level of the Amu before the planting season. 'The jesters would come beforehand,' he says. 'They had bells on their wrists so as to warn the people of the khan's approach. They had their kneecaps removed as children to make their special wobbly walk, then the khan would look after them until they were grown up – I suppose it was the fashion then. Then rich, clever people would bring pans of *pilau* and stand at roadside holding them aloft as the khan came through. He had a glittering coat, I remember it sparkling. A riderless horse came behind him. He would lean from his horse and take a little from each *pilau*.'

The khan's authority, Qader remembers, was total. 'He would hang you or shoot you if your crime was big or beat you with a stick and imprison you and shackle your legs. I remember them binding three planks together to make a gallows, hoisting the criminal on a cart and taking him around the city for all to see before they hanged him. The bazaar was full of his officers, I remember. And after he went, it did not change much. We were still afraid of the lord of the land – *obkom*, they called him. Before, they forced us to the mosque. Then they forced us not to go. If they say "hang!" we will be hanged, if he says "beat!" we will be beaten. He is the shepherd, we are the sheep. What should we do? Use guns?'*

The insecurity of the times dislocated thousands of people's lives, regardless of their political views. Ikrama, the daughter of the court

* This interview was conducted by Adiba Atayeva of the BBC Uzbek Service in 1999

scribe of Shahr-e Sabz, was about twenty at this critical period. She could read and write, and was a woman of some substance. Her adult life had begun in the old world, when she was about thirteen and her parents took her to a strange house and left her there. When a 'big naked man' came into the room, Ikrama took fright and escaped to the stream, where she spent a peaceful day fishing with her little brother. Only when the man's mother fetched her back was Ikrama made to understand that she had become a married woman, and was expected to stay. She grew fond of her husband, and eventually bore him a dearly-loved son who died when he was five years old.

The new world arrived violently in Shahr-e Sabz. As a married woman Ikrama did not go outdoors, but she had the evidence of her ears. She heard shots from the main square near her father's old house – five to ten every day, she recalled – and men's voices cursing the infidels in the only private place they had left: the wash-house behind the mosque.

'Then a friend of my husband's came to our house as a guest. He had become the police chief. He had dinner and left. Then he denounced my husband as a *kulak* and had him sent to Siberia. He confiscated the house. I had nothing, and nowhere to go. So when he offered to help me, I went to his house. He raped me, and so I became his wife. He was a brutal man, and all four of us wives hated him. We used to sit in the house and smoke *kuknor* [opium] in the *chillim* [water-pipe] and talk about how terrible he was. One day he caught us, and beat us all terribly. He caught me by my plait and threw me around and punched me. He could do whatever he liked with us.'

Ikrama was by no means the only woman to be 'redistributed' in this way. The Muslim tradition as interpreted in Central Asia allows a man four wives and as many mistresses as he can support even-handedly; many local men who became communists unveiled their women and sent them out to work, making it possible for them to maintain more. The police chief – who later trained as an agronomist – unveiled Ikrama and put her to work outside. He ended with seven women; another party grandee kept ten. More unusual than Ikrama's situation is the frankness with which she has talked of it. Her hair-raising stories, passed on to her grandson, record the daring of some unveiled women who, with no parental home to return to, actually left their violent husbands and made their own way in life. The eldest of the police chief's wives took her younger daughters and walked out when she saw that her eldest – a fourteen-year-old – was pregnant by him. The girl bore him nine sons altogether: her mother never returned.

Ikrama lived to a ripe age, long enough to think Gorbachev a handsome chap and to shout 'Up the Reds!' at hockey games, which she had learnt enough Russian to follow on television. She earned the name of a hard woman, shocking parish ladies with her blunt language and disregard of humbug. When the police chief finally died, Ilhama caused a scandal by arriving late at the house and, instead of weeping in the proper way, declaring that she hoped he would find no rest until judgement day.

What became of Ikrama's first husband and approximately forty thousand Central Asian '*kulaks*' and 'class enemies' like him is no more recorded than are the fates of the six million or so other Soviet citizens sent into internal exile. Many were sent to Siberia. A great number of Uzbeks were used in the labour gang – half a million strong – deployed on the first gargantuan Soviet construction project, the canal from Lake Onega to the White Sea. The perpetual light of the Arctic Circle summer was an additional, excruciating hardship for Muslim prisoners during *ramazan*, as they could not eat until after the sunset that never came.

Thousands of families who had hung on, wanting to give the Soviet Union a chance, packed up in the late 1920s and the 1930s and followed the earlier émigrés across the Amu. Many were educated people; some had had high hopes of the fall of the dilapidated old regime and the coming of the new. Some had stayed behind as an act of courage, believing that their country needed them and that only cowards run away. Two relatives of Sadr-e Zia – uncles of his small son Muhammadjan – left for Afghanistan in 1929. This pair of brothers had been successful greengrocers in Bukhara, but found life impossible after the demise of the New Economic Policy. The same year, an uncle of Hindustani's new wife set out from Kokand with his young son and crossed the Amu.

The *kolkhoz* experiment was a catastrophe. Famine arrived in Ukraine, southern Russia and Kazakhstan in the winter of 1932/3.

Word of what was going on, particularly in Ukraine, did reach the outside world, mainly through foreign visitors and journalists, and there is no doubt that officials in Moscow and Leningrad knew how desperate the situation had become. But outsiders were forbidden to travel to Central Asia, from where there was no news at all.

'There were great long lines of people queuing for bread in Bukhara, huge lines,' remembered Muhammadjan Shukurov, son of Sadr-e Zia. 'I was about seven and I queued for so long, hoping to get 400 grams of bread for my parents. But when I got to the front they would not give me anything because the bread was only for workers, and my parents were not workers.'

Sadr-e Zia had lost his job at the library when the People's Republic of Bukhara became part of the Uzbek Republic created in 1924, and was living quietly at home, writing and reading. 'We had black tea in the morning and in the evening we ate *piaba* – that is, onions, salt, water and a little oil,' remembers his son. 'Sometimes we had lentils, as they were cheap.' Bukhara was transmogrified from the busy merchant city of 1909. 'I remember empty streets, empty houses. Almost half the city was abandoned. People had sold up and run, to the mountains, to Afghanistan . . . anywhere they could.'

Many of the old families who had stayed on lost the last of their possessions in the early 1930s. Muhammadjan Shukurov tells how workmen wrenched inscribed marble tombs from the graveyards to lay as paving stones, and how men dressed in black went from house to house, confiscating gold 'for factory-building'. When they came to the house of his aunt – Sadr-e Zia's sister – they bundled her bracelets and ear-rings and necklaces together in a tablecloth and took them away. She asked boldly for a receipt, but did not get one.

Outside the major cities, food shortages were even more acute. Ikrama, the new wife of the police chief of Shahr-e Sabz, remembered how the kitchen gardens in the hills, on which every Shahr-e Sabz family depended for survival, were deemed to be 'luxuries' and requisitioned, so that despite her husband's job the family had to rely on the pittance Ikrama could make by working in the bazaar. 'Each morning before work we used to clear the corpses from the streets, usually ten or fifteen,' she said. 'Often they were children, left by their mothers as their strength gave out. The spring was even worse than the winter, because people ate shoots and roots, and then they died. Once I saw a corpse in a tree, someone who had climbed up after leaves.'

Ikrama understood how famine put the whole world out of joint, she said, when a falcon that should have been afraid of humans dropped out of the sky and snatched a scrap of meat from her cupped hands. Starving animals went wild. 'One night I heard what I thought was a dog or cat scratching to get in the house,' she recalled. 'In the morning it was quiet. I opened the door and found a dead man.'

Ikrama's baby son was born while she was baking ('he cracked his head on the floor, but he was all right') and she managed to keep him alive by grinding locusts for flour. A woman in Tashkent related how she caught mountain tortoises and picked out the meat for her children. Like most people, she neither knew nor cared whether it was Stalin or some amir, shah or tsar in power. Many walked, then crawled, then died beside the railway tracks, having gathered there in the muzzy hope that people might throw bread from passing trains. By the summer there were fewer bodies by the wayside, then almost none.

Collectivisation continued despite its terrible beginning. In 1933, about ten years after tractors reached the villages around Moscow, farmers along the Amu received a first delivery of three-wheeled metal contraptions from the north. One farmer remembers that he and the other men brought out all the barren women of the village and circled them around the tractor, assuming that it would bring fertility. The tractors did not transform the land to a cornucopia of grain – very many arrived already broken – but at least the summer of 1933 brought a harvest.

Fear of failed crops, requisition and starvation continued for many years after the great famine of 1932/3. Ilhama's daughter has an early memory of men knocking at the door for an axe to chop up a dead donkey they had found in the street. Only many years later, after the death of Stalin in 1953, did some people find out that they had come through a Union-wide famine in which about seven million people had died: the worst disaster of its kind ever recorded. There was no way most people could have known this at the time. Newspapers were forbidden to report it, no outside aid was allowed in, and even the use of the word 'famine' carried the risk of three to five years in prison – that is, almost certain death.

To many ordinary people, famine became a benchmark by which to measure life. The availability of wheat and fat was the litmus test for the next two generations, and beyond. Famine also became a glass through which to see all subsequent events. Nothing could ever be as bad again. No price was too high to pay for a quiet life in which there was enough flour to keep baking, and no authority more respected than one that could keep the peace and provide.

Being part of the Soviet Union transformed everyday life in all its detail. Geography changed – Central Asia swivelled from being the north-east of the Muslim world and its bridgehead to Russia to being the southern rim on a new map. Aspirations changed – the mulla to the last khan of Khiva retrained as a *kolkhoz* manager. Even the way one named and recorded the world was different. The year 1348 became the year 1929 on the Gregorian calendar (a shift some older people found tiresome all their lives). The rouble came and, later, the kilo and kilometre. Surnames were introduced outside literate, city circles, as they had been in Iran and Turkey. Many country people picked a handy epithet – the surnames Mirza (scribe), Khal (freckle), Yuldash (companion) are all common, as well as Baba (Grandfather), Babakalan (Great-grandfather), and Muslim names, especially Muhammad and Abdullah. People added on the suffix 'ov' or 'ova' (for women), meaning 'of', just as, under the Arabs, they had included 'ibn'.

Muhammadjan Shukurov became one of the first Soviet children of Bukhara. 'I remember when passports came in, and all us children had to have identity papers. Of course, very few of us knew our birthdays, so there was a big commission sent to organise us. An official checked my teeth and felt my arms, and said my birthday was 30 October 1926. I said "No! I know I was born in 1925!" But he wrote it down, and there it was. They changed my surname at the same time. So in five minutes I had a completely new identity.' Looking back over seventy years, Muhammadjan Shukurov laughs.

Muhammadjan learnt to write from left to right in the new Latin alphabet, which he still uses for private notes, introduced in the Central Asian republics as the script of the revolution in 1930, as it was in Atatürk's Turkey. The Arabic or Persian script, the marrow of Muslim learning for twelve hundred years, was banned. At a stroke, the new generation was severed not only from the rest of the Muslim world but from their entire literary canon, from the seventh century onwards. Using the old script became the act of an outlaw, which is one reason why it is impossible to evaluate claims that, until the coming of Soviet secular education, only 2 per cent of Asian Muslims could read. In the tense political atmosphere of the middle 1930s, any hint of adherence to the old could prove dangerous. Anyone with a religious background was at risk, as was anyone in possession of books. Some parents hid their literacy even from their own children. And so another secret joined the others in the family box.

One day in 1932 the police came for the elderly Sadr-e Zia. The charges against him and his wife were never explained. They locked him up in the madrasa in which he had studied as a boy. Muhammadjan Shukurov remembers that the two-storey building was crammed with prisoners. Mothers, grandparents and children like himself, bringing food and clothing for their relatives, filled the main road outside all day long. There was such a noise, he says, of all those people crying and praying. 'Then I remember them coming to tell us that my father had died in the prison. They said it was typhoid fever. We went to wash the body for burial – my mother, my uncle, two neighbours and myself. We had no one but each other. I was eight years old.'

When Muhammadjan Shukurov's mother died the following year of tuberculosis contracted in prison, he became the ward of his uncle, the poet Habibullah Awhadi, with whom he lived.

Hindustani's work at the Qizil Mehnad mosque in Kokand did not last long. 'They called the mullas "the enemy within" and many lost their jobs,' Hindustani's account records. 'I went to prison for a while, and when I got out I took a job in a silk factory.' His position there was precarious. Not only was he a mulla of note but, having lived abroad, he could easily have been fingered as a spy. After a few uneasy months, he took his young family away from Kokand, across the mountains to the town of Angren.

Hindustani's written account records the move with characteristic brevity. The detail comes from his stepson Ubaidullah, who was then about five. 'We set off on two donkeys and a horse, my mother, my father, myself and the baby,' he recalled in old age, sitting with his wife beneath the trees in their peaceful garden. 'We were so afraid that my father would be taken and shot. We had a tent made of skins, two plates and a pan, and my mother would bake a little flour in the pan for bread. There was nothing else. Other people ate weeds, and their stomachs swelled and they died. After a week we arrived in Angren, where my father met two friends in the mosque and they gave us a house. It had everything in it but people! Everyone had gone, or was leaving.'

The family moved from house to house during this time. Sometimes they decamped into the mountains, hiding among red rocks glittering with ore (Angren comes from *ahangaran*, meaning iron-workers). Sometimes they stayed with friends. And so Hindustani taught the word of God until 1936, which Ubaidullah remembers as the year his little sister was born.

'Soldiers came to Angren, and my father went away. We stayed behind. One night a man came to us and told us to be ready in the morning and he would take us to a safe place. He put us in a cart and took us to Tashkent. When we got there and saw my father, he said he had had enough. He said that from now on, he would not be a mulla, he would be a peasant like everyone else.'

Hindustani got a job as a cashier in a *kolkhoz*. It was 1937, and the world was changing at astounding speed. More and more young men were wearing the short jackets and narrow trousers of Europeans. The zip-fastened shirt had arrived in Bukhara, where a Gastronomical Co-operative sold tinned food near the Mir-e Arab madrasa. The Red Star film studio was going strong, and Russian girls with permanent waves tittupped to offices in the growing Soviet-built part of town. But Ubaidullah remembers 1937 for other reasons.

He has not forgotten the day the political police came for his father. They also took the family books, Hindustani's writings on the poet Bi-del and some medicines he had learnt to make in India. He was denounced as a religious agitator and sentenced to four years in a prison camp. For a while his wife and children took him food and clothes: but one day he was gone.

Hindustani was sent to Sverdlovsk, on the edge of the Urals, and set to work as a logger. Few prisoners survived more than two years in the timber camps, but Hindustani, his family says, was saved because something he had learnt in India at last came in useful in the new world. The guards, spotting his skill at chess, took him off the labour-gang to coach them. These respites made Sverdlovsk survivable. After a year, however, there came news that Hindustani was to be transferred.

It took sixty days to cross Russia by wagon to Tygda, a desolate spot across the river Amur from where north-east Mongolia meets the Russian Far East. Tygda was a hard-labour camp, and Hindustani was put to work making railway sleepers for a branch of the Trans-Siberian railway. There are not many accounts of what became of the relatively few Asian prisoners at Tygda, though one Russian survivor recorded with horror how the Muslims of the hot, dry south keeled over 'like dolls' in the cold. Most of them understood little Russian. When they were taken to hospital, modesty prevented them from undressing for the doctors. When prison guards yelled orders and beat them, they were silent. Very few came home from Tygda: of those who did, many were ill and died shortly afterwards. Hindustani's wife and children heard no news.

Faizullah Khujayev, wool-merchant's son, leader of the revolutionary committee in Bukhara and first President of Uzbekistan, fell in Stalin's purges of 1937. He was accused of having buried his brother according to Islamic rites, and charged with having nationalist tendencies. Sceptics said his luck ran out with his gold. Khujayev was among those convicted in the famous Moscow show-trial at which Bukharin made his last appearance, and went to the wall in 1938.

That same year, some Turkmens crossed the Amu and made for Bukhara with a package for Muhammadjan Shukurov's guardian Habibullah Awhadi. Inside was a letter from the poet's two greengrocer brothers who had despaired of doing business at home after the end of the NEP and left for Afghanistan almost ten years before. Life on the other side was good, they said, and they encouraged

Awhadi to join them. 'My uncle said he would not go. He had always been a reformer, and had done many good things for Bukhara. He said he had nothing to fear,' remembers Muhammadjan Shukurov. The police took Awhadi anyway: his offence was to have opened the letter.

Awhadi died in prison in Siberia. There was no one else left in Bukhara to look after Muhammadjan Shukurov. A grown-up cousin, however, agreed take him; she had lately left the city for the mountainous new republic of Tajikistan. Many Persian-speaking families from Bukhara, Samarkand and other broken old cities were packing up and doing the same. Most had lost fathers or mothers, brothers or sons, in prison, starved, vanished to the camps, or in exile beyond the Amu. There has never been a day of reckoning, and people could only judge the scale of what befell them in the early Soviet years by counting the gaps in their own family or street. The poet Aini, Sadr-e Zia's protégé, thrown into prison by the last Amir of Bukhara, Alim Khan, wrote that of his own circle of twenty-eight, four were killed outright by the Amir, ten by the Soviets and eight beaten up and imprisoned. Some people have hazarded a figure of one in eight Bukharans missing during the early Soviet years, but it is impossible to say for sure.

Tajikistan seemed like a good place to start life again. In 1939 Muhammadjan Shukurov, aged fourteen, found himself heading out of Bukhara for the first time in his life, bound for the town of Dushanbe.

4

A town called Monday

'And that winter was long-drawn-out and the chill of the air
and the violence of the cold were such that all of the climes
were like "the lands of snow"... and all the forces in that
region, whether Turks or Tajiks, put themselves in readiness.'

M UHAMMADJAN SHUKUROV arrived in Dushanbe to find a fresh
partly-built town set in a half-circle of mountains between the
Zarafshan range and the Pamir. Elegant pale yellow and blue stuccoed buildings stood along the one made road, Prospekt Lenina. The
tilting streets behind, cobbled with mountain stones, gave on to small
mud-built houses with apricot and pomegranate trees in even smaller
courtyards. River water rushed through the *ariqs*, the canals on either
side. The air was clean and the water sweet.

Food was a little more plentiful than it had been in Bukhara and
the incomers were able to cook most of the dishes they had known at
home. Each morning, Muhammadjan Shukurov and his aunt drank
chai sher, tea with hot milk, butter, powdered walnuts and pepper.
'After the dust of Bukhara, Dushanbe was green and full of trees and
flowers,' Muhammadjan Shukurov remembers. 'I suppose it was provincial, but I did not feel it to be so.'

'Dushanbe' means 'Monday', and probably comes from a weekly
market held at this modest, natural trading point between the Afghan
border and Bukhara. Weavers, tanners and iron-workers lived there
in the nineteenth century, when the village was part of the Bukharan

bekship of Hisar. When they were pressing on into the outposts of the emirate in the spring of 1921 the Bolsheviks had counted 3,140 inhabitants; by the time they secured control, there were only about three hundred. Dushanbe seemed a perfect site for the capital of Tajikistan. It was just about well-placed enough to control the mountain territories, in so far as that was possible. Best of all, it was a clean canvas: Dushanbe, the boast went, would be the first city in Muslim Asia without a mosque.

New Dushanbe was conceived in the Bauhaus manner, as the curved cinema building opposite the Post Office on Prospekt Lenina shows. It was designed by a couple named Adler, German architects who came to Tajikistan full of enthusiasm to help build communism. Later plans were tamer, but numerous original and handsome neo-classical buildings rose against the mountain backdrop, elegantly painted, with columns and friezes picked out in white. Telegraph wires marched along the roads, and the Russian officers' hotel had lights powered by the new electricity plant. The effort and expense involved were enormous. Local building materials – mud and straw – were not used. Poplar wood was too soft to support buildings on a grand scale, and gnarled juniper unsuitable. Each pane of glass, each nail, even timber, was procured elsewhere in the Union, packed into trains and freighted often thousands of miles to the railhead at Termez. Here everything was strapped to camels and hauled along the last leg to Dushanbe over roads so rough that each plank report-edly lost a yard in length, and so dangerous that Red Army guards rode alongside for fear of attacks by bandits. Food, tools and disman-tled machinery came the same way.

The city grew in leaps and bounds. In 1924 there were two cars in all Tajikistan – the year the first school primer in Tajik came out. In 1925 the first edition of the newspaper *Eid-e Tajik* (Tajik Holiday) rolled off the first printing press, and was delivered on horseback along Prospekt Lenina. Two years later the first documentary film was shot in Dushanbe. It records some interesting details of life at this important turn of history. The shaky scene is of an ordinary bazaar – men are selling grapes and melons, a blacksmith is shoeing a horse and a *darvish*, a pious indigent, begs for alms. But there is already one figure dressed in the European-style short shirt and narrow trousers that gradually became standard wear for the modern young man.

In 1929 crowds lined the brand-new railway track (every sleeper dragged from a Siberian forest) to see the first train, driven by an Armenian, steam into brand-new Dushanbe station. That year Tajikistan gained the status of a Soviet Socialist Republic separate from Uzbekistan. As Dushanbe – renamed Stalinabad to mark the occasion – was still very small and the republic both weak and unstable, adjustments were made to the Central Asian borders. The old city of Khujand in the Ferghana valley was taken away from Uzbekistan and added to Tajik territory. Khujand – renamed Leninabad – was far more urban and richer than the rest of Tajikistan and, as an early Russian conquest, had a few factories and made roads. The inclusion of Khujand made Tajikistan just about viable economically. It also made sure that Tajikistan stayed, if not under, close to the thumb of Tashkent. Khujand was connected to the Tajik mainland only by a tenuous track over the 3,372-metre pass at Anzab: a ride of several days in summer, and impossible in winter. A made road ran the much shorter drive – only sixty miles – between Khujand and Tashkent, however, thus reinforcing the link between the Uzbek capital and Dushanbe.

Half an hour's ride beyond the capital the scene was very different. 'Houses and other buildings are destroyed and ruined. Walls are levelled to the ground . . . Fields, gardens and melon patches are full of weeds and fallow,' noted a Soviet committee sent to make an assessment in the countryside in the 1920s, and the 1930s brought little improvement. In the highlands and on the plains between Dushanbe and the Amu, whole villages had been deserted. Around one house in two stood empty in the old market town of Qurghan Tappa; fifty villages around it were abandoned. Little more than fourteen thousand people lived in the town of Fakhrabad; there had been thirty-five thousand before the revolution. Irrigation canals had been destroyed, and the amount of land under cultivation was half what it had been. As much as a third of the population of the plains had disappeared; of these, Soviet accounts estimate, about half had gone to Afghanistan and half had been killed. Few parts of Central Asia had been hit so hard by the establishment of communism.

In rural Tajikistan, the shadow of the *basmachi* wars lingered on far longer than it did elsewhere. Years after the execution of Ibrahim Bek in 1932, parts of the mountains were thought unsafe for travellers. The republic had a reputation for being lawless and unruly that it never wholly shook off. Not surprisingly, considering the level of destruction and insecurity, it also had a name for backwardness, and for only superficial loyalty to the USSR.

Muhammadjan Shukurov enrolled at the handsome new Pedagogical Institute in Dushanbe as soon as it opened in 1941. The young teachers were mainly Persian-speaking Bukharans, and the class also rapidly acquired Russian, as the new language of advancement. They learnt the Cyrillic script that replaced the Latin in 1940: the second alphabet change in a decade. Students studied Maxim Gorky and other big names in the new Soviet literature, as well as the transcribed writers of their forefathers. Some boys came to school in Russian-style clothes. 'We were not trying to be modern,' Muhammadjan Shukurov said. 'We dressed in what we could get.'

Soviet officers combed the mountain villages for the brightest and best children and brought them down to Dushanbe, where they were given free schooling and warm clothes. These hand-picked children were intended to become the modern men and women of the future: secular teachers, doctors of a new type of medicine, lawyers who knew nothing of the shari'a, people as avant-garde as the city they were to live and work in. Some village boys who heard about the opportunities on offer made the journey from the mountains themselves. Other eager pupils in the early Soviet classrooms were the many orphans left by the wars – it was from the orphanages that the first leaders of the Tajik Young Pioneers (the communist children's organisation) were recruited.

When Muhammadjan Shukurov came to class for the autumn term of 1941, there were already gaps in the ranks of teachers and older students. In the small hours of 22 June German forces had launched a huge multiple assault on the western Soviet Union. Before dawn broke, Minsk, Kiev and Sevastapol were all under attack from the air. Until the bombs actually fell, Stalin had believed in his pact with Hitler: Operation Barbarossa brought the USSR into the Second World War.

Far away in Dushanbe, Muhammadjan Shukurov and his friends heard anxiously of the rapid German advance. 'Every morning we listened to Moscow Radio for news from the front. We understood clearly what was happening. We were very patriotic.'

It was a grim winter. Leningrad was surrounded; Ukraine fell, and the march on Moscow began. The Soviet government decamped. The embalmed body of Lenin was quietly removed to safety on a special refrigerated train. Muscovites in their thousands abandoned their homes, and a state of siege was declared. The most remote Soviet-allied peoples joined in the defence of the capital. When Mongolian cavalry rode at advancing Germans across an open snowfield, two thousand were wiped out by machine-gun fire. Not one German was killed.

'It was very, very cold and the snow fell and fell. In November my shoes split,' remembers Muhammadjan Shukurov. 'There were some clothes and shoes in the bazaar, but they were terribly expensive because of the war. So I wrapped my shoes in rags and bound them with string, and went to class as early as possible and sat at the furthest corner and didn't go out at break. But my teacher Abdughani Mirzayev saw under the table and called me out and asked about my shoes. I said I had not had time to buy new ones. He looked at me.

'"Who is your father?"

'"I have no father."

'"Who is your mother?"

'"I have no mother."

'Abdughani Mirzayev told the director about my condition, and he ordered up clothes for me: a warm coat padded with cotton, and boots. They were big, fine soldier's boots and I wore them for four years! The next day when I went to class all the boys were teasing. "Look at you! What happened? Did you get married or something?"

'It was desperately cold in Russia too. The Germans were at the gates of Moscow, but because of the desperate cold they were stuck, so that was good news.' On 5 December 1941, in deep snow, the Red Army began to fight back.

Returning to college after the winter holidays, Muhammadjan Shukurov found that Abdughani Mirzayev had been called up. Like many educated Tajiks, the Persian-speakers of the Soviet Union, he was sent to interpret in Iran, which had been invaded by Soviet and British forces in August 1941 to secure an allied base in the east. The Trans-Iranian railway – the Persian Corridor – running between the

Gulf and the foothills of the Caucasus was a lifeline for desperate Soviet troops. Along it travelled vast amounts of supplies, especially radio equipment, Studebaker trucks, boots, belts, wheat, corned beef from Chicago and tinned pork – 'Spam'. The route was far less risky than the sea convoys to Archangel in the Arctic. The Tajiks' unique contribution to the war effort was to help keep the Corridor open.

Other young teachers from the Pedagogical Institute went to fight, and the literature class dwindled. Still tuning in to the news every morning, the remaining students grew ever closer. They were much impressed with one of their professors, Abbas Aliev, a big, handsome Bukharan in modern clothes. His lectures were so popular that students typed them up and spread them from class to class.

Aliev proved wonderfully diverting in the bleak days of 1942. Instead of discussing the front-line news and politics, he enjoyed the film then playing in the cinema hall over the new Aini theatre: *The Three Musketeers*. 'We loved it, and Abbas loved it. Every day he sent a student to buy the tickets for the four o'clock show, and seven or eight of us went with him. For a month, maybe two, we went! We knew all the moves and the words, and we could act out whole scenes.' Aliev, who had spent time in prison in the 1930s, never mentioned communism or ideological matters. He barely even mentioned the war. 'There was only one battle about which he said, that was a good victory for the USSR. I think that was the first and last time he mentioned it.' The battle was Stalingrad.

Hindustani of Kokand did not die in the labour camp in Tygda, but finished his sentence and in 1941 returned to Kokand, where he took a humble job in a cooking-oil factory. All around him, great numbers of men were working on the home front. Two days after the USSR entered the war, a tremendous operation began to save those Soviet industries that lay in the path of the German advance – that is, in the most developed part of the Union. Almost three thousand industrial complexes had been dismantled down to the bolts, packed on to trains, and reassembled in Siberia, the Urals, Kazakhstan and Central Asia by the middle of 1942. Most of those transplanted to Central Asia went to Uzbekistan, mainly because it was relatively close, the land was flat, and the railway system, though limited, much more extensive than that of Tajikistan.

More than twenty-five million workers and their families came with the factories, including significant numbers to Uzbekistan. Many were billeted with local people – that was how many Uzbeks encountered Russian women and children for the first time, and how countless Russian civilians first set eyes on Central Asians. The many labouring jobs provided by the industries drew in thousands of farmers from the villages, and new Uzbek-inhabited suburbs spread out around several towns, especially Tashkent. The coming of the Ilyushin aircraft factory to Tashkent gave the city a renewed power and prestige that lasted into peace time. Munitions works, especially the parachute factory, and the mines at Kentau ('We dug the lead for every bullet fired at Stalingrad') in southern Kazakhstan, transformed the landscape. Coal and oil extraction were developed to fuel new industries, and the first big electricity plants opened. Chests greased with mutton-fat against the cold, Uzbek boys swam a river with components for the Farhad power station south of Tashkent. They became an abiding image of human endeavour.

Uzbeks were also called upon to house great numbers of evacuees, especially orphans from Ukraine who were sent to Tashkent. They took in many thousands of Polish families too. Stalin had sent about two million Polish citizens to prison camps and special labour zones following the division of Poland in accordance with the Molotov–Ribbentrop pact of 1939. In the desperate year of 1942, however, he granted an amnesty to those Poles who were not Jewish or Ukrainian – those remained in the camps – and offered them free passage out of the USSR. They were directed south to Iran to join General Władysław Anders, a Russian-born Pole who had been released from Lubianka specifically to form a Polish unit to fight against the Germans.

Hundreds of thousands of Poles from camps in the Arctic circle, Siberia, the Urals and Kazakhstan began to make their way south towards Uzbekistan. An aristocrat, Anna Mineyko, arrested in the middle of lunch at her country house at Brzostowica, had watched Red Army soldiers throw Dürers and Rubenses into waiting lorries before they took her away in a muck cart ('As we passed, people made the sign of the cross in the air . . .'). After three years making clay bricks in a hard-labour camp in Kazakhstan, Anna got away by giving her daughter's hair ribbon, two sheets and a hundred roubles to a nomad in exchange for a ride in an ox-cart across the steppe to a made road. (No Kazakh would buy the pearl earrings she had treasured, as they had no colour and therefore no worth.)

Three weeks later, on 24 July, Anna, her mother and her children arrived at the mustering point of Yang-e Yul, south of Tashkent, where they met General Anders and heard Mass under a blazing sun. The Poles boarded with local families, who remember them with much affection. Many worked in the *kolkhozes*, and kept alive by stealing potatoes. The heat and the unfamiliar environment were often too much for those weakened by years in the camps.

Jan Sulkowski, a Polish accountant, wrote to his family from an invalid's home in Uzbekistan before moving on to Iran.

July, 1942
Bukhara, USSR

Beloved!

I feel an urgent need for contact with you – I really haven't received anything from you except the telegrams which are full of worry and a stranger's words. Don't expect to get my letter too quickly as communication between us is far and difficult. The impossibility of a quick reunion terrifies me – if the time comes when we can be united, a very long journey awaits you. The trip will be very traumatic and there's no knowing what we'll live on – maybe from the sale of your remaining bits and pieces. I can't think calmly, not knowing where Janka is – it's beyond us to settle this question . . .

I usually rise at five in the morning and buy myself some milk, which I have with bread. Dinner consists of a litre of water with dumplings, or sometimes watery soup, and donkey meat, which can be tasty if the animal is young, otherwise it's a bit tough. Yesterday I ate a cucumber and grapes for the first time (but carefully). So far I haven't tried an *uruk*, which is an apricot. I tried to buy some eggs, but they're too expensive.

They promised me new clothes in a few days (American gifts) but what I'll get I don't know.

The heatwaves are awful – which terribly affects us, who are unacclimatized, and most of whom also have dysentery. Children are dying like flies. The little cemetery near our nursery is growing daily: twenty-two new crosses since the middle of April, not counting those who died in hospital, about a dozen. Usually the process is as follows: the child returns from the hospital after being 'cured' of dysentery, and dies after two or three days. It simply extinguishes itself as it grows weaker and weaker by the hour, until there's just a corpse. With adults it's not much better – there are no medicines, no proper nourishment (a complete lack of animal fat and protein).

Impatiently I await your letters – to find out what's going on! Big, big kisses for all of you,

Your Father.

More than a hundred thousand Poles made it to the Caspian coast and sailed from Krasnavodsk to the Iranian port of Bandar-e Pahlavi. 'We raced down to meet them,' remembers an elderly fisherman at the jetty, then a ten-year-old, 'with milk, bread and eggs, but a lot of them were too ill to eat. The British marched them up to the bath-house. They burnt their clothes and shaved their heads and put them in camps.' Scores died there as the Christian graveyard near the harbour shows. Surviving civilians were moved on: thirteen thousand Polish children grew up in special boarding schools in Isfahan alone. Many grew up to marry Iranians – often Armenians or other Christians – and learnt Persian. They opened pastry shops and introduced the *piroshki* dumpling to Iran, where it is still popular though few post-revolutionary Iranians know its origins. In 2001 there were still twenty or thirty Polish survivors, almost all grandmothers, living in Teheran. 'Of course it's nice to visit Poland,' said one, Henrika, who crossed Uzbekistan as a fourteen-year-old, 'but Iran is home now.'

The Polish military continued their odyssey, travelling with the British Army to Lebanon, Egypt and British Palestine. Some Jewish Poles who had slipped out with the rest despite Stalin's injunction absconded in Palestine. Among them was Menachem Begin, son of a tsarist timber merchant from Brest-Litovsk, who went on to become the Prime Minister of Israel.

Some Tajik and Uzbek farm boys from the most remote places were selected to serve in the élite corps of the Soviet Army. 'Salam from Grozny!' begins Rahmatullah Azimov's letter home to Kulab, on the Tajik–Afghan border, in 1942. Written on a long narrow strip of wrapping paper, the letter is carefully decorated with turquoise and pink ornamental capitals.

To my brother, sisters and friends!

I am in the North Caucasus, in Chechnya at the flying school. I am learning a lot here and I'm fine, my health is good. How is the weather at home? I miss you all so much, I miss my country, my son and the warm weather. Every week I write two or three letters to you, but perhaps you're not getting them. In any case, I am getting none from you. Please say hello to all my friends and – brother dear – do not send boots for me as I've got some.

I don't know when this training will finish – perhaps I'll be away another six months or so. Then we must go to the war, to the front. But don't worry, everything will be fine.

Please send my best regards to all. I've made this letter especially beautiful for you – which is hard because one can't find paper or ink! When I began at the school here I bought a pen. It cost me twenty sums and I still have it safely.

Your loving little brother.

Azimov was sent to fight soon afterwards. His plane was shot down over the Barents Sea and he never came home. He was probably about twenty-two, young enough to write in Cyrillic – many Central Asian letters home from the war are in Latin script – and young enough to have sent his family a little drawing of a plane with 'Hello!' across the wings.

Many Central Asians went to the front to serve behind the lines, digging trenches, cooking and carrying supplies – at least in the early stages of the war. There was a reluctance to use many Uzbeks and Tajiks, especially those from the countryside, as combat troops – partly because of language difficulties, but also because the Red Army had not been restructured to take into account the diversity of the Soviet Union. The officer corps was almost entirely Russian, or drawn from other Slav groups. However, after the catastrophic loss of Soviet life between 1941 and 1943, far greater numbers of Central Asians were called to fight. There were still loopholes in the border with Afghanistan, and a few young men determined to escape conscription managed to reach the Amu, where they hid in caves until they could slip out of the Soviet Union. The majority were called up, and shepherds, factory workers and farmers left in their thousands for the front.

One farmer, a boy of thirteen at the time, remembers the warning shout of '*Kafer! Kafer!*' as the conscription officers swept into his mountain village. 'The soldiers closed the bazaar and rounded up the men. One managed to run away, and they shot him. There was another with no understanding of the war. He just knew he was meant to fight for the *kafer*. He went off. Then his family got the black letter, the one they send when the boy is killed.'

Many, probably most, of these conscripts had never before seen a laced boot or a modern gun, let alone a tank. Some felt utterly degraded by having to eat the impure food in the army rations, like the Spam which reached them from America by way of the Persian Corridor. A few absolutely refused to do so. The urgency of the military situation meant that training officers were forced to cut corners. One month of training, sometimes none at all, instead of the stipulated six, was even less effective because many recruits did not properly understand the language in which orders were given. There was no time to teach them Russian before sending them to fight, and no time for them to practise using their weapons. Some Central Asian conscripts blew themselves up with their guns. Many lost their hearing. Russian contemporaries remember how air-raids in particular seemed to disorient the Central Asians. One soldier was aghast to see a row of poorly dressed Turkmens, straight from desert temperatures of 50 centigrade, collapse from their horses into the snow.

After the famous Soviet victory at Kursk in the summer of 1943, the news on the radio began to seem a little less terrible: the Germans had lost much ground, and many men. The expanded Red Army pressed on towards the western territories lost at the start of the war. Hindustani, by then an elder of fifty, was conscripted into the labour gangs formed to do the jobs left by those who went to fight. 'I was sent to Kazakhstan, to Semipalatinsk,' he recalled later. 'The wheat was ripe, but all the men were gone. There were only women. We harvested the wheat, and the hay for the animals, and in the autumn we returned to the city.' In November, the Red Army regained Kiev in triumph. Only one Soviet capital was still in German hands – Minsk, in Belorussia. Without warning and without any instruction at all, Hindustani found himself on a train heading west.

None of the men involved in the campaign to regain Minsk were told where they were going. Even the train drivers were given only the number of the engine they were to operate. The plans for the advance were so secret that only five Red Army officers knew their whole scope, and they were forbidden to communicate with each other. Radio stations were closed down. Dummy armies complete with fake tank bases were sent to the north and to the south. The real Soviet forces attacked in late June 1944. Hindustani of Kokand was among them.

'We arrived at Minsk and very soon afterwards the Germans attacked us. It was heavy fighting and some of us were killed straight away. Others were wounded, and I was shot in the arm. I was put in hospital, and a week later they collected all the wounded soldiers and put them on the train to Moscow.' The bullet that passed between Hindustani's wrist bones may have saved his life.

Hindustani might have played a part in the successful battle for Minsk, but he was still counted as an enemy of the Soviet people. After several months of recuperation he was sent to Kemerovo, an 'extreme' labour camp in the Russian Far East, where he was put to work as a shepherd in charge of a flock of five hundred. As a life-long pacifist, he thanked God for allowing him to go to the camp. 'I loved the sheep and cared for them,' he wrote later. 'They always came when I called them. Being a shepherd teaches mercy. I used to take them into the woods, and while they grazed I would recite the Quran to myself, all the way through every three days. Of course I had no books at Kemerovo, and I was all alone, but I knew the scriptures by heart.' Hindustani made such a good shepherd that he was rewarded with a coat, fifty roubles and a small plot of land to grow potatoes on. Each day the cowherds gave the shepherds a basin of milk, and so Hindustani lived out the remaining months of the war in Kemerovo, on a diet of potatoes and milk.

Meanwhile, in Central Asia, the military introduced in semi-secret a measure inconceivable at any other time. They had already called up the men, even to the elderly mullas in the labour camps. But still more troops were needed, so in the spring of 1945 a number of Muslim women were taken into the mountains, 'to a place where the *basmachi* once had their camp. We learnt how to take cover, how to strip a gun, and fire and so forth. Only very modern women went,' one remembered. 'Our husbands were away at the front, or missing somewhere.' Training went on from March to May, but the women never had to use their skills. In the early hours of 9 May 1945, victory was announced in Moscow. Crowds filled Red Square and the streets around. A million people pressed into the capital, then two million, perhaps three. Evening fell, and a thousand-gun salute boomed out.

By the time the European war was over, a quarter of a million Tajiks and perhaps two and a half million Uzbeks had served at the front. Figures can never be accurate, but official records indicate that approximately three hundred thousand were killed or never returned: that is, about one in nine servicemen, and one in twenty-four of the population – a rather smaller proportion than the national average. Soviet Central Asia was never bombed, so nearly all the casualties were military rather than civilian.

One remarkable and almost forgotten role the Central Asians had in the war was that played by the Turkestan Legion – a special Muslim unit of the German army. The legion was founded in Berlin by two Central Asian nationalists from the Ferghana valley, Vali Qayum Khan, who had been sent to Germany to study before the war, by the Soviet authorities, and Mustafa Chaqai Bek, who had headed the short-lived autonomous government of Turkestan in Kokand from 1917 to 1918 and lived in exile in France for many years.

The Legion, said to have numbered about two hundred thousand, recruited from the great numbers of Central Asians taken prisoner by the Germans. Many chose to join rather than take the greater risk of staying in detention camps, where many, especially Uzbeks, were apparently mistaken for Jews because of their colouring and because they were circumcised. Agents also recruited among the Uzbeks and Tajiks of the north of neutral Afghanistan. Large numbers of families who had emigrated across the river Amu in the 1920s and 1930s were consequently moved away from the border regions to the central province of Baghlan. (Agents tried at the same time to aggravate grievances among the Pashtuns of Afghanistan, their object being to tie down the British at the gate of India while simultaneously undermining the USSR on the border of what both the Germans and many Russians believed to be potentially disloyal peoples.)

The Legion did not fight on the Soviet front, but it did take part in German campaigns in Italy, Greece and North Africa (as the Uzbek and Tajik graves there show) and its soldiers also served behind the front lines, as dog-handlers, guards and cooks at concentration camps.

Baimirza Hayit of Namangan, a young Uzbek captured early in the war, became prominent in the Legion and its chief recorder and historian. He stayed on in Germany, as did Vali Qayum Khan, who preserved a personal photograph collection documenting the lives of the young men he knew. Some show them at prayers, with their mullas (some Central Asian, some Turkish, some specially trained in madrasas in Dresden and Göttingen) facing lines of young men kneeling piously in uniform – standard German military dress with a crescent moon on the collar. Others capture more private moments – an acrobatics competition outside some wooden huts, a boy playing a trumpet, a game of backgammon. Very few, possibly none, of the people in the pictures ever went home.

Norman Lewis, a British officer who later went on to fame as a travel writer, crossed paths with one group of 'collaborators' in 1944, when he was given the task of escorting three thousand Tajik Turkestan Legion prisoners by ship to the Iranian Gulf port of Khorramshahr, whence they were to be delivered back into Soviet hands. Although the Tajiks had been wearing German uniforms when they surrendered to the British, their officer told Lewis that, at the last minute, they had turned on the Germans and attacked them. During their ten-day voyage together, Lewis enjoyed the company of the Tajiks. 'Every day was a party,' he remembered. The Tajiks composed poetry, and turned zinc water bottles, mess cans, toothbrushes and combs into stringed instruments and drums. Gas capes and camouflage webbing became costumes for Tajik theatre, and so the prisoners played and sang their way to the dock at Khorramshahr. Lewis saw the Tajiks put into cattle trucks on a rainy day in the marshalling yard. He was certain they were being taken away to their deaths.

Most Tajik and Uzbek servicemen returned home, however, and many became great Soviet patriots. They were among the first Central Asians, outside a tiny élite, to see anything of the Soviet Union beyond their own republics. They had met and fought alongside men of other Soviet nationalities, Muslim and Christian together, and made friends among them. Of necessity, they had learnt Russian. 'We called the Russians "pigs" and they called us "sheep",' one man recalled. 'But the front was the front and life was the same, really, for everybody.'

It was the common cause of war that cemented the Central Asians into the Soviet Union, rather than the Agitprop films that local communists were supposed to drive from village to village in the post-war campaign to increase political education – most of these films were quietly dumped in any case, in favour of thrillers from which the showmen could make a few illicit kopeks on the side. The Tajiks won fifty thousand military and civilian decorations, and were praised for contributing horses, sheepskins, butter and jam to the war effort. Safar Amirshayev, of the village of Zargar in Kulab, who single-handedly blew up two tanks in the battle of Kharkov, had a street in Dushanbe named after him.

The much-respected and even loved republican leader, Babajan Ghafurov, went to Moscow and personally talked Stalin into declaring an amnesty for the remaining *basmachi* and their families, some of whom had fought bravely for the Soviet Union. A huge metal 'V' for victory, known locally as 'Donkey Ears', was erected in Dushanbe to mark the contribution of the village-turned-capital.

The post-war period brought a shift in fortune for Hindustani and his family. His release from the labour camp in 1946 coincided with the coming to fruition of an important political decision taken some years earlier. During the dark days of the German offensive, Stalin had permitted the opening of some Orthodox churches and the limited celebration of Mass. The carefully-vetted priests used the pulpit to raise money for the war effort and even blessed tanks on their way from the factory to the front. Having permitted the public expression of their faith to Orthodox Christians, Stalin also allowed the restoration of some mosques. Muslim practice in all the Central Asian republics and in Kazakhstan was put under the control of the Tashkent administration, Moscow's main regional partner.

In 1943 the first 'Red' Mufti opened his offices at the Barak Khan madrasa in the heart of old Tashkent. Ishan Ziahuddin Babakhanov was a sufi from the Ferghana valley (his son and then his grandson succeeded him, and the job was thus kept in one family until the last days of the Soviet Union). Babakhanov and his Red mullas soon proved their worth by drawing sackfuls of money and food from their congregations for the war effort. In 1945, for the first time since the revolution, a few carefully selected believers were allowed to go on hajj. The Red Muftiat was accorded only limited respect in religious circles, because it was government-run and tainted from the start by its closeness to the secret police. 'The KGB had their people from the top to the bottom of every Red mosque, even to the doormen,' a top official in the Muftiat said much later. It was up to the Muftiat to train mullas and appoint them as it saw fit.

Hindustani was offered a job. It was in Dushanbe, at the Yaqub-e Charkhi mosque, famous for its giant plane trees that were older by far than the city around them (the boast that Dushanbe was to be the first Muslim capital without a mosque proved no more than that). Once he had settled in, Hindustani invited his family to join him. His stepson Ubaidullah, an observant five-year-old when the family first fled Kokand, was now in his early twenties. 'The Kokand we had known was gone. It was all the same to us where we went. We came to Dushanbe. We had a small mud-built house, and we built a little wooden house for summer, too. It seemed like such a nice town. I didn't speak Tajik then, but I learnt soon enough. All the people around us were good Muslims, and the air and the water and the earth were good. We are farmers, we people from Kokand, and if there is good earth and water we can live.'

In 1947 Muhammadjan Shukurov visited Bukhara for the first time since leaving the city as a fourteen-year-old. He was now a married man in his early twenties and a rising scholar of modern Tajik literature, in particular the works of the Samarkandi poet Said Ahmad Ajzi. He walked the streets in which he had once waited among weeping crowds with food for his imprisoned parents, in the company of a chattering official who was keen to show him what strides Bukhara had made since the collapse of the old order. 'He said, "Look at this new shop where the madrasa used to be! And here's a hospital instead of that old mosque," and so on. I told him he had built the commonplace and destroyed so much that was irreplaceable.' A few lumps of mud were all that remained to show where the city wall had been. Beneath the vaults of the most beautiful and oldest bazaar stood a statue of Lenin.

The family had been forced to bury Sadr-e Zia in the big public cemetery at Khuja Ismat instead of in the family plot, and Muhammadjan Shukurov went to pay his respects at his father's grave. He walked to and fro but could not find it. The tomb had been made of good bricks and they had been stolen during the war.

The one bright spot of Muhammadjan Shukurov's first return to Bukhara was some unexpected good news. When Sadr-e Zia's possessions were sold after his death in prison, Muhammadjan's uncle had put the proceeds on deposit in the bank in his nephew's name, but Muhammadjan had been too young to claim it when he left Bukhara. He now made enquiries about the money and, astonishingly, it was still there – three or four thousand roubles.

The windfall could not have come at a better moment. 'I took it back to Dushanbe and my wife and I – we had nothing – we were so excited, and at once we made a shopping list. We would have shoes! Clothes! Everything we needed! We were listening to the radio, and the news came on that the rouble had been devalued, and there was to be "monetary reform". We didn't understand everything they said, but my wife rushed to the shops to spend it all at once. It was too late. All the shops were shut, except the bookshop. She bought what there was – an ink-stand with a tray for keeping pens and so forth, and seven little stone elephants. Each was smaller than the next, and they stood in a row on our shelf. That was what I inherited from my father Sadr-e Zia!' Remembering, Muhammadjan Shukurov laughs and laughs. It just goes to show, he says, what happens when people get worked up about inheritance.

Muhammadjan Shukurov does have two treasures to remember his family by, however. They are his aunt's commonplace book from which she used to read poetry aloud, and Sadr-e Zia's *tasbeh*, his prayer beads, of green stone shot with red, cool to the touch. Some of the hundred beads have been lost along the way but, restrung, the *tasbeh* look as fine as ever.

5

'A paradise on earth'

'. . . every light that shineth because of the darkness is exceeding
marvellous and wonderful . . .'

HINDUSTANI'S STEPSON UBAIDULLAH planted a garden at the new
house in Dushanbe in the early 1950s, and put in grape vines
and pomegranate trees. He loved the work, and so began a passion
for flowers that has lasted all his life. Ubaidullah rode with the times.
He learnt Russian, and managed to get on to a typography course in
Leningrad by keeping quiet about being the son of a convict.
Entranced by the parks and botanical gardens that flourished there
despite the short summers, he grew eager to try out some of the new
plants he saw, like forsythia and amaryllis, in Dushanbe. On a book
jacket he found the name of an eminent botanist, and went boldly in
search of his house.

'I saw a tall Russian with long hair working in a greenhouse full of
flowers. When I walked in and said hello, he turned and started to
laugh, and he said something to his daughters. I was wearing our
usual hat [a black and white embroidered cap], and I thought
perhaps he was laughing at me. Later, he told me he was just surprised to see an Asian fellow in his greenhouse. It was the first time
someone like me had come to ask his advice. He was very kind, and
we had a long, interesting conversation. He said I could take whatever seeds or cuttings I needed without charge, and he wished me
luck.'

When he got back to Dushanbe, Ubaidullah joined forces with two friends, an Armenian and a Russian, and embarked on a plan to make the green city greener. They planted an arboretum, and they travelled around the Soviet Union in search of new plants, supported by a small municipal grant. Gradually the business expanded, until Ubaidullah and his friends had two flower shops and five hectares of nursery land. They travelled to the Baltics, to the Caucasus and to Kazakhstan, and brought home flowers and saplings never before seen in the south.

Political repression was much less acute than it had been in the 1930s. None the less, any religious figure was vulnerable, even a Red mulla. In 1952, on *eid-e qurban*, the holy day of sacrifice, the police came for Hindustani. Ubaidullah remembers that they accused his father of anti-Soviet activity and, for the third time in his life, destroyed the family library. The NKVD* men, schooled in the Cyrillic alphabet, were unable to tell one book in Arabic from another, and would not have known what they burnt even if they had wished to. 'My father had absolutely no interest in politics. They had no evidence against him. All they could say was "You went to Afghanistan! You went to Hindustan!", as though those things were crimes. But sixteen other people from the mosque stood up and bore witness against him, and my father got a sentence of twenty-five years. He was sent to Karaganda, in Kazakhstan. I wrote to Stalin. I wrote several letters, but nobody answered.'

When Stalin died the following year, factory hooters from Siberia to Turkmenistan summoned the people of the Soviet Union into the streets for parades of public mourning. Some village elders held prayers for the *padshah* as was customary on the death of a king, however distant. Over the next months and years, thousands of political prisoners were granted amnesty, among them Hindustani. When he eventually got back to Dushanbe in 1956 he did not resume his job at Yaqub-e Charkhi, and gave up being a Red mulla altogether. Not one of his colleagues from the mosque had helped his family, or even visited them, during his absence. Hindustani decided to teach privately. He opened his house to small numbers of students, with whom he expounded the works of poetry, literary Arabic and Muslim doctrine with which he had been engaged since the age of

---

* People's Commissariat for Internal Affairs (1934–53).

eight. Even in the easier political atmosphere that followed the death of Stalin, the pursuit of religious understanding and pre-Soviet culture had to be conducted discreetly.

The men who sought Hindustani out were mostly mullas of the old tradition with roots similar to his own, middle-aged scholars who had kept their faith through long periods of exile and incarceration. One such was Sami Adinzada, called Damulla Sharif, of the Shurabad district of Kulab in the far south of Tajikistan, also lately released from jail.

Born in 1906, Damulla Sharif had fled to Afghanistan in 1927, along with perhaps half the population of Kulab. He took a chance and re-crossed the Amu in 1934. The OGPU* caught him three days later. Before he was taken away Damulla Sharif himself made a hurried bonfire of his hundred-book library, rather than give them the pleasure. He spent the next twenty years in and out of prison, accused at one point of writing 'anti-Soviet poetry'. By the time he was finally released in 1955 Damulla Sharif could neither see nor walk properly, and was tormented by the memory of his burnt books. He resumed his studies none the less. On returning to Kulab from Dushanbe, Damulla Sharif worked as a night watchman while teaching and writing poetry in his free time. In his house he kept a blackboard on which he demonstrated Arabic calligraphy to a handful of students. There were no public signs of this private life. Very lame, a little bent, Damulla Sharif could have passed as any quiet Kulabi elder.

Hindustani approached old age with vigour. Despite failing eyesight he kept up his interest in science, and continued his amateur practice as an apothecary. He tuned in every day to the news. It was on a Kabul radio broadcast one day in the 1950s that he heard of the death of his best friend and classmate from the old days in Mazar-e Sharif, Mulla Faqer, whom he had last seen on Hajj in Mecca almost thirty years before. 'He was still interested in everything. He was still very good at chess,' said one of his grandsons. 'He could win in three moves! All the boys round here used to peep in at his room, and if Hajji Baba was alone they would come in and play chess with him. Then he'd give them kopeks and sweets.'

* United State Political Administration for the struggle against espionage and counter-revolution (1922–34).

During the course of his travels, Hindustani had become fluent not only in Uzbek and Tajik but in literary Arabic, literary Persian, Turkish, Pashtu, Urdu, Hindi and Russian, and could switch easily between four alphabets – Arabic, Cyrillic, Latin and Hindi. He was thus able to earn money doing some translation work in the Ancient Manuscripts Department at the new Academy of Sciences on Prospekt Lenina. Muhammadjan Shukurov had been at the Academy since its opening in 1951, continuing his work on modern Tajik literature, but if his path and Hindustani's crossed there, they did not know it. Hindustani was a scholar, an Uzbek, and a religious; Muhammadjan Shukurov was an intellectual, a Tajik, and a rather reluctant member of the Communist Party. In the Bukhara they had both once known, these distinctions might have counted for less. But that had been in a different world.

In the late 1950s Dushanbe bore little resemblance to its pre-war self, let alone to the village it had been a generation before. It had quadrupled in size and had, in the centre, mains electricity, piped water, a 'modern restaurant' and (according to the official data of the day) sixty-one hospitals and thirty-seven dental clinics. The enormous change of scale and character had been brought about mainly by the arrival of some of the millions of Slavs, Europeans and other Soviet nationalities who moved to Central Asia before, during and after the war. These incomers arrived for a variety of reasons. Very many had been deported from the Western Soviet Union, ostensibly for fear that they would collaborate with Nazi Germany or prove anti-Soviet in some other way. These groups included Pontic Greeks, Ingush, Chechens, Mesketian Turks and others. Other incomers, especially scholars and doctors, were banished individually to Central Asia. Great numbers of others chose to try their luck in the south, drawn by the prospect of a warm climate, jobs on building sites and in factories, and more plentiful food than there was at home. The immigrants turned the Soviet Asian capitals from small towns into international cities immediately recognisable as Soviet.

Dushanbe benefited in particular from an enormous influx of Germans. The narrow steeple of the beige and icing-sugar plaster

Lutheran church in the south of the city stands as a monument to the fifty thousand Germans who, more than any other single group, literally built the modern city, and at one point made up almost a quarter of its population. Some of them were prisoners-of-war who never returned home, as the lines of German graves on the bank of the river testify. The great majority, however, were among the half-million Soviet Germans deported from the Odessa and Volga regions of Russia to the periphery of the Soviet Union in a single week of September 1941. Some were taken directly to Tajikistan, many arrived in search of work after years of exile in Siberia.

Ella Ivanova lives in a threadbare two-roomed house on the steep bank of the river Dushanbe. When she was two, Stalin ordered the evacuation of her village, Arlovka, in Saratov, about four hundred and fifty miles south-east of Moscow, a solidly German corner of Russia ever since the first pioneers arrived at the invitation of Catherine the Great in the eighteenth century. Ella's particularly blue-eyed looks give her origins away, and she still speaks a few words of German.

'My mother and sister told me what happened,' she says, sitting in her spick-and-span living room, drinking tea. 'We were given twenty-four hours to get out. We had to leave our cow, and all our things but the clothes we wore. We killed the pig, cut it up and took it with us in a can. We were put under guard in a special train and sent to Novosibirsk in Siberia. Father was taken to the labour camp, and mother brought up us four children on her own in a one-room hut.

'It was absolutely terrible, even by the standards of the time. It was freezing and we were close to starving. My mother was almost killed once in a fight over a radish – just a radish! There was no hospital. There was a teacher who boarded in the settlement, and that was our school. When this teacher finished her term a new woman was supposed to replace her. She set off – it was a ride of about six miles – but she never arrived. Wolves ate her on the road. She must have stopped to light a fire in the snow, we think. Wolves hardly ever attack humans, and it tells you how hungry even they were.'

After Stalin's death the family were at last able to leave Novosibirsk. Ella's father reappeared, and her parents decided to head south to Dushanbe, where they heard there were jobs going.

'We found a paradise on earth here!' Ella says, laughing for the first time since she began her story. 'There was mud up to your knees on Prospekt Lenina then, but Father found work as a builder and brought home a bag of flour, one of rice and one of sugar. I thought he was the richest man in the world. I took big chunks of sugar and stuffed them in my mouth. My mother said she hated to see it, but I suppose I needed the sugar after all that time. In Siberia, children used to shout "Fascist! Fascist!" at us, but in Dushanbe all that stopped. When relatives came from Russia to visit they went home with tales of bazaars full of fruit.'

The Germans were received warmly, by and large, and earned themselves a reputation for honesty and industry. They established their own quarter, Sovietsky, and in the easier political climate of the late 1950s were able to revive their German-ness. Ella's family celebrated Christmas on 24 December in the German manner and went to church every Sunday; afterwards, they would sit around the table for German-speaking family meals. 'I still remember a couple of recipes my mother taught me,' Ella says. 'One was a dish of very thin, flat noodles – like paper – to eat with chicken soup, and also a pork and cabbage dish.'

Exiles and evacuees opened new windows on the world for the city people of Soviet Central Asia. A German, Konstantin Redlich, founded the botanical gardens of Dushanbe, and his ambitious plantings eventually included specimens from every continent, and glasshouses with coffee bushes and banana trees. The Navai opera house, built by Japanese prisoners-of-war, made a handsome centrepiece to Tashkent. Carrot salad hot with chilli spread through bazaars far and wide with the Koreans, the first wave of whom had stumbled across the Kamchatka peninsula into the Russian Far East to escape famine at home in the early twentieth century. Stalin moved 172,000 of them from Vladivostok to Soviet Central Asia, presumably for fear that they would collaborate with the Japanese. There they were joined by many more through the 1940s and 1950s, until half a million lived in Uzbekistan alone. At one point, as many as one Tashkent resident in five was Korean.

Many of the big names in Soviet theatre and cinema lived in Tashkent at some time or other, because several film studios, including Mosfilm of Moscow and Lenfilm of Leningrad, moved there for safety during the war. All the main characters in Alexander Solzhenitsyn's *Cancer Ward* (set in the Tashkent hospital where their exiled creator was treated) are migrants. Tashkent gradually took its place on the map of the Soviet arts circuit. The American jazz clarinettist Benny Goodman played to an invited audience of Party men there in 1962.

Some intellectuals enjoyed the slow pace of southern life, the feeling of walking on ancient stones and of being out of the mainstream. Mikhail Bulgakov's widow Elena managed to hide the manuscript of his extraordinary last novel *The Master and Margarita* in Tashkent, keeping it safe until its publication in 1967. The collector Igor Savitsky was able to amass a tremendous number of banned (non-Socialist-Realist) works of art, including anonymous drawings on matchboxes smuggled out from a women's prison camp, and impressionist pieces that he saved from artists' attics. 'I remember him rushing into our house in the night with paintings under his coat,' recalled the woman who grew up to become the curator of his collection. In Russia, the secret police would have closed him down. Only a few lackadaisical officials ever made it out to the desert at Nukus, near the Amu delta, where the doors of a small-town museum open on to a dazzling display.

Little by little a generation of Tajiks and Uzbeks began to emerge with no memory of the non-Soviet world, born to parents who remembered it vaguely if at all. This generation, the first truly Soviet Tajiks and Uzbeks, was born within the system and reaped its rewards. They were the first children since the 1917 revolution not to worry all the time about getting enough to eat or what to wear when the snow came; the first, if they were lucky, to have shop-bought toys. For this deliverance, their parents thanked God and the Soviet Union.

Growing up in the 1960s and 1970s in or near the city meant growing into a new shared world that connected young Soviets from Vladivostok to Krasnovodsk. A fortunate child might visit the circus, on tour from Tashkent or even Moscow as a mixed troupe of daredevil Russians and local tightrope and stilt walkers. Zoos, another long-standing feature of the Russian city, appeared in Central Asian provinces as well as in the capitals (Khujand zoo housed even an ele-phant in the 1970s). Dushanbe zoo, opened in the early 1960s, boasted three thousand visitors every weekend, admiring local exhib-its such as the cobra, desert monitor, snow leopard and Bukhara red deer as well as the hippopotamuses and kangaroos shipped from across the world to Moscow and distributed to the republics.

Most fun of all, however, was an evening at the cinema. Major cities had several. They screened by no means exclusively Russian-made films, and as the post-Stalin period gave way to that of Brezhnev they explored an ever-widening range. The Tashkent Film Festival became an international showcase for work mainly from China, Cuba, Soviet-friendly Middle Eastern countries and Africa, and was at times probably the foremost non-English-language event of its kind.

In *kolkhozes* in richer parts of Central Asia the highlight of the summer was the arrival of the mobile-projector van and the rigging of the outdoor screen with its ear-splitting loudspeakers. Whole village populations, young and old, thronged to watch Indian box office hits, whose mixture of romance, skulduggery and seductive song and dance routines was wildly popular. For millions of Tajiks and Uzbeks, the 1970s are captured by the mingled sensations of ice-cream, sunflower seeds, and Raj Kapoor, super-star of the Bombay screen, belting out numbers from *Samgan* and *Shri 420* on a hot, black night. The ability to sing show-stoppers all the way through in Hindi without understanding the words became and remained a character-istic of the Central Asian Brezhnev generation.

'I thought, we want for nothing,' says one young man who grew up a *Shri 420* child. 'The only thing I longed for was to see Russia. I wanted to walk in dark green birch forests dripping with rain, like on television. I wanted to go skating at an ice-rink. I wanted to see the sea and sit under a little beach umbrella – those umbrellas were magical to me. I had seen such things in books. I thought the Russians must be absolutely marvellous people, shining with good-ness. I loved their language and taught myself. I wanted to go to Moscow and stay in a tall apartment building. I planned how it would be – how I would come down in a lift and make my way to school with my friends. I would go to Red Square and see the domes. I would go to the mausoleum of Lenin.'

This new generation had unprecedented opportunities within the Soviet horizon, opportunities which opened up the lives of girls particularly. Tajik girls in neat pinafores and ballerina-style hair-ribbons trotted to school hand-in-hand with Slavs beneath the now mature planes of Prospekt Lenina in Dushanbe. They learnt the curriculum taught in all Soviet cities (country schools were less structured), gymnastics, dance and volleyball. Farsi was offered as a foreign language. History was Soviet-Russian history, with supplementary lessons on medieval Muslim poets and scientists, depending on the school. Shining role models appeared. Aziza Azimova became one of the first Tajik dancers of the Russian ballet. Ulmaskhan Davlatova made local history when, in 1954, she made a parachute jump.

Many girls, including some from villages, cut their hair, put on dresses without trousers underneath, and went to university in the towns. A great number of educated women then found that there were no jobs at the end of the road, or that their parents would not allow them to work away from home. Still, they married at twenty-one instead of seventeen, and often had some say in the choice of husband. Those who did find jobs often continued to work after marriage. There was two years' maternity leave on full pay per child, free health care including infant inoculation, and a guaranteed place at a nursery for every child between the ages of three and seven. 'I felt I was the luckiest girl in the whole world,' a secondary-school teacher who grew up in the 1960s remembers. 'My great-grandmother was like a slave, shut up in her house. My mother was illiterate. She had thirteen children and looked old all her life. For me the past was something dark and horrible, and whatever anyone says about the Soviet Union, that is how I see it.'

The *lingua franca* of the new multi-national cities was Russian, the only language of advance in the USSR, despite the existence of Tajik-medium and Uzbek-medium schools. Boys who had not learnt Russian at school (or taught themselves, as the ambitious did) learnt it in the army, where they served for two years unless they could dodge the call-up. To promote internationalism, servicemen were sent to the furthest parts of the Union, even to the extremities of the Soviet bloc, where they lived in mixed-race brigades, were obliged to eat canteen pork, and often learnt to drink vodka – though many Tajiks and Uzbeks resisted this, or tried it only once.

Those dispatched to the German Democratic Republic drew the long straw, and came home with travellers' tales of shops bulging with food and 'honey everywhere'. The majority served at the most basic level, as builders, painters and garrison cooks in Siberia and Kazakhstan. They had next to no military or any other kind of training, but they did learn barrack-room Russian.

Russian was not exactly a leveller, since very few Uzbeks or Tajiks came to speak it as Russians did. Yet enough people spoke it well enough to make it the common tongue of the city centre, and Russian words like those for diploma, suit, skirt, chair, suitcase, train, telephone, refrigerator, document, hairdresser passed into everyday Tajik and stuck. So did military language and prison slang (jails, like the army, were melting-pots of Soviet nationalities). Less explicable were the arrivals of the Russian words for zero, pen, cheese and lunch. Some city families spoke only Russian, first to push the children to get ahead, and gradually because their declining Tajik seemed inadequate for what they wanted to say. Many people came to believe that Tajik was intrinsically unsuited to the modern world, useful only for such old-fashioned things as poetry and the language of love. From knowing only the Russian word for, say, matches, it was an easy step to the assumption that had the Russians not come there would have been no matches.

The relationships between Moscow and the peripheral south, grounded in empire, flowered as such and remained entirely on Russian terms. Russians learnt Tajik so rarely that the exception was considered a marvel, and Uzbek almost never. Internationalism meant, in practice, the adoption not only of the Russian language, at least in public life, but of habits and values drawn from the Russian tradition. A successful city man – one, say, who belonged to a Party family – slept in a raised bed, sat on chairs not quilts, and ate from a table not a *dastarkhan*, with a fork not his fingers, a meal that might include European vegetables (cabbage, tomatoes) and sausage (not 'really' pork) instead of aubergines and spinach, pheasant and ptarmigan. His wife (only one, in principle) and daughters very often joined the men after cooking the meal on their gas stove and setting it out in tempting little dishes. The modern family home was probably not a house but an apartment with large windows, and looked into a broad, straight un-walled street or a communal courtyard filled with trees. An evening of high culture might be spent at the opera house listening to works played on European instruments, led by a conductor, from a written score, without improvisation. Very often, in the case of local compositions, these pieces took on an Eastern flavour through the use of micro-tones or distinctive melodies.

Politically, the people of Central Asia remained last among equals. Slavs on their way up the Party ladder might well serve in one or other of the Afghan frontier republics, but Central Asian Muslims hardly ever took senior posts in other republics, or in the Union-wide apparatus; nor did most Central Asian-born Slavs. Mistrust of the southern republics had not been laid to rest despite Muslim participation in the Second World War and all subsequent demonstrations of loyalty. Very few Central Asians became senior officers in the army. Foreign tourism was even more tightly restricted than in other republics. 'The experience of the USSR has smashed the racist theories, the age-old lies of the colonialists about the causes of the backwardness of certain peoples,' said Anastas Mikoyan, President of the USSR, addressing the faithful massed in the Dushanbe opera house on the fortieth anniversary of the founding of the republic in 1964. When he spoke, there was not one Muslim among the eleven members of the Presidium of the Central Committee, the highest authority in the Soviet Union.

Central Asians did not become pilots or, usually, doctors or nurses. Jobs that involved interaction with other parts of the Union (hotel receptionist, telephone operator, Intourist guide) generally went to Slavs; so did disproportionate numbers of teaching jobs. Factory jobs went to Slavs. So did jobs in engineering. Women's hairdressers were almost always Russian. The differences between how Slavs and Central Asians lived, outside the urban super-élite, was built into everyday life so completely that many people either did not notice it, or thought it reflected some sort of natural order. Rather than prickle at unfairness, many ordinary parents thanked their lucky stars when their child got a 'real' Russian as a class teacher rather than a Tatar or a local.

Relations between the smaller Union republics crystallised during the boom years. Uzbekistan, from the outset the seat of Russian and then Soviet power in Central Asia, grew to have more influence than ever over Tajikistan. Tashkent was the fourth biggest city in the USSR by 1960. There was a measure of development in Tajikistan –

gold and rubies were mined in the mountains, chemical, porcelain and aluminium factories were built in the plains – but if Dushanbe wanted gas or schoolbooks or buses, Tashkent was the main supplier. Physical geography made it impossible for Tajikistan to build roads to anywhere but Uzbekistan: the Chinese border was closed, and routes to Afghanistan limited. Quantities of dynamite were used to blast the Pamir highway from Osh in Kirgizstan through the mountains, but this road was not especially useful for people outside the Pamir region and was often closed by snow.

Dushanbe was also shackled to Tashkent through its political leadership. After the retirement of Babajan Ghafurov, all republican leaders were chosen from his home region of Khujand, the sliver of northern territory tacked on to Tajikistan in 1929. The classical colonial device of favouring one region over others had extra leverage here because Khujand was so geographically close to Tashkent. Much of the political élite was Uzbek by origin and did not even speak Tajik.

None the less, the high degree of local autonomy held out fine prospects, and while the Union prospered, there was no need to dig at its roots. Very many young urban Tajiks looked at their lives, found them good, and embraced all that was Soviet. Having brought birthdays, the Russians also brought cakes, scalloped with icing, with which to celebrate them, and sweet fizzy wine. Walking along Prospekt Lenina, past the opera house and the smart nine-storey Hotel Tajikistan, it was easy to share the commonplace view that, had the Russians not come, 'we would have been living in the dust'.

Outside the cities lay another Central Asia, the one which the great majority of people knew. Between seventy and seventy-five per cent of Tajiks lived in the countryside, a figure that stayed constant while Dushanbe and Khujand, the main city of the north, expanded. City people often characterised the countryside as a bastion of old-fashioned, unchanging conservatism. Yet when challenges to the moral authority of the Soviet Union appeared, and with them political alternatives to the Soviet world-view, the earliest and some of the most important came from the Tajik countryside.

Along the road south out of Dushanbe, the elegant stuccoed buildings and small apartment blocks give way to farms and roadside bazaars within a few miles. As the road leaves the city limit it cuts through an outcrop of rock pitted with tiny holes, each one hiding a bird's nest. From this wall of twittering song one can see green hills dotted with horses and brown fat-tailed sheep, sharp as cut-outs in the clear light. This is the Fakhrabad pass, the gateway between Dushanbe and the rural south.

Fakhrabad is a point from which to get one's bearings. To the east rise the mountains that eventually become the Pamir, to the west is the Uzbek border. Straight ahead lies the river Vakhsh, the main tributary that runs from the hills to the plains until it reaches the Amu and the Afghan border. The flatlands on either side of the Vakhsh support scores of farming villages grouped around market towns that were old a thousand years before Dushanbe was any more than a village; Qurghan Tappa lies a couple of hours' drive south of the capital. Continuing south one reaches Qabadian, then Shahr-e Tuz, the last town before the frontier.

The villages of the Vakhsh valley, built on ancient sites, look as though they have stood forever. Formed from the dust of the plains the houses, each with its courtyard, fruit trees, women's room (*dukhtar-khana*), guest room (*mehman-khana*) and domed outside oven, differ only in the detail from those of five hundred years before. Most, however, actually date from the 1950s, when tens of thousands of Tajiks from the mountainous regions of the republic were forcibly moved to the valley as part of a massive expansion of the cotton plantations between Dushanbe and the Amu.

Compulsory migration had begun in the 1920s, as a means of moving labour to where it was needed, and of mixing communities within the republic. These labour-gang settlers chopped down woods, dug canals, and turned the cotton fields along the Amu into plantations. After the Second World War, however, came an enormous rise in the need for cotton to clothe the beggared Soviet Union, and the Vakhsh valley, with its long hours of sunshine, seemed a suitable spot to expand the plantations further. The local population was nothing like large enough to support the plan. Rather than import even more Slavs and Europeans, as Stalin had first intended, the republican leadership decided to move whole villages of Tajiks to the plains. The great *mahajarat-e ijbari*, or forced migration, began in 1952 and lasted well into the 1970s. (In 1978 a foreign tourist trekking in Afghan Badakhshan close to the Tajik border at Ishkashim saw a procession of forty or so Pamiris with their flocks cross the river from the Tajik side and make their way down the path into Afghanistan. They were, they told her, escaping deportation to Vakhsh. In principle, this border between Tajikistan and Afghanistan had been shut for more than forty years.)

The first to be evacuated were the very highest villages of the Pamir, like those of Yazgulam, which cling to the mountain walls at over four thousand metres. Then came highland regions like Bartang, Darvaz and Gharm. Whole village populations were ordered to collect their things and walk down to the road, where they would be met by trucks. 'We were told we were going to a *gulestan*, a flower garden, where there were streams and grass,' one man remembered. 'We were going to build a fine, new country and bring to life new lands for Tajikistan.'

Said Abdullah Nuri, who later became a symbol of the anti-Soviet challenge in Tajikistan, was six when the order came. His family was one of the last to leave the highland village of Sangvar, seven thousand feet up the Pamir, in November 1953. 'We were fine people. We had a horse, three cows and eight or nine sheep, and an orchard on the hillside with pear trees, mulberries and apples. Life was good. We had everything but pomegranates in our village. We had no use for money,' recalls Nuri's elder brother Asadullah. 'We knew there was no paradise waiting for us, but we were thankful that all the family was alive and we were all together. We came by truck to Dushanbe, where they put us on special trains and sent us to Vakhsh. The livestock came by road.'

Asadullah was right. There was no *gulestan* in Vakhsh. Nor, in the early years, were there any houses, food or clean water for the fifty thousand or so people who were brought here to break new land. More than a quarter of the mountain people – perhaps more – died in the first few months, mainly of dysentery and heatstroke. Children and elders could not breathe properly. Like many others, Nuri's family scraped a hole in the ground, and in this they survived – Nuri, his parents, his seven brothers and sisters and his grandmother. Of the sixteen families in other dug-outs nearby, three died in their entirety. People killed their animals and ate as much as they could before every single head of sheep and cattle perished in the heat. The wages they had been promised did not come through, in many cases, until 1958, six years after the deportations began.

Despite these catastrophic beginnings, deportations to the Vakhsh valley continued in various forms for the next twenty years or more. The later stages were better organised, and migrants often moved in with relatives who had gone before them so there were fewer fatalities. The manner of deportation, however, changed very little. The last mountain people to be rounded up were the Yagnobis, a people living in a long, narrow fold of mountain above Dushanbe. From the main road it takes four days by donkey to reach the inner Yagnobi villages, which are built of the rock of the mountain and cut off for more than half the year. The deportation officers waited until deep winter, when the huts of the Yagnobis were banked in by snow, then they suddenly dropped military helicopters into the valley. The Yagnobis were given an hour to pack their quilts and pots, then put into the helicopters and flown to a *kolkhoz* on the banks of the Amu. They were set to work in the plantations in one of the hottest inhabited places on earth, and forbidden to return to their mountain homes for fifteen years.

Those who survived the deportations put down new roots in the villages they built, which were generally given patriotic Soviet names, like Rah-e Lenin (Lenin's Way), Oktyabrsk, and Bolshevik. Naturally, people of common origin stayed clustered in village groups. Many people from Hait, for instance, went to Qumsangir; from Tajikabad they went to Shahr-e Tuz; many people in Kolkhozabad started life in the Gharm valley. There were so many people from Gharm, which was a trading centre of substance before the Soviet time, that 'Gharmis' became a short-hand name for all incomers, regardless of their actual origins.

The mountain peoples added new pieces to the old mosaic of the plains that run all the way to the border with Uzbekistan. One distinctive group in this mosaic is the local Arabs, who believe that they can trace their descent to the first Arabs who crossed the Amu at Termez in the seventh century, and whose elders still speak a spoonful of Arabic; they still live near the road from Termez, mainly around the village of Auvaj. There are also local Tajiks. There are Kirgiz who had arrived as nomads and settled as farmers, and there are Turkmen shepherds. There are great numbers of Uzbeks, especially in the borderlands, in addition to the thousands of other Uzbek families who had been brought from the Ferghana valley in smaller very early forced migrations – so many that Uzbek was the language used in schools around the town of Panj until the mid 1940s.

'At first there were language problems, of course, but gradually this became less, and slowly, slowly people began to marry into other families,' remembers Nuri's brother Asadullah, who still lives in Yakum-e Mai – First of May – the village the family and many other people of Sangvar helped to build near Qurghan Tappa. Yakum-e Mai is typical of the plains: one lane of mud-built houses. A stream lined with white hollyhocks and wild yarrow runs along one end of the village: only a few feet from the water the flowers stop, and the yellow ground is parched. By June the straw crackles underfoot and the oven-like air is thick with chaff as village boys spread the ripe family wheat in the lane and the girls pluck the grain from it. This is poor man's harvesting. As Asadullah talks, the women of his extended family cook meat and potatoes on a spitting open fire outside the *dukhtar-khana*.

Nuri and his brothers became *kolkhoz* boys, attending the village school and, from the age of eleven, working in the cotton plantations through the summer and autumn, as was usual. Like most rural children they were born to parallel lives. At 'Russian' school they learnt mathematics, the Cyrillic alphabet and Soviet history and geography: the skills that, if they persevered, could give them access to the shared Soviet world of the city. At home, they followed the prescriptions of an older time. The 'Gharmis' of the *mahajarat-e ijbari* were proud that they had kept alive many religious and cultural traditions since fallen out of public use among city people.

'When we were very young my father did not let us see him praying, because it would have been dangerous for us,' says Asadullah. 'But our law says a Muslim must learn the scriptures, and our father taught us the Quran and to read from the poets, especially Ferdausi. All our family – daughters, sons, aunts, grandfathers – all thirty-two of us learnt the scriptures.'

Nuri's father, Nuriddin Saidov, was born around 1900. His family owned land around Sangvar, and he was studying at a Bukhara madrasa when the revolution came. The family tried to get away to Afghanistan, but though they managed to send some possessions on ahead, they were stopped by soldiers at the Panj crossing. Nuriddin returned to the relative safety of Sangvar where, as a literate man, he managed to get a minor position in the Soviet system. He continued to read prayers 'under the blankets', and married Khasiat, the daughter of an educated family. For thirty years Nuriddin hid his small library under the hay in the shippon, and during the *mahajarat-e ijbari* managed to bring his books with him to Vakhsh.

By the time Nuri was seven he was learning the Quran, and all the boys of the village – 90 per cent of whom were deportees from the mountains – attended illicit lessons at his family house. Nuri won a name for studying while the others played about, and raced ahead in learning Arabic. His mother Khasiat thought him the sharpest and most diligent of her children. 'He learnt the old alphabet before the Russian one. He studied and studied: after school he'd come back and read here. I was afraid all the time in those days; the communists could have beaten us and thrown us into jail if they had found out.' There were very many families like hers, Khasiat says. 'There isn't a Tajik or an Uzbek who doesn't know Islam in some way.'

Teaching one's children 'the right way' according to Muslim precepts was at the marrow of Tajik country life, as central to one's sense of self as offering hospitality to guests and respecting elders. To do otherwise was simply not an option. 'The right way' gave detailed rules for life in all its aspects – from the days on which it is impermissible for a man to shave to the recommended hours for sleep (not before evening prayers).

'The right way' was just as compelling for the great numbers of country families who were also pleased to be Soviet citizens. 'There were dreadful wars and then a huge repression and then came the big war. And then things were all right,' one elderly farmer put it, summing up the half-century. He had been a boy during the *basmachi* period and though he thought the *basmachi* and the Bolsheviks were as bad as each other, he was immensely grateful to the Soviet system for bringing peace. He gave thanks too for the asphalt that made it possible to ride into town in the winter, should someone become dangerously ill, and for the electricity that saved on lamp-oil. Like almost all Central Asians, he could only compare his life to the imaginary, and was under the impression that Muslims outside the USSR had no modern amenities at all. Soviet belief had it that Pakistan, in particular, having been colonised by the uncaring British, was full of virulent diseases. Kindly people like this farmer felt desperately sorry for his brothers beyond the border, and in fifty years of back-breaking labour on the *kolkhoz* never uttered a complaint. Nor did any element of this make him any less a Muslim. Every dawn he said his prayers, his ten children copying the sounds softly behind him.

Although Soviet policy could no more stop Tajiks being Muslims than it could stop them being Tajiks, campaigns to promote atheism struggled fitfully on, concentrating on appearance rather than substance. Shrines were concreted over. Officials forbade people to tie votive rags on holy trees, and explained patiently what everyone had always known – that many 'holy men' were charlatans. An official report of 1968 expressed angry concern that rural Tajiks would not lend their knives to Russians to cut pork sausage. Such campaigns to change the look of things naturally did nothing to dim the mind's eye. A pilgrim at Chel-u Chahar Chashma, where the forty-four springs said to flow from the fingerprints of Imam Ali form gentle waterfalls just outside Shahr-e Tuz, spoke for many when he said how nice it was that the Soviets had smartened up the holy place by making a spa and a children's playground there.

The newspaper *Kommunist Tajikistana* reported in 1951 that a torn map hung upside down in a tea-house was the only sign of ideological life in all Kulab, and that even a colonel in the regional interior ministry, who had studied Marxist-Leninist theory for three years, did not know when the Communist Party had been founded (the same paper noted that there was not a single copy of *Das Kapital* in the main library in Dushanbe).

Even at death, compromise was possible. Some élite families, unwilling to be seen to bury a prominent Party member in accordance with Muslim rites yet unable to bring themselves to comply with the communist – that is Russian – tradition of interment in a coffin, trod a middle path by carrying the body in a coffin as far as the grave and there removing it, to bury it wrapped in a winding-sheet, as a Muslim.

Official atheism, however, could and did degrade the level of religious practice in the scholarly sense, as it did with every religion in the Soviet Union. Many people were only semi-literate even in the Cyrillic alphabet they had learnt at school, and could not begin to read the hundred-year-old books written in Arabic they treasured as heirlooms. Isolated from the mainstream Muslim world, they knew little more than snippets of doctrine. They passed down a faith rich in folk-tales and superstitions – such as the widely held belief that a baby taken from the *gahvara* too young will become 'a Russian'; that is, not a 'real' Muslim. 'We knew to fast during *ramazan*. We learned the old alphabet, at best. It was hardly profound,' remembered one man whose grandfather, ostensibly an illiterate doorman, hid his Bukhara education for twenty years. 'Our knowledge became so thin that we considered a man to be a big mulla if he knew the Quran! Our faith *was* faith: we simply believed in God.'

Most children in the Vakhsh valley followed the conventional course. A boy came home from military service to marry a girl straight from school and resumed work on the *kolkhoz*. 'There was no way out, except for a tiny few,' said a farmer from one of the poorest regions. 'We came home, we looked at our fathers and we knew what we were going to be.' On the ladder of secular education or entre-preneurship, the determined and lucky climbed out of the village into the city and got jobs in Qurghan Tappa or Dushanbe. With strong family networks behind them, those 'Gharmis' or mountain Tajiks who did well often did very well indeed. The farms their parents had planted as destitute deportees eventually yielded not only the best and most valuable cotton ('Egyptian' long-staple) in the Union, but also citrus fruits that fetched high prices in the city, and eucalyptus which was used for medicines. The Gharmis won a name for working hard and prospering, within the limits of the possible. Their families still drank from the *qanat* and lived in mud houses, but many courtyards opened on to a *mehman-khana* with a television set. Families bought carpets and gold jewellery for their women as invest-ments, and married their daughters well. Cars appeared in the dusty lanes.

Nuri's brother Asadullah became auditor of the *kolkhoz*, another brother went to agricultural college. Their father chose his most dili-gent son to follow him in helping keep alive their faith. 'Father said he must continue to study Islam and we must do everything to support him,' said Asadullah. 'We had to keep him out of the army in case they broke his spirit. We told everyone he was studying accoun-tancy but he was not, he was studying Islam.'

By the 1970s, religious revival had become a pressing concern for those who cared about such things. Two generations had passed since the beginning of official atheism, and most mullas with a pre-Soviet education were long since dead. Their successors were mainly Red mullas, or self-taught celebrants of family rituals without formal learning. Nuri gravitated towards other young men who, much like himself, wanted something more. The town of Qurghan Tappa was their natural meeting place. 'We wanted to shake out some of the fairy-tales and revive our faith, to get young, educated people interested,' says a friend of the time. 'We knew Arabic and we tried to get back to essential sources, the Quran, the *hadis* [the sayings of the Prophet]. The more you read, the more you know. We were young – some of us were very young – and we wanted to revive Islam along proper lines.'

'I wanted to know some simple things,' recalled a less scholarly member of the group. 'It was the custom in our village to give a carpet to the mulla when he came to say prayers for the dead. Was that a correct Muslim practice? We needed to live our lives properly. We needed to know.' There were not many men who could answer such questions with authority. But there was one. Nuri went to Dushanbe and sought him out.

By the time Nuri began to attend his classes in Dushanbe, Hindustani had been teaching privately at home for a generation, staying faithful to the old syllabus he had studied in Afghanistan. In times of political tension the class would move around the city, deciding each day where to meet the next. In times of ease, his students would gather at his house. In summer Hindustani returned to the old village at Chahar Bagh, and often visited his old students in other parts of Central Asia, travelling by aeroplane, which he enjoyed. He worked constantly on interpreting the poems of the seventeenth-century poet Bi-del, and on his masterwork: a translation of and five-volume commentary on the Quran in Uzbek, begun at the age of seventy-five. Hindustani kept up a lively interest in the outside world. He listened to foreign radio broadcasts, and never missed the Moscow evening news programme, *Vremya*. 'He especially liked watching Anatoly Karpov play chess on television, and called out advice to him,' a grandchild remembers. 'He praised his mind, even though Karpov was not a Muslim.'

Nuri was an enthusiastic guest in Hindustani's house. 'He was bright, confident and very serious about his faith,' recalls a contemporary. 'Actually, I thought of him as a boy! He used to get so excited. But there is no doubt he was serious.' Nuri made friends with young men from well beyond the Vakhsh valley. One was a cleric, Abduvali Mirzayev, who had come from the Ferghana valley in Uzbekistan to study with Hindustani. Nuri helped Mirzayev learn Persian, and returned with him to his home town of Andijan on visits.

Contemporaries remember how they all enjoyed the feeling of exploring a wider world. 'We became interested in the news. We listened to foreign radio stations from Arabic countries, Iran, Afghanistan. Of course the KGB watched us, and monitored who was listening, but listening to foreign stations was not actually forbidden. We made friends with students from Muslim countries friendly to the USSR who had been sent to technical colleges here. Knowing them helped us a lot.'

In the late 1970s Hindustani's students listened avidly to the news from Iran, which as Persian-speakers they could easily understand. Striking students paralysed campuses in Teheran while liberals, communists and clerics spoke of justice and the end of repression and corruption. Men and women marched in demonstration. Soldiers fired on them. Riots broke out in city after city. Muhammad Reza Shah left Iran for the last time on 16 January 1979. Far away in Moscow, Brezhnev applauded the 'anti-monarchical anti-imperialist' revolution, the first in this part of the world since 1917; but his cautious approval did not last long. The Iranian revolution set soon afterwards as 'Islamic', and the gaunt image of Ayatollah Khomeini emerged as the face of the new Iran.

From the holy city of Mashhad and the Caspian town of Gorgan close to the border with Turkmenistan, revolutionary Iran began special radio broadcasts in Tajik and Turkmen. Some programmes called directly on Soviet Asians to revolt against their godless oppressors. Many took the form of question-and-answer sessions on points of doctrine, designed to reawaken religious sentiment. 'We did not really know much about what we were doing,' one man involved remembers. 'We knew the Soviets were trying to jam us, and we did not know whether people could hear. We did not know if they were interested, even! After all this time, we did not know who these people really were . . .'

'Of course we were fascinated by the news from Iran and we listened to whatever we could,' recalls one of Hindustani's students. 'There had been a revolution in the name of Islam, so naturally we welcomed it, even though we are Sunni and they are Shi'a. But we were not interested in politics as such – elections, parties, that kind of thing. The KGB harried our people and said we were anti-Soviet, but very few of us thought in those terms.'

The eventful year of 1979 drew to a close. Then in the last days of December came a quiet piece of news that was soon to resound around the world: the Soviet Union had invaded Afghanistan.

6

'Why were we there?' – Afghanistan

'. . . when the time of the decline of their fortunes was arrived,
neither craft, nor perseverance nor counsel could aid them; and
neither the multitude of their troops nor the strength of their
resistance was of any avail.'

WHEN SOVIET TROOPS first went into Afghanistan, Leonid
Brezhnev, General Secretary of the Communist Party of the
USSR, was seventy-three years old and went nowhere without his
doctors for fear of a repeat of the heart attack that had slurred his speech
and made a mask of his face five years before. By the time the last soldiers came home he was dead, as were his successors Yuri Andropov
and Konstantin Chernenko. In the interim, perhaps a million Afghan
civilians had been killed, five million more had fled their country, and a
war had been set in train that was to continue into the next century.
About fifteen thousand Soviet troops were also dead, or missing in
action. The Cold War had reached its end-game, and the Soviet Union
was in the hands of a new man with a new style, Mikhail Gorbachev.

The decision to send the first-ever concerted Russian-led military
force south of the river Amu was taken by a coterie of generals and
perhaps four members of the Politburo. The full Politburo and the
Foreign Ministry were not properly informed. The over-riding
purpose behind the decision was the least confidential part: the time
had come, from the Soviet point of view, to do something about the
growing disorder in Afghanistan.

On 27 April 1978, a group of Afghan communists had seized
power in a *coup d'état* and proclaimed the establishment of the

Democratic Republic of Afghanistan. The Soviet Union gave the coup leaders full support and poured economic and military aid into Afghanistan while the United States cut back its assistance, thus between them ending the Afghan position of non-alignment that had held for the past fifty years. In the months after the coup the leader of the most radical faction, Hafezullah Amin, became more and more powerful and led 'Marxist' reforms as crude and self-serving as the worst excesses committed north of the Amu two generations before. Along with literacy campaigns and gun-point land confiscation, the communists arrested, tortured and murdered those they considered their adversaries, including, inevitably, disproportionate numbers of educated people. According to official figures, twelve thousand people were killed in the main jail in Kabul – Pul-e Charki – alone. Beyond the capital, as one survivor put it, all Afghanistan 'became one big prison'.

The regime had all the weaknesses of government by fear. It was detested by much of the population, especially in the countryside, where some men – early *mujahedin*, or fighters – took up hunting guns against its officials. More pressingly, his frequent purges of the officer corps meant that Amin could not count on his generals. Matters started coming to a head in March 1979, when army garrisons began to mutiny, most famously at Herat in western Afghanistan, where some Soviet advisers and their families were killed. Herat lay just a short drive from the border of Iran, and it is possible that Iranian revolutionaries were involved. In the following months, almost every Afghan garrison revolted, including that of Kabul. Amin and the other leaders of the coup called again and again on their ally, the Soviet Union, for help in the form of troops.

Top-secret preparations for a response went on in the Soviet Union through the summer of 1979. The Cold War was at its height, and senior army officers genuinely felt the security of the Union to be at stake. Some believed that if the Soviet-friendly government in Kabul failed to restore order the United States, in the shape of the CIA, would try to take the helm in Afghanistan – a move that appeared all the more likely because Washington had just lost its old regional ally the Shah of Iran, and it was hard to predict what might happen in the Islamic Republic of Iran. If the Soviet Union were to 'lose' Afghanistan it might, according to the simple domino theory common at that time, next lose authority in the Afghan borderlands of Central Asia – that part of the Union always least known and trusted by a Soviet military in whose senior ranks Uzbeks, Tajiks and Turkmens were so thinly represented.

Among the field-agents it sent into Afghanistan to lay the ground for the Soviet response the KGB chose many Central Asians because of their ability to blend in. Tajik and Uzbek officers grew beards and adopted Afghan clothing; some went on courses designed to weed the Russian words from their speech, to help them pass more easily as Afghans. These agents concentrated mainly on intelligence-gathering while various schemes for what to do in Afghanistan were under discussion. In the autumn came two events that set the Soviet course more firmly. In September, Amin became President of the Afghan Revolutionary Council, after ordering the assassination of his predecessor, Nur Muhammad Taraki, who was arrested on his return home from a visit to Cuba and smothered with a pillow soon after-wards. Then, on 4 November, Iranian revolutionary students seized the US embassy in Teheran and held hostage fifty-two diplomats and other personnel. Moscow became more worried than ever that Washington might use Afghanistan to make good its losses in Iran.

When Hafezullah Amin appealed again for military help from his allies, Moscow took steps – or so it appeared – to ensure Amin's personal safety. His Soviet advisers asked him to move from his offices in the Ark in central Kabul to the old royal palace of Darulaman; being on the outskirts, it was said to be easier to defend. To ward off any attempt by Amin's many enemies to kill him by infiltrating his staff, the new palace guard and the cook were to be Soviet Uzbeks and Tajiks dressed as Afghans, as well as Afghans. The palace was reno-vated at Soviet expense, and in early December Amin and his family moved in. Their security was now entirely in Soviet hands.

On the morning of 27 December 1979, Amin invited his inner circle – ten or so men, with their wives – to a luncheon party to welcome a colleague who had lately returned from Moscow. When the clear soup was served only this man, Dastagi Panjshiri, refused it, saying that his doctor had forbidden him fats – although as one guest pointed out, consommé was hardly fatty.

Doctor Alexey at the Soviet Embassy got an urgent call and rushed to the palace. 'There were people strewn around everywhere,' he said.

'Some were still in their chairs, some on the floor. There was one man on the floor with his leg up on a chair. They were all poisoned. Amin was the worst. His breathing was terrible. He was gasping for breath and his face was sagging.'

Amin was carried to his private quarters and put to bed. His wife (some Afghan women do not use their given names) later told a well-known Afghan journalist, Zaher Tanin, what happened next. 'Several doctors came and injected serum and medicines into my husband and his condition improved. At seven o'clock I heard heavy shooting start on the west side of the palace. I ran into my husband's room and at that moment he sat up and asked what was happening. I told him we were being attacked.' Amin staggered up and reached for a telephone. The line had been cut.

Amin and his wife went out into the corridor, where they were joined by other members of the household. 'The shooting got much louder and was coming from all sides,' said Amin's wife. 'We all moved down to the second floor and sat in the corridor. My son Abdu Rahman, a relative of ours and a guard took up position on one of the staircases, and I brought weapons for them. We still did not know who was attacking us, so my husband sent the head of the guards upstairs to look out. He came back. "It appears to be Russians," he said. Amin just said "No". It was unbelievable. We held out until our ammunition was spent. Then they came in, shooting all around the palace. They went to my daughter and said, "Where is Amin?" "Why are you attacking us?" she asked. "Amin is here." Then they spotted him sitting on the floor. They shot him dead.'

As Soviet troops mounted their attack against the palace at seven o'clock (shooting some of their own fake presidential guardsmen in the belief that they were Afghans), other agents blew up Kabul communications centres. Troops stormed the Ministry of Internal Affairs, the Security Service and Pul-e Charkhi prison. By the following morning all important positions were under Soviet control, and Soviet military aircraft were landing in and near Kabul every two or three minutes. One, direct from Moscow, flew in Babrak Karmal, the man chosen to replace Amin. The Kremlin considered Karmal, one of the original coup leaders, a more reliable ally than Amin, and it was hoped that his smoother style would make the communists more acceptable. In the sensitive period of transition – so the idea went –

Soviet troops would be deployed temporarily in Afghanistan, joining forces with the Afghan army.

That day, 28 December, the United States National Security Advisor Zbigniew Brzezinski recommended in a memorandum to President Carter that Washington should support Afghan resistance to the Soviet invasion through the *mujahedin* who had opposed the Afghan communists all along. This recommendation was only the official expression of plans that had already been laid by the CIA as détente disintegrated over the past year. Yet the wording was memorable. 'We now have a historic chance to give the Soviet Union its Vietnam,' wrote Brzezinski, in a phrase that would resonate for a decade to come.

The Soviet ground force used for the invasion, the 40th Army, had begun to move into Afghanistan a few days before Amin's luncheon party. The bulk of the troops crossed the river Amu on the Soviet-built Bridge of Friendship into the Afghan town of Hairatan from Termez, the Uzbek river port that was the headquarters of Soviet military operations throughout the war. A smaller contingent took the desert route through Turkmenistan to Herat. The 40th Army, recruited locally, included large numbers of Uzbeks, with some Turkmens and Tajiks. The officers were almost all Slavs.

'It was late at night. Nothing was announced but the news spread from village to village. Each *kolkhoz* told its own people that we were going into Afghanistan.' Rajab Ergashev, now middle-aged, is the guardian of the shrine of al-Hakim Termezi and lives only a few yards from the Amu. 'People did not think "We are Muslims invading a Muslim people like ourselves." They did not think about it at all.' Ergashev looks across the scrubby sand to the bank on the Afghan side, less than a mile away, where shepherds, their trousers hitched up to the knee, are wading their flock to the low, reedy islands midstream. 'Ordinary people did not know what country was there: maybe they found out later, when they went. But mostly I think they did not. We did not know, and did not understand. I was young. I was a school teacher and a member of the Communist Party. I had no choice but to believe. I supported the invasion.'

*

Muhammad Sharif, an Afghan carpet maker, watched the 40th Army arrive at Hairatan. 'I heard on the radio that Amin was dead. And that night they came,' he said. 'In the morning I saw them climb out of their trucks. In their uniforms they all looked alike, but when I looked closely I could see they were Tajiks, Uzbeks, Turkmens, Kazakhs, as well as Russians. They came and spoke to us in our languages and said they were our friends. Friendly! Of course we knew who they were!'

'Sons of Lenin, what are you doing here?' demanded a leaflet picked up in the bazaar on the other side of the country in the southern city of Qandahar in early January 1980. Such *shabnamas*, or nightletters, handed out after dark, called for mass resistance to the invasion. As dusk fell one misty evening, hundreds of people in Qandahar climbed on to their roofs and for hour after hour called 'Allah-u Akbar' – 'God is Great'.

The protests reached Kabul on the night of 21 February 1980. In the old city and on the west side, people went to their roofs and shouted 'Allah-u Akbar' over and over again. The journalist Zaher Tanin remembers that everything was shut when he went to the university the next day, and that the campus was far emptier than usual. Then, 'About a hundred people burst in. Some of them had guns and sticks. They killed two or three Communist Party members. The protests were organised by *mujahedin* groups but they had real popular support. People were so angry about the invasion. The Russians misjudged completely how Afghans would respond.'

What was supposed to have been a smooth relay of power, completed by midsummer, slid into disaster. The Afghan army, far from being strengthened by the Soviet presence, fell apart even faster than before as so many soldiers deserted. The press-gang was called out and filled the gaps with teenaged boys, many of whom, picked off the street as they were, ran away. Afghan government troops were quickly outnumbered by Soviet soldiers. *Mujahedin* guerrillas in the countryside ambushed Soviet–Afghan forces where possible, armed with the Kalashnikov rifles that had been bought covertly by CIA agents in China and Egypt and dispatched to Afghanistan through Pakistan. (Kalashnikovs, being of Soviet make, could pass as captured Soviet guns if need be.) In the towns, students called strikes and demonstrated against the invasion. The number of Soviet troops rose to more than a hundred thousand, and stayed there.

Babrak Karmal's government concentrated on holding the cities as best it could by means of a coercive Soviet-style administration. KGB advisors were flown in to build KhAD, the Afghan secret police force which, like its model, conducted surveillance of people's lives, set up a network of informers and compiled loyalty dossiers. As it had in the Soviet Union, and in Afghanistan under Amin, spying proved an extraordinarily effective tool of social control, spreading mistrust, then paranoia, then complete dislocation of judgement among friends and even inside families. Like the KGB, KhAD also had powers of detention, and could torture people and 'disappear' them with impunity.

Red stars, slogans, portraits of Lenin and other communist paraphernalia appeared in city schools. Educational advisers were brought in to the universities to lecture on Weber and Marx; predictably, they were often KGB agents, many of them products of the Oriental Institute of Tashkent. Membership of the Communist Party was encouraged for teachers, doctors, and anyone connected with officialdom. Conscripts in the Afghan army found out by checking their payslips that they too had paid Party dues and thereby become members.

Great quantities of Soviet aid and retail goods flowed into Kabul and other cities, creating economic reliance on the USSR while presenting it as a friendly land of plenty. Oil, sugar, schoolbooks, medicines, wide-bottomed nickel kettles, Russian television sets and electric wiring, together with Eastern Bloc construction engineers, arrived along the Salang highway which runs from Hairatan to the capital, as did growing numbers of troops, weapons and ammunition.

Keeping open the Salang and other supply roads was an absolute imperative for the communists. Already by February 1980, only weeks after the first ground troops had crossed the Amu, Soviet–Afghan helicopter gunships and bombers had begun in earnest to subject the countryside through which these roads ran to extreme, punishing violence. In the province of Kunar, whole villages were wiped out. Then came offensives in the mountainous north-east, Badakhshan and the Panjshir valley. Then came the bombing of Baghlan, Takhar and Ghazni in central Afghanistan.

Civilians began to flee first their villages, then their country. Hundreds of thousands from the western provinces crossed the border into Iran. Those from the east fled across the long frontier into Pakistan. 'They [the Soviet–Afghan forces] made a base in our village and searched our house,' says Muhammad Sharif, who had watched the tanks roll in across the Amu. 'They beat an elder and picked up the young men for the army. We were in a *mujahedin* area and two of my cousins were killed.' He and the rest of his family ran from the village near Aqcha that had been their home since 1921 when his father, a Turkmen weaver and tailor, drove his small flock into Afghanistan to escape the Bolsheviks in Kerki. Thousands of other families from the frontier towns of Aqcha, Ankhui and Qunduz, several headed by elderly refugees of two generations before, removed to camps outside Afghanistan, mainly in Pakistan. Many young men then walked back through the mountains to join what they saw as the only available means of getting the occupiers out: the *mujahedin*.

The *mujahedin* were, in the early 1980s, developing rapidly into much more than the poorly armed anti-communist fighters they had been two years before. Military aid, initially tens of millions of dollars per year, came primarily from the United States but also from Pakistan, Saudi Arabia, and Britain – all countries with some interest in the proxy war of the superpowers being waged in Afghanistan. As weaponry grew more sophisticated, CIA and other agents flew to Afghanistan to supervise instruction in its use. *Mujahedin* commanders came to the Welsh and Scottish borders to train with the British SAS.

Numerous *mujahedin* political parties and groups, mainly based in Pakistan, organised the fighters on the ground and were both conduits for and beneficiaries of the prodigious wealth in weaponry and humanitarian aid being pumped into Afghanistan. Of these groups, the two most famous had both been founded long before the Soviet invasion. Hezb-e Islami (the Islamic Party) was heavily influenced by Pakistan. It drew its main support among the Pashtuns, the largest ethnic group in Afghanistan, and was led by a Pashtun, Gulbuddin Hekmatyar from Qunduz. The young men of many émigré families originally from the Ferghana valley in Uzbekistan – the Ferghanachis who had settled in Qunduz in the 1920s and 1930s and stuck together ever since – also followed their community leaders into Hezb-e Islami.

Jamiat-e Islami (the Islamic Society) found its support largely in Tajik areas in Afghanistan. It was headed by Burhanuddin Rabbani, a theological scholar from the mountainous region bordering Soviet Tajikistan, but it was the military leader of Jamiat who commanded a real following inside Afghanistan and became the most famous face of the *mujahedin* in the outside world: Ahmad Shah Mas'ud made his headquarters in the Panjshir valley in the mountains north-east of Kabul. Communist forces launched campaign after campaign against the Panjshir, but they never held the valley consistently.

Most people inside the Soviet Union knew nothing of all this, even – perhaps especially – those living in the border areas of Central Asia closest to Afghanistan. 'We saw loads of cooking oil and flour and medicine crossing the Amu every day and we were very proud to see that we were helping the poor Afghans,' says a young man from Termez. He was nine when the tanks went in to, as he saw it, protect the aid convoys from 'bandits' who were trying to steal from 'the people'. The war was not declared or acknowledged – officially, it did not exist: 'Shipment 200' was the code for the covert delivery of corpses back to the USSR, and it was even against the law for Soviet families to inscribe 'in Afghanistan' on a dead man's grave.

Sleepy Termez, where men snooze beneath the palm trees in the heat of the day, had become a bustling military camp more intimately engaged in the war than anywhere else in the Soviet Union. As a 'closed' city, Termez was off-limits to outsiders, even those from other parts of the Uzbek Republic, and as much labour as possible was drummed up locally. Every Termez family was in the war in some way or other. Boys went to the army, girls went as nurses (to the extreme distress of their parents).

Termez families packed into special shopping buses and drove across the Friendship Bridge into Afghanistan, where the border base of Hairatan was promoted as a model 'communist' Afghan town. Hairatan shops were rich with Russian commodities on their way to Kabul – and European-made goods not available in the USSR. 'We bought nice things like wardrobes there. Things that we could not get at home. And we thought, of course the Afghans are happy,' said one boy.

And traffic came the other way, too. Cheerful 'Welcome' signs in Arabic script decorated Termez as the point of entry for the thousands of Afghan children transported to schools and children's homes in the Soviet Union. The Homeland Nursery sent girls and boys between seven and nine to special institutions, mainly in Central Asia, to be brought up as the first Afghan cradle-communists, intended as the nucleus of future Party cadres. It was an organisation headed by Babrak Karmal's wife Mahbuba, ostensibly intended for orphans (children of the 'martyrs of the revolution'), including those who lost their families in Soviet–Afghan air-raids; but many poor families say that soldiers picked up children from bombed villages without proper checks being made.

Provision was made for secondary-school and university students to study in the USSR: several hundred were flown every year to Russia, Siberia, Ukraine and other parts of the Union, mainly to study technical subjects, especially engineering and military-related skills. The majority of students stayed on in Central Asia, however, where they were put into classrooms alongside local Tajiks and Uzbeks. They learnt Russian and the rest of the standard Soviet curriculum, and attended special religious knowledge and literature lessons.

The projects in Afghanistan sponsored by the USSR seemed proof enough that the Soviet presence was warmly welcomed by ordinary Afghans as greatly to their advantage. The calendar for the summer and autumn of 1981 alone speaks volumes: 12,500 tons of Soviet sugar made their way through Hairaton; 100 computers were sent to Afghan polytechnics; the farmers of Balkh received fertilisers worth 11,400,000 Afghanis; credit was allocated for a tannery in Herat, a fruit factory in Qandahar, a brickworks, a fruit-juice factory, a battery farm and two fish hatcheries; the Watan Plastic Factory reached a production level of 7,000 pairs of shoes a day; Afghan citrus fruit and olive oil was exported to the USSR; a tractor exhibition opened in Kabul.

On the cultural front, Soviet ping-pong and tennis teams, artists and photographers gave displays in what was now called the Democratic Republic of Afghanistan. Film-makers put on a Soviet festival. The Hungarians sent musical instruments. The 'children of Tajikistan' sent schoolbooks to the children of Hairatan. A centre for Afghan philologists opened in the Ferghana valley of Uzbekistan. A Lenin Museum was founded in one of the royal palaces in Kabul, and the reminiscences of the Soviet war hero Marshal Zhukov were translated and disseminated.

Afghan officials attended the Inter-Sputnik space conference in Havana. Religious scholars went sight-seeing at shrines at Uzbekistan and Tajikistan. Envoys of Nicolae Ceauşescu of Romania and Fidel Castro of Cuba flew to Kabul, as did Soviet advisors on higher education, trade, transport, irrigation, hospitals, paediatrics, science and culture. Afghan ambassadors presented their credentials in Ulan Bator, Baghdad, Tripoli and Ankara.

'We felt we were bringing freedom and democracy to Afghanistan,' one Uzbek man remembers, 'especially to women. We felt we were liberating them from their miserable past.' Like many people, he did not fully understand that there was a war going on in Afghanistan; still less did he have any idea of the political and historical context in which it was happening. Most Soviet citizens believed themselves to be 'advanced' and the Afghans 'backward', and looked no further. That the first transmissions had spluttered out of Kabul Radio in 1925, that mass vaccination was well established by 1938, that Kabul University in the 1970s was one of the most successful in western Asia, were as unknown to most people as the fact that the livelihoods of the poorest Afghans – the very people whom they thought they were helping – were being destroyed by mines and helicopter gunships.

The widespread idea that the Afghans were a needy people who could not 'go forward' unaided had a deep and special significance among Central Asians, who looked in the mirror of Afghanistan and saw what looked like their own good fortune. Afghans, as imagined by most Uzbeks and Tajiks, were a people like themselves yet somehow trapped in the past, at the point they supposed they themselves had been when the Bolsheviks came: 'To cross the river Amu is to cross from one century into another' runs an old Soviet saw (the number of people who knew both sides well was tiny). It was an axiom of Soviet Central Asia thinking that without Russian help, Uzbeks and Tajiks would have stayed in this past 'like Afghans' – caught, as figures in a daguerreotype, in a world through which time had ceased to march, in which women were still wrapped to the eyes in horse-hair veils and the nightwatchman still swung shut the gates of Bukhara at dusk.

Many of these messages were enforced by feature films set in Central Asia in the early Soviet period. The most famous was a poignant love story of 1971, *Beloye Solntse Pustini* – 'White Sun of the Desert' – which starred the Tajik actor Ata Muhammadjanov as the leader of a gang of improbably dressed *basmachi* who double-cross one another in an imaginary Bukhara filled with heaps of spice and Turkish-restaurant-style belly-dancers. The hero – a Russian Bolshevik – does not get the girl, but this rather poignant film drew the crowds none the less. It says much about modern Soviet Central Asia that such films were very popular.

The word *basmachi* came into new service during the Afghan War to explain the *mujahedin* away as religious fanatics and charlatans who were detested by the population at large. 'Party members throughout the country volunteered to fight reactionaries and defend the revolution' ran a typical account of the Kabul press-gang: it might have been written in the 1920s. Naturally enough, the involvement of the CIA was given much publicity and, for reasons of geography, spread particular alarm among Soviet Central Asians. Many people, especially around Termez, believed disguised American troops to be in action only a stone's throw from their villages: if these men were to prevail and invade the Soviet Union, as was their supposed ultimate purpose, it would be Central Asian dead who filled the river Amu.

Words fail Rajab Ergashev, the communist school teacher of Termez, when he tries to explain how severed from reality he now feels he was during the Afghan war. He holds up his hand to show a silver ring.

'You think this is a plain ring.' He turns it to reveal a dark green stone. 'You wouldn't think there was a stone *unless you already knew*. Afghanistan was like that. The truth was *absolutely* hidden from us. Perhaps one person in a thousand understood what Afghanistan meant. I did not, no one I know did, but perhaps there were some.'

Muhammadjan Shukurov was one such in a thousand. Never a man to be blinded by propaganda, his response was clear and bold. 'I knew the war was a terrible thing for Afghanistan, and for us too. I could see that it would turn the mullas against the Soviet system. I went to Moscow to explain to the newspaper editors what the result would be – this was before Gorbachev – and some of them listened and agreed. One editor who was in the Central Committee agreed. But it was too late.'

By 1986 the United States was openly spending more than half a billion dollars a year on the Afghan war. Saudi Arabia, the main finan-cier of the *mujahedin* from the Muslim world, reportedly at least matched that amount. Soviet expenditure reached perhaps five times these totals put together, and Afghanistan became probably the largest recipient of personal weapons in the world. Each contributor spent many times more – fifty times, in the case of the USSR – than it had given in pre-war development aid. Yet the Soviet–Afghan army was no closer to controlling the countryside than it had been five years before. It was clear that it had no chance of 'winning' the war – whatever that might mean – unless Moscow committed significant numbers of new troops, trained them in mountain warfare (a radical idea for the flat-land, tank-bound Soviet army), and committed them for the duration of a war that had already lasted six years longer than anticipated.

In February Mikhail Gorbachev, new Secretary General of the all-Union Communist Party, broke the official silence by calling the Afghan war a 'bleeding wound', and began the long process that would lead to the phased withdrawal of troops. The decision ushered in the most deadly year of the war. The Soviet–Afghan air force carpet-bombed large parts of the countryside, especially in the border areas. Most of the tens of thousands of people killed as a result belonged to poor Afghan farming families. Villages, animals, fields, crops and irri-gation canals were smashed to pieces in an attempt to destroy the supply base of the *mujahedin*. Refugees continued to leave, until a point was reached when about half the population of Afghanistan was abroad or internally displaced. Vast numbers of landmines not only killed (mainly) civilians, but wrecked the land behind them.

Shamshad, a Soviet Uzbek from a lemon-growing *kolkhoz* in Termez, was seventeen when he was parachuted in to Kabul in 1986. 'That's how I got this,' he says, pulling back his shirt to show a jagged scar in his shoulder. Shamshad had never left Termez before the call-up came, whereupon he was sent to Romania (where he fancied the local language was probably English) for military training – in Russian, with translation into Uzbek. 'I stayed two years in Kabul.

Even boys of eight and nine were in the war. They'd stand on the roofs and offer you a cigarette or invite you into a shop and it could blow up in a second. We were young and we didn't know anything. We did not really understand that it was all for nothing.'

Morale in parts of the army was exceedingly low. Many Soviet and Afghan soldiers mistrusted one another and lacked confidence in their officers, some of them Second World War veterans schooled in the belief that expenditure of lives eventually wins the day, as it had at Stalingrad. Official reports papered over a series of calamities, mainly caused by failures in military intelligence: Soviet troops were blown up by landmines laid by Soviet troops who had gone before them; they dropped bombs on their own people by mistake; on one hot day, a single battalion reportedly lost seventy men as they sat on a river bank for a cigarette break, having been told that the ground above them was in Soviet hands: it was not.

'Nothing about Afghanistan was what it seemed to be,' one officer said much later. 'They used to say the *mujahedin* were very cruel and cut off the ears and noses of their prisoners. Actually, it was we who did it; I knew the people who were detailed to mutilate the dead. Others said the *mujahedin* were very pure, very good Muslims, but most of them were in it for the money. We used to send back "corpses" to the USSR, and really it was hashish inside the coffins. Afghanistan was all secrets and lies.'

That which could not be spoken of found expression in haunting camp-fire ballads. These Russian songs, sung to the guitar, gave voice to defeats that never officially happened and opened agonised questions about the purpose of the war. One begins like this:

People often ask me this question:

'Were you there? Tell us about it truly.
Did lots of our lads die,
Giving their lives for someone else?
Open our eyes, tell us the truth,
Did you see your friends die?
It must have been hard to die,
Of course it was hard to say goodbye.
Answer us, tell us. Why were we there?'

So much sorrow has visited all our homes,
Will the truth ever see the light?
We shouldn't have sent our lads there.

'Did lots of lads lay down their lives,
In those far away Afghan mountain passes?'

Of course, none of us wanted to die,
When we've lived so little of our lives.
And eighteen isn't any age at all,
And twenty also seems much too soon,
But death took them all in,
All those lads who'd taken their oath.

So don't believe the rumours, they're not true,
They come from an enemy spirit.
Someone needs us to be there,
As though Afghanistan was stuck in their throat.
And what can I say in reply?
We're given our order to go forward, not back,
We can't argue with that.
That's the fate of a soldier.

By the late 1980s there were few Soviet Central Asians in the 40th Army in comparison with the great numbers who had been sent in with the first ground force. Local reservists had by now served their time, and their places had been taken by other nationalities. There were widespread and tenacious rumours, however, that the Central Asians had been withdrawn because so many had proved unreliable and betrayed the Soviet army to the *mujahedin*.

Such rumours fed the tensions inevitable inside a multi-racial army, especially one in which different races dominated different ranks. Because so many Central Asian soldiers were poor, semi-literate teen-agers, some of whom spoke such bad Russian that they had difficulty following orders, disproportionate numbers served as cooks, drivers and camp orderlies rather than as active combatants, let alone officers. This opened the way to charges that they were not pulling their weight in a war that was supposedly being fought on their behalf, inasmuch as it was a war to preserve the borderlands of the Soviet

Union. Many veterans recall fist fights and worse between different ethnic groups, Kazakhs beating up Muscovite Russians in particular. No hint of such friction was supposed to reach the Soviet Union from Afghanistan. As early as 1981, all photographs of the Afghan campaign published by the Defence Ministry had to include a Soviet Muslim face, every report to mention a Muslim name.

A handful of Central Asian soldiers did turn coat and fight as *mujahedin*. One group of Soviet Tajik deserters is said to have particularly unnerved their former comrades by keeping their old uniforms and changing back into them for ambushes.*

Some Central Asian soldiers sold or gave away information and equipment while staying in Soviet ranks. One Hezb-e Islami fighter of Qunduz, whose father had migrated from the Ferghana valley, recalled striking a no-attack deal with Soviet Army Uzbeks, themselves from Ferghana, who had carried with them to Afghanistan old photographs of relatives who had crossed the Amu in the 1920s (it was not uncommon for Central Asian soldiers to carry photographs or lists of names of relatives they were hoping to trace). 'They used to tell us about their operations and we arranged that, when they left, they would bury their weapons and tell us where to find them. In return we used to send them bread and cigarettes. I can honestly say that, at times, we never would have managed without the Uzbeks.' He gives convincing details of names, places and times. As well as cigarettes, he and other Hezb-e Islami commanders gave the Soviet soldiers pamphlets of Quranic verses to take home. 'It wasn't any sort of CIA plot,' he said. 'We were the men on the ground, not Pakistanis or Americans. We gave them books because that was what they wanted.'

Many of the transactions were purely commercial, especially during 'leaving sales' at which soldiers disposed of everything they could before going home, including warm jackets, kettles, and camp equipment like television and refrigerators. Afghans often paid with

* According to Brigadier Muhamad Yousaf of Pakistani Intelligence, such deserters joined in 'probably the most secret and sensitive operations of the war': covert raids in Tajikistan and Uzbekistan that were designed to undermine the Soviet Union from the inside. Yousaf claims that hundreds of *mujahedin* trained especially for this purpose crossed the Amu in rubber dinghies, mainly to distribute religious books, including Qurans printed in Uzbek in Cyrillic script. The idea, he alleges, originally came from William Casey, head of the CIA, who saw the books as the forerunners of arms that would eventually take the war north of the Amu. These operations culminated, according to Yousaf, in an audacious *mujahedin* attack on the Tajik river port of Panj in March 1987.

hashish, which was in great demand for both personal use and resale. One Tajik remembered that the *mujahedin* coming to his camp offered farmland. 'Of course it was not only us who bought and sold stuff; many, many Russians and others did it too,' he said, 'but it was easier for us, because of the language.'

Very many Central Asians who served in Afghanistan gained a greater sense of being Soviet than ever before. They improved their Russian, made friends of different nationalities, often for the first time, and felt all the camaraderie of fighting men with a shared enemy, as their fathers had in the Second World War. To have served in Afghanistan became a mark of prestige – there were plenty of garrison cooks who, once back on the *kolkhoz*, found themselves respected as hard-bitten fighting men. Asians in the Soviet Union, in Afghanistan some had felt like Europeans – the heroes of a thousand feature films, not the losers. Some veterans kept their Russian-style nicknames – Saids became Sashkas, Nuris became Yuris.

Some Soviet Asians, however, came home more questioning of the world around them than before, mainly those who had gone to Afghanistan not to fight but, as civilian translators, to assist in the spread of Soviet ideology as the campaign for hearts and minds laboured on. 'The minute I arrived I understood that no one wanted us there,' said one Tajik flown to Qunduz in 1986. 'We didn't say anything, of course, but when we interpreters were brought in from the regions to Kabul we used to meet and compare notes.' Like many of the interpreters, he had a weak grasp of – and little interest in – the ideology he was supposed to be disseminating. The theories of nineteenth-century Germans, the idea of a command economy, seemed not the basis of enlightenment but absurdly out of step with modern times. One, possibly apocryphal, story that did the rounds for years was of a young man who stalked into a village house and ripped down a picture of Karl Marx, judging it by the beard to be of Ayatollah Khomeini.

Some of these translators were profoundly changed by their experience in Afghanistan. One such was Muhyeddin Alemov, a dynamic journalist and photographer originally from a mountain village near Aini in Tajikistan. Muhyeddin at once fell in love with Afghanistan. He rejoiced to meet Persian-speakers like himself, and to discover more about the roots of his culture. He took quantities of photographs, recorded hours of Afghan music and learnt Arabic script avidly. When his term was over he went back to Afghanistan voluntarily, spending seven years there all told. He became one of the first Soviet Tajiks to drop the Russian suffix from his surname and replace it with a local one: Alemov became Alempur, the name by which he later became well known.

Muhyeddin was full of vigour and bounce. He made friends easily. At a shop in Mazar-e Sharif in the 1980s he met two old men who recognised him as a Tajik and invited him in for tea. Learning that he was from Dushanbe, they asked whether he had heard of a relative they had there: the son of Sadr-e Zia, last Qazi Kalan of Bukhara. The intellectual circle in Dushanbe is small and Muhyeddin, who knew Sadr-e Zia's son very well, took home with him a letter.

Muhammadjan Shukurov was delighted to hear from the family of his greengrocer uncles who had fled Bukhara in 1929. 'It was full of news: that so-and-so had married, and so-and-so's daughter had gone to America. Of course, I had never heard of any of these people, and it was difficult for me to read the writing. But it was wonderful to get it, and to know that I had relatives all round the world.'

About half a million Soviet citizens had served in Afghanistan in some capacity or other by the time withdrawal began on 15 May 1988. The stories they brought home had spread inexorably across the Union. An Uzbek, then a schoolboy, recalls boasting in an essay that he wanted to serve in Afghanistan when he grew up. 'When my teacher read it she said, "What do you want to do that for? I thought you were meant to be clever!" I was so surprised.' It was not long before gaps appeared in the Saturday rota of school-children who were supposed to wash the local Lenin statue. 'I felt sorry for Lenin with bird droppings on his head. No one could be bothered with him any more.'

On 15 February 1989, General Gromov walked alone out of Afghanistan, across the Friendship Bridge and into Termez. The Commander of the defeated 40th Army, Gromov was also the last Soviet soldier out of Afghanistan. The latest Afghan communist leader, Muhammad Najibullah, was still in place in the presidential palace in Kabul; from now on he would receive considerable financial support, but no more Soviet soldiers would be sent to Afghanistan.

It was a sign of the times that the Russian journalist Artem Borovik was able to overcome opposition from the military censor and publish, in Moscow, his haunting analysis of the past nine years in his book *The Hidden War*.

> We were obsessed with our own messianic mission and blinded by arrogance . . . We thought that we were civilising a backward country by exposing it to modern bombers, to schools, to the latest models of tanks, to books, to long-range artillery, to newspapers, to new types of weapons, to economic aid, to AK-47s. But we rarely stopped to think how Afghanistan would influence us – despite the hundreds of thousands of Soviet soldiers and officers and the scores of diplomats, journalists, scholars, and military and political advisers who passed through it.

Borovik went on:

> In Afghanistan we bombed not only the detachments of rebels and their caravans, but our own ideals as well . . . In Afghanistan the policies of the government became utterly incompatible with the inherent morality of our nation. Things could not continue in the same vein.

7

'What is to become of us?'

'. . . despise not the determination of the humble man, for the
tree-trunk is set on fire with chips of wood . . .'

MANY SOVIET INTELLECTUALS remember the late 1980s as being
the most exhilarating time in their lives. All over the Union
and its satellite states, the cultural landscape, frozen for so many
years, began to thaw. Radical young historians in Moscow tried to
reclaim the past by putting on an exhibition of Stalinism at which
ordinary people were invited to tell their stories and show their
family photographs. They used an off-beat, underground location,
the electric lamp factory, and this became the venue for all manner
of alternative events. When makers of the film *Assa* – featuring the
pop song 'I want things to change' – were stopped at the last minute
from releasing their film in a cinema, they held the première at the
lamp factory.

Though the wind of change blew far more softly in Central Asia,
there was still a new sense of freedom, especially among the young
and educated. Many bright and imaginative people were inspired by
the idea of rediscovering themselves, their culture and their history.
For some non-Russian nationalities, there was more than just the
Soviet system to question – deep, subtle and sometimes excruciat-
ingly painful doubts were raised about the whole colonial order.

On the snowy morning of 24 February 1989, demonstrators began
to gather under the biggest statue of Lenin on Prospekt Lenina in

Dushanbe to demand that Tajik take the place of Russian as the state language of Tajikistan. Fresh snow and sleet stormed out of a grey sky, yet hundreds of people turned up, stamping their feet and swinging their arms – one held a banner reading 'Bukhara! Samarkand!' 'We did not care how cold it was,' a young journalist remembers. 'We all thought there were marvellous times ahead for us Tajiks.'

The most respected intellectuals in Dushanbe came to the square. Muhammadjan Shukurov of the Academy of Sciences came as a speaker, his overcoat stuffed full of petitions from students. Muhyeddin Alempur came. So did the well-known man of letters, Muhammad Asimi. Police cars and fire engines stood ominously on both sides of the square. 'We were scared that they might break up our gathering even though we had permission to hold it,' said Muhammadjan Shukurov. 'This was the first demonstration in Dushanbe organised by society itself, not by the government. It went peacefully and well. We discussed our demands, about language and about freedom of the press. And we discussed how to have meetings like this, what was the culture of a political meeting. We thought we should be patient. You see, all this was completely new for us. I looked down from the platform and I could see the square was absolutely full.'

Muhammadjan Shukurov was at the forefront of the revival of the Tajik language. For years he had done his best to keep Tajik alive in his own family. He had gone to some lengths, for example, to find a Tajik nursery-school for his son Rustam – only to find that the children spoke Russian in the playground anyway. As soon as his sons were old enough, he began taking them to Bukhara in the winter holidays – the summers being intolerably hot. As the family no longer knew anyone in the city, they stayed in a hotel. The new generation of Shukurovs had a sense of being grounded in something other than the Soviet Union. Rustam, as a student in Moscow in the 1970s, translated and published a thirteenth-century Persian manuscript on philosophy: the start of a career in scholarship.

'But if Rustam had published the manuscript here in Tajikistan he would have been banned from Komsomol!' his father says. 'We were still so restricted. That was how people had become removed from their language, their culture. I was very worried about Tajik. When a language stands idle, it dies. And not only that. Tajik children learnt Soviet history – that is, Russian history – and they had such a weak grasp of their own story and even geography. That sort of ignorance is very bad, very dangerous.'

In 1987 Muhammadjan Shukurov had fallen ill. Characteristically, he took advantage of his stay in hospital to write some newspaper articles. One, 'Who knows his own language?', caused a big stir in Moscow. 'In it I explained what had happened here: that a language a thousand years old was in decay. Everything I wrote was within Leninist precepts: it was not anti-Soviet in any way. I got letters from all different parts of the USSR agreeing that this was terrible, that it was happening in their republics too, especially the Baltics. Tajikistan was really in the vanguard of the language issue.'

Muhyeddin Alempur, the journalist who spent seven years in Afghanistan, was especially keen on reviving links between Tajikistan and other parts of the Persian-speaking world. He had a brainwave that made his a household name for many years. He launched a television show, *Setaraha-e Sharq*, 'Stars of the East', which introduced to a Tajik audience Persian singers from Afghanistan and Iran. The dry fact of sharing a mother tongue with millions of people outside Soviet borders came to life when it meant listening to a foreign song and understanding all the words. The music of the Afghan pop star Ahmad Zaher became popular all over Tajikistan, taped and re-taped in the bazaars. Even the Teheran dialect of Persian with its borrowings from French and English was easy to pick up in pop songs. The songs of Googoosh, the Iranian pop queen of the 1970s, enjoyed a renaissance in Dushanbe.

> Love came
> And pitched its tent in the desert of my heart,
> And set a chain around the foot of my heart.
> If love does not heed the cry of my heart,
> Oh my heart, alas! 'I have come,'
> says love . . .

sang Googoosh in her syrup-sweet voice. Some Iranophiles stuck her picture up next to that of Ayatollah Khomeini, whose revolutionary government had banned Googoosh, and all female singers, from performing in public. 'There were Tajiks who didn't even *know* that the Iranians spoke the same language as us until they heard Googoosh!' Muhyeddin said.

Some Iranians also took advantage of the new, freer atmosphere of the USSR of the 1980s and joined Intourist excursions to see the cities they had heard so much about in poems and at school, Samarkand and Bukhara. One such tourist describes spending a hot day trailing around the Ark of Bukhara, restored as a museum of the revolution, before repairing to the hotel bar and a quiet beer. It slowly dawned upon him, as he gazed into his glass, that the music he could hear was a Googoosh number. 'Then I realised that I understood what the barmen were saying to each other. Of course, I knew Bukhara was a city of Persian culture – but I somehow hadn't taken in that it still was. I went and said hello and we talked a lot. They told me that they hated the Soviet Union. They kept a special box behind the bar, and every time one of them said a Russian word, he had to put money in.'

Freedom of language and of speech were inseparable. Tajikistan, the poorest republic in the Soviet Union, nevertheless managed to turn out possibly more independent newspapers than any other, despite having very few presses and a chronic shortage of paper. Some estimate that as many as forty independent Tajik titles went into print in the late 1980s. One reporter for *Javanan* (Youth), a newspaper with about 40,000 readers, described a desperate hunger for truth after all the lies. 'People needed to say things, about Gorbachev or Afghanistan or whatever they liked. *Javanan* was a state paper, but the editor put out one issue with blank columns. It was a protest against censorship: very powerful for its day. We talked a lot about what it meant to be Tajik. Every Friday we printed poems from Tajikistan or from Afghanistan or Iran, and we ran specials on Persian history, calligraphers, architects, and the memoirs of literary men. We talked about sending Persian books to Samarkand and Bukhara, where people had been under Uzbek rule for so long. We wanted to understand ourselves again. We wanted a Tajikistan full of fresh air!'

A young newspaper journalist in a remote district of Kulab became fascinated by the story of Damulla Sharif, the teacher and calligrapher who in 1934 had burnt his own library before the OGPU took him away. Damulla Sharif was still alive, and still teaching at his house. 'The KGB warned me off the story but I did it anyway!' the journalist said later. 'I went to Damulla Sharif for an interview. He was too afraid to talk, but I got enough about him from his friends.

After that he agreed to see me. He was reassured when he saw how un-Soviet I was. We didn't use words like "glasnost" in my village! I just did it because I wanted to.' Someone showed the article to Hindustani, who was delighted to discover that his student of so long ago was not dead after all.

Freedom of expression also took the form of religious revival, especially in the countryside around the Vakhsh valley. Said Abdullah Nuri and his circle had been critical of the war in Afghanistan from the start. 'It was an act of aggression against a fellow Muslim country. We said nothing in public, but of course we were dissidents,' says one of the study group who met at Hindustani's house. Hindustani had listened to all the news he could from Afghanistan, but made no comment except that to say that what was happening was absolutely dreadful. Some of his young students were less reserved. Contemporaries remember that Nuri and others toured the villages, praying and giving private homilies against the war in people's houses. Nuri won an audience among families who had lost their sons for reasons they did not understand in a country only a couple of hours' drive away.

The 1980s were a critical time in the rural south. A few people had become rich, though it was often not the sort of wealth that an outsider passing through the village would easily spot. The family whose children played outside barefoot might well have wealth in gold. Other people remained as poor as their fathers had been. Boys who had seized the opportunities of the Soviet system with both hands and got themselves to university found there were no decent jobs waiting for them afterwards. 'There were almost no Tajik officers in the KGB,' said one man who was trapped in the ranks. 'Now why was that?' Born in the mountains, he grew up in the Vakhsh valley, and got to an élite KGB training college in Moscow through hard work and ability. Yet for all that, it seemed impossible to progress.

Some did their military service and returned to the *kolkhoz*, as ever. 'I wanted to be a pilot,' says one man from Kulab. 'The Russians trained plenty of Afghans to be pilots – so they could kill their own people. But us? Practically none.' 'We were the trash at the bottom of the heap,' says one man who dreamed of becoming a doctor but ended up back in the cotton fields. 'My father worked all his life on the *kolkhoz* and did not know we had nothing, but I knew and so did my friends.'

After three generations of communism, rural Tajikistan still came a steady last in all Soviet development indexes, year after year, except when Turkmenistan scraped in even lower. For example, the Union-wide statistics office calculated the percentages of new rural houses with a sewage system, running water and heating in 1985. Azerbaijan came top with a hundred per cent, with the three Baltic republics close behind; 30 per cent of Russian rural houses had all these modern amenities. Tajikistan ranked far and away last at only 4 per cent: 72 per cent of new Tajik houses had none of the three.

At the same time, the rural population had grown and was grow-ing at a tremendous speed. Tajik women in the countryside gave birth to more children than the women of any other Union republic, and to far more than most women anywhere in the world: forty-six per thousand of the population in an average year. Improved infant survival rates meant that most of them lived. As a result, while in much of the Soviet Union the urban population grew as country people migrated to the cities, this was not at all the case in Tajikistan or, to varying extents, the other Central Asian republics. Between 1951 and 1987, the population in the Russian countryside shrank by more than 30 per cent. In Tajikistan, it almost tripled.

Bored sons of the overcrowded *kolkhoz*, often hectored into un-wanted marriages, disappointed by lack of opportunity, angered by spending pointless years in the army, cast about for new horizons. Some clubbed together, bought cars, and rented themselves out as private drivers. Some started going to the mosque. Security officials – worried as ever about the appearance of things – wrote troubled memos not about the shortage of jobs but about the reluctance of Tajik youth to listen to Russian pop music, and the craze for having large, golden mottos – 'May God Protect Us!' – written in Arabic across windscreens. Some who had served in Afghanistan found it hard to re-adjust. 'The *mujahedin* seemed so dashing and free com-pared to us *kolkhoz* boys,' one ex-soldier put it later. 'Some of us thought the *mujahedin* were fighting for an Islamic state that would include us one day. We thought how fine it would be if the borders were all opened. Then we could make masses of money by travelling freely and selling televisions and so forth.' Some of these young men became interested in the new independent-minded mullas who proliferated in the villages, and seemed to care more about them than the state did.

In the late 1980s the name of Said Abdullah Nuri became distinguished from the others, mainly because of a chain of events that had begun in 1986. On 24 June of that year, the KGB launched a dawn raid on the flats and houses of about forty known religious figures. They found no anti-Soviet material, but they detained all the suspects. Nuri, his friends say, was driving that morning to the mountain town of Yavan, where he had business in the building firm for which he worked in Qurghan Tappa. The police were waiting on the lonely road, and detained him without taking him first for questioning or making any public statement. It amounted to a disappearance while in police custody, and Nuri's supporters were worried that if they did not draw attention to it, he might quietly vanish altogether. Family, friends and relatives held an illegal rally in the main square of Qurghan Tappa – the first unsanctioned demonstration of any size held in Tajikistan. The Afghan war was still going on, and a young teacher who was there said he saw the demonstration as dovetailing with other worries. 'Four coffins had just arrived from Afghanistan. You know, first comes the letter, then comes the coffin. All the dead were local boys. Maybe a hundred or a hundred and twenty people came, mainly relatives, and held a mourning meeting. Then a thousand more people came and wrote a petition, demanding that their sons be brought home from Afghanistan. Because Nuri was against the war, it looked like a demonstration for him, and he grew stronger then because people did not trust the authorities any more.'

Nuri went on trial for anti-Soviet activities. The customary array of 'witnesses' gave pre-trial evidence against him to the prosecutor. Then a remarkable thing happened: when the actual public trial began, every single witness recanted. Only a lesser charge of possession of marijuana – a standard Soviet charge against subversives – stuck, on police evidence, and Nuri was sentenced to eighteen months in a prison camp at Khabarovsk, in the extreme east of Siberia. As the only cleric of his generation to be punished in this way, Nuri now appeared, in the eyes of his followers, to be the direct spiritual heir of the mullas sent to the camps in Stalin's purges fifty years before. His time in jail set Nuri apart from scores of other young clerics. 'The Soviet Union was getting weaker, we could feel it,' said one supporter. 'People wanted a mulla to follow, they looked around, and they found Nuri.'

Nuri came home from prison in 1988 to find Muslim revival growing by the day. On a national level, it was led by the highest official religious authority in Tajikistan. Akbar Turajanzada was made Qazi Kalan, a post that came back into being when the old Red Muftiat of all Central Asia and Kazakhstan was broken up in that same year of 1988, possibly to prevent the formation of cross-republic religious parties. Each Central Asian republic got its own independent Qaziat, except Uzbekistan, where the position and title of Mufti were retained. Turajanzada had been, briefly, a student of Hindustani, and had met Nuri and his friends for the first time in 1983 or 1984. On Nuri's release from jail, Turajanzada gave him the job of editing the Qaziat newspaper *Minbar-e Islam*, 'Tribune of Islam'.

Akbar Turajanzada was a young, vigorous official cleric of a kind never seen before. Under his leadership, the number of mosques in Tajikistan shot from seventeen to about three thousand within three years. He had *éclat* and confidence and said what he thought. He talked openly about how the Muftiat of the past had been rotten with spies. He joked with journalists where others shied away; he was witty, trenchant and a natural public speaker. He also had the newest and most conspicuous premises in town. Work began on a Friday mosque (the biggest or main mosque of a town or city) and madrasa complex, the seat of the Qaziat, on the site of an old mosque on Prospekt Lenina. Very soon, a great silvery dome began to rise above the plane and pear trees in the heart of Dushanbe – only five minutes' walk from the Central Committee of the Communist Party building.

Born in 1954, Turajanzada grew up in a scholarly and pious household in the village of Turkabad, about fifteen miles east of Dushanbe. His father Ishan Turajan was a highly respected sufi whose ancestors had migrated from Samarkand seven generations before, and whose

own father had been exiled by Stalin to Siberia.* The older generation had been early deportees to a sugar-cane growing *kolkhoz* in
southern Tajikistan, but there were such terrible water shortages
there that they left the plains after only two years. By the time
Turajanzada was born, the family was settled. He studied the Quran
and Persian language and poetry with his father and maternal grandfather, a middle-ranking mulla. Turajanzada remembers a happy
childhood home full of conversation and guests, many of them his
father's followers, or *murids*.

Turajanzada joined the Pioneers, as a matter of course, but refused
to move up to Komsomol at fourteen. The story he related is characteristically unexpected. 'I told the teacher that I did not believe in
Komsomol, I believed in God. He said, "So you think the whole
class will go to hell and only you will go to heaven? Won't it be dull
in Paradise all alone?" And I answered back that it would be nice if
some girls came to heaven with me. It was the first and last time I got
slapped at school . . . that teacher, he is still alive and now he says his
prayers five times a day . . .' Turajanzada finished school with top
marks and decided on a career in Islamic jurisprudence within the
official system. At eighteen he went to Uzbekistan to study at the
Mir-e Arab madrasa in Bukhara, still probably the most prestigious
seminary in Central Asia.

After graduating in 1976, Turajanzada moved to the Institute of
Islamic Studies in Tashkent. He studied for two more years while also
starting work as a translator in the foreign relations department of the
Tashkent Muftiat. His native Persian came in especially useful when
there were official guests from Afghanistan to be shown around the
sights of Central Asia, such as Bukhara, Samarkand and Khiva. 'I
talked to them and listened to them, and I went to Kabul to translate
for senior delegations,' he says. 'I knew what was going on in
Afghanistan; what errors were being made and what risks were being
taken there.'

---

* Sufis are mystics, an *ishan* a sufi with a strong personal following. The Naqshbandi strand of sufism
originated in Bukhara, another strand, called Qaderi, in Baghdad. There are differences in the ways the
Naqshbandi and Qaderi pray, but few Central Asians make much of the distinction. Many adepts
describe themselves as both or either. Ishan Turajan's family were close to a famous sufi, Qalandarshah,
who migrated from Qandahar, in Afghanistan, in the nineteenth century. The family are the guardians
of a thousand-line sufi history which they kept safely throughout the Soviet time.

In November 1982, at the time when martial mourning music was booming out for the death of Comrade Brezhnev, Turajanzada became one of only a handful of the Central Asian élite to leave the Soviet Union for more than an official trip when he went to Jordan to continue his studies. He arrived in Amman, aged twenty-eight, at a time of great upheaval in the Middle East. Israeli tanks had just invaded West Beirut, hundreds of Palestinians had been gunned down in refugee camps, Hosni Mubarak had recently become President of Egypt after the assassination of Anwar Sadat. Turajanzada absorbed with interest the new world around him, and read as a matter of course the publications put out by the Society of the Muslim Brothers.

Founded in Egypt in 1928 by a secondary-school teacher, Hasan al-Banna, the society had played a significant part in ending British rule in Egypt and elsewhere. The values it originally expressed found an echo in those of the informal groups whose meetings Said Nuri attended in Qurghan Tappa in the 1970s.* While there was little common ground between the Muslim Brothers of the 1980s and the Central Asian religious-national revivalists, it was natural that the Society and its history should have been of interest.

'I became part of a little circle of liberals; Mufti Muhammad Sadeq of Uzbekistan was there, and Allah Shukur Pashahzada of the Caucasus. Of course there were KGB spies in our classes, but we used to tease them.'

Turajanzada returned to Central Asia in 1987, speaking greatly improved Arabic as well as his Tajik, Uzbek and first-class Russian. When he became Qazi Kalan in Dushanbe two years later, it was as a man whose experiences went far beyond those of even the very top government ministers. He knew the Soviet Union and the world outside it, he had spent time in countries at political turning points, he had absorbed and assessed different schools of thought. His was the face of the bold and the new; he was also a deputy in the Tajik Soviet. With one foot in the establishment and one out, Turajanzada understood the workings of power in a way many did not. His

---

* Hasan al-Banna wrote: 'You are not a benevolent society, nor a political party, nor a local organisation having limited purposes. Rather, you are a new soul in the heart of this nation to give it life by means of the Qur'an.' (Quoted in Mitchell, *Society of the Muslim Brothers*.)

obvious intelligence, his access to channels of authority, most of all his confidence, made him a powerful figure, and he was loved and loathed in about equal measure.

Hindustani of Kokand did not at all approve of the course some of his former students were taking. He felt that they had become politically ambitious, and that it was always a bad thing to confuse politics and religion. Having witnessed mortal aspiration on a monumental scale for the best part of a hundred years, Hindustani had had time and reason to reflect upon the nature of how things should be. His beliefs were simple. 'My father thought that parents should bring up their children to do right and to study at school. He thought that people should live properly, have enough to eat, and not force their views on one another,' says his stepson Ubaidullah. 'He used to tell a story about a tiger who lived in the far, cold mountains. Once, when the tiger came close to a human settlement, he saw a light and went towards it. A dog began to bark. "Why are you barking at me, dog?" he asked. The dog said that it was his job to bark, and that he got food and shelter in exchange. The tiger thought the dog must have a fine life. It was only after he had indulged those envious thoughts that he noticed the big chain around the dog's neck. He changed his mind and went back to the mountains, hungry but free.'

Hindustani in extreme old age let his grandchildren film him at a tea party. In grainy monochrome a broad, strong-looking old man in heavy spectacles and the velvet hat he always wore sits propped up on pillows, laughing and talking energetically. His family thinks that the lively discussion around the couch was about Bi-del, the seventeenth-century poet he had studied since the time of his first arrival at Bukhara in 1909.

Hindustani had a heart attack and died shortly afterwards, on 17 October 1989. He was officially ninety-seven years old. From his birth in the old world to his death in the new, he had spanned the Russian century and – almost – outlived the Soviet Union. He left behind a great volume of work, including his Uzbek Quran and commentaries and a mass of interpretative writings on Bi-del. His only regret was that they had remained unpublished. 'People came in their thousands to pay their respects,' his grandson Hamidjan remem-

1. Tajik women and girls on the border with Afghanistan at Qalah-e Khumb

2. Tajik interior, Qurghan Tappa

3. Uzbeks at a Tashkent bazaar

4. Women picking cotton, Andijan

5. Amir Abdulahad of
Bukhara and Crown Prince Alim

6. Hajji Parman (*left*) crossed the Amu
into Afghanistan aged 7 in 1928. He
lived at Aqcha until the Soviet invasion
of 1979, when he and his family fled to
Peshawar. His neighbour (*right*) was
born just after his pregnant mother
reached Afghanistan

7. Sadr-e Zia and his circle at Bukhara, 1911

8. Muhammadjan Rustamov –
'Hindustani' – on his return from
Afghanistan

9. Sadr-e Zia in his library with his baby
son Muhammadjan, 1926

10. The Ministry of Labour: one of the first Soviet departments to open in Dushanbe

11. Ibrahim Bek: the triangular badges may be amulets of a kind still used in Central Asia

12. Trial of a Basmachi suspect, probably in Dushanbe, 1920s. The prisoner stands in the centre, his hands bound. The official seated left wears 'revolutionary' clothing − a European-style suit, laced shoes and black and white hat

13. Ibrahim Bek under arrest, 1931

14. Literacy campaign, Tajikistan, 1940s

15. Blasting the Osh–Khurug road, 1940s

16. Uzbeks and Tajiks in the Turkestan Legion of the German army, 1940s. Note the crescent insignia on their collars.

17. Second World War veterans, Dushanbe

18. Kabul shortly before the Soviet invasion

19. Soviet troops returning from Afghanistan rest on the Tajik side of the Amu

20. Shahidan Square demonstration, Dushanbe

21. Azadi Square demonstration, Dushanbe

22. Tajik refugees arrive in Afghanistan

23. Imamali Rahmanov

24. Said Abdullah Nuri

25. A Russian woman and her daughters leave Dushanbe

26. Post-war *buzkashi* match outside Dushanbe

27. Tajik refugees return home to Shahr-e Tuz

28. Central Tashkent: the memorial commemorates the Tashkent families who took in orphans from all over the USSR during the Second World War. The glass building (*left*) is a post–Soviet office block

29. Soviet-era flats, Tashkent: domestic architecture was given an eastern flavour by the inclusion of characteristic closed balconies derived from the classical *aivan*. The mural is of Ibn Sina

30. The Tashkent–Kokand road

31. Islam Karimov

32. Abduvali Mirzayev

33. The shrine of the Caliph Ali, Mazar-e Sharif

34. Ahmad Shah Mas'ud

35. Abdul Rashid Dustam

36. Trial of the Tashkent 'bombers'

37. Female relatives mourn during an 'Islamic' trial in Namangan

bers. 'They had to triple the number of buses from Dushanbe airport. There was no room here at the house so we sent them on to the mosque. There was never before such a funeral here, and probably never will be.'

Maulavi Qari Muhammadjan Rustamov called Hindustani was buried at the Yaqub-e Charkhi mosque in Dushanbe, where a white marble tomb stands to his memory under the giant plane trees. 'I am glad,' said his grandson, 'that people honoured him at last. I am also glad that he did not see the wickedness that came after.'

Muhammadjan Shukurov went to have his hair cut on Prospekt Lenina on 11 February 1990. 'I sat in the chair, and through the barber's window I saw something odd. There were a lot of very young people about. I wondered what they were doing, what they wanted. Nobody seemed to know.' Muhammadjan Shukurov went home.

Next day, he went back into town for a meeting at the Writers' Union building. When he heard a commotion outside, he thought it must be children playing with fire-crackers. After the meeting, he walked out of the building to find that crowds of young people were charging down Prospekt Lenina, smashing windows. 'Their eyes were bloodshot and they looked angry. Some of them were carrying things in their hands. There were buses burning and an ambulance racing to and fro.' Muhammadjan Shukurov managed to get hold of a car and dodged through the backstreets to pick up his wife from work. That evening they sat at home with the telephone cut off and two buses in flames outside the front door. They could hear clearly the sound of tanks rolling into the city from the west side.

The demonstration that rocked Dushanbe on 12 February was something completely new and, to most people, extremely frightening. About five thousand young demonstrators had suddenly turned up outside the Central Committee of the Communist Party on Prospekt Lenina, many worked up by a street rumour that Armenians were to be brought to Dushanbe following riots against them in Azerbaijan. The Armenians never appeared, but such a rumour was enough to aggravate tensions caused by the severe housing shortage in Dushanbe. When Qahar Mahkamov, First Secretary of the Party

Central Committee, came out to speak to the demonstrators, a protestor threw a stone. 'Then someone pulled off a shoe and threw it,' remembers a reporter who was in the thick of the crowd. 'Suddenly they were all throwing things. Someone shouted "Mahkamov, resign!"'

Government troops opened fire into the crowd without warning. 'It was hard to grasp what was happening even when we saw that eight or ten people had been shot. We just stayed rooted to the spot. Then they fired the tear gas,' remembers the reporter. Young men pelted away along Prospekt Lenina, smashing and looting as they went.

Dushanbe was left shaken. Muhammadjan Shukurov wrote an open letter of apology to the people of Armenia and received a warm response, and a bottle of brandy as a present. Many other people were also shocked by the sudden eruption of violence in a peaceful city. People who were now taking an interest in politics, however, also felt indignant that no one was brought to book for ordering the shooting of young demonstrators armed with sticks and shoes. The official inquiry into what happened was inconclusive. The KGB files on the shootings were burnt in a fire that has never been fully explained. It was not the city authorities but local journalists who counted the dead and put up a memorial stone carved with twenty-three names. The square where they fell was renamed Shahidan, or the Square of the Martyrs.

In the months that followed, several reformist movements were founded or grew in strength, all in one way or another interested in the idea of greater fairness or openness and rooted in the revival of Tajik-ness. One, named Rastakhez, popular among intellectuals, was dedicated to Tajik culture. Founders of the new Democratic Party argued for a free press, a just political system and a modern economy. 'For seventy years gold from Tajik mountains and cotton from Tajik fields had gone to Moscow,' one enthusiast put it. 'We had rubies, copper and hydropower and we felt we should have been rich, not the poorest part of the USSR! We were tired of being a source of raw materials for others to profit from.'

Said Abdullah Nuri and other young clerics formed their own political party. The Hezb-e Nahzat-e Islami, or Islamic Renaissance Party, was founded on 6 October 1990 at a meeting which was held in the village of Chahar Tut outside Dushanbe to prevent interference from officials. The party was declared to be a branch of a Union-wide Islamic organisation announced at a congress in Astrakhan, in Russia, four months earlier, but its roots were firmly local. The Hezb-e Nahzat-e Islami wanted to look afresh at what shape the new order should take – what should be preserved from the colonial past (trains, telephones), what should be rejected (lack of religious education in schools). Eventually, it aimed to work towards the gradual introduction of laws suitable to a modern Muslim country, whatever they might prove to be. Akbar Turajanzada did not join the party, though naturally he and its leaders shared some common ground, and the silvery Friday mosque on Prospekt Lenina became the informal headquarters of what amounted to an anti-communist alliance, or opposition. Their meetings were far more lively and unrestrained than those permitted elsewhere Central Asia – or in most parts of the Soviet Union.

Across the border in Uzbekistan, many of the same kinds of movements and parties were also forming, albeit more cautiously. Two secular nationalist movements, Birlik and Erk, held public rallies and drew a following among urban intellectuals. Nuri's friend Abduvali Mirzayev reclaimed as a house of prayer the medieval Friday mosque in Andijan, which had been used as a Soviet museum; he did not ask permission of the Muftiat, but simply did it. Religious revivalists talked about forming an Uzbek Islamic Party. In Tashkent, bastion of Soviet power, things began to happen that would have been unimaginable only a year before. 'Some Christian missionaries came to the House of Culture and showed a film about the life of Jesus. My friends and I were interested in everything at that time so we went to see it,' remembers a student. 'It was a nice film and the missionaries – I don't know where they were from, Sweden, Switzerland, some European country – handed out booklets to go with it. Suddenly men jumped up from their seats, ripped up the booklets and shouted "*la elah ella-allah ashhad-o an muhammadan rasul-allah* – there is no God but God and Muhammad is his prophet."'

Ubaidullah turned sixty-five in the year after the death of his step-father Hindustani. An elder in his own right, he was now also head of the family. Like Hindustani, he had no interest in politics and saw himself as a simple *dehqan* or peasant. His passion for flowers was undimmed. 'No one realises it now,' he says, smiling, sitting in the garden he planted forty years ago, 'as they walk around this city and smell the roses – thirty-five varieties – and the sweet Williams and the forsythia, that we went to Riga and Tallin and Minsk to bring back the seeds. I even brought the cuttings for the Canadian maples.' To supplement his income, he had worked in numerous odd jobs over the years, as a cook, butcher, tanner, driver, weaver, and type-setter.

Ubaidullah decided to go on hajj soon after the first anniversary of his stepfather's death, an occasion of great import in an Uzbek or Tajik family's calendar. In the early spring of 1991 he travelled by aeroplane to Mecca on what he described as a 'magical' journey, accompanied by his fourth son, Nurullah. Arriving at their hotel, they made enquiries for their relatives on his mother's side, a man and his young son, who had fled Kokand in 1929 intending to make a new life in what they called Arabistan. 'I had brought with me the photograph taken before they left and the hotel staff, you know, they found the son of the boy,' says Ubaidullah. 'I was so happy.' The son, Yunus Khan, at once took Ubaidullah and Nurullah to his house, where they met his family and stayed for two days before carrying on with their pilgrimage. Having fulfilled their Muslim duty they returned to Dushanbe, and so were among the very first Central Asians to make the Hajj in modern times.

On 19 August 1991, two thousand miles away from Dushanbe, Mikhail Gorbachev's rivals in Moscow staged the *putsch* that finally brought down both him and themselves. For forty-eight hours, the fate of the Soviet Union seemed to hang in the balance. Most repub-lican leaders – and those of the opposition – waited to see what would happen before speaking up for one side or the other. The great majority of people in Uzbekistan knew nothing about the attempted coup, though a few had a hunch that something was awry when they saw the old Soviet cover-up, *Swan Lake*, on television. Tajikistan was far more aware politically: as soon as the coup failed, opposition leaders challenged Qahar Mahkamov to say whose side he had been on.

Mahkamov's account, delivered to parliament, claimed that he had heard, on the morning of 19 August, only the gist of what was going on in Russia. He had tried to find out more but no one in Moscow had answered his phone calls. 'I rang Lukyanov [Speaker of the Supreme Soviet] and was told that he couldn't talk. Then I rang Yanayev [Vice-President of the USSR]. In vain. Next I talked to Nazarbayev [of Kazakhstan] and Niazov [of Turkmenistan], who didn't have complete or reliable information either. Later in the day I didn't manage to speak to anyone either.'

That evening, a telegram arrived from Moscow summoning Mahkamov to a Central Committee Plenum, and he set off in the usual way. 'When I arrived in Moscow I was told that the plenum would not take place,' he claimed. 'And still I kept on trying to find someone, anyone, to talk to. They were all in the Kremlin. Unfortunately I did not manage to speak to any of them.' Mahkamov returned to Dushanbe on the night flight.

Mahkamov's story did not convince his opponents. His days, and those of the USSR, were numbered. Mikhail Gorbachev resigned as leader of the Communist Party and dissolved the Party organisation on 24 August. Ukraine declared independence the same day, and one by one the republics broke away from the atrophied spine of the Union. Even staunch Uzbekistan issued a declaration of independence, on 31 August 1991. Tajikistan followed on 9 September.

On the night of 21 September thousands of demonstrators gathered at Lenin square on Prospekt Lenina. They had been bussed into Dushanbe specially by the Hezb-e Nahzat-e Islami, mainly from the Vakhsh valley and from the mountainous regions whence the party leaders came. They were *mu-e safeds*, farmers and shepherds, factory workers and the unemployed. They unrolled their mats on the tarmac, made little fires, brought out their kettles and cooked rice in huge pots. Some had never seen the capital, and it was the first time the modern, Soviet city had seen so many of them. 'I saw them praying all together,' said one resident. 'It was astonishing for us to see them in their robes, crowds of them, reading the Quran right in front of Lenin!' After prayers some settled to sleep, many others recited the poem that caught the mood of the time:

The East is no more than a trail of dust,
Nothing but a dying breath.
Awake! Awake from this deepest sleep.

In every corner of this earth, life stares without hope.
Awake! From India, to Samarkand, to Iraq and Hamadan,
Awake! Awake from this deepest sleep.

Muhammad Iqbal's song of Muslim resurrection had been written under British rule in what is now Pakistan. Some of his Persian poetry fitted perfectly the mood in Tajikistan eighty years later. Tajiks knew what Iqbal meant when he called Afghanistan the heart of Asia from which discord or harmony could flow, or when he wrote:

To the new flame old nations are like sticks on a bonfire;
Followers of the last messenger are consumed in its flames.

The crowd watched and chanted as men hoisted a rope around the Lenin statue. A crane tugged to and fro through the small hours. At half-past six, the statue toppled over and broke: the first Lenin monument in all Central Asia to fall. Someone shoved the head into the chest and loaded the pieces on a trailer. Someone else scrambled up and scribbled 'Death to the USSR!' on the plinth in Cyrillic letters. He turned, grinning for the video camera. By the time the first trolley-buses of the morning were rattling down the avenue, Lenin had been towed away. The men from the villages picked up their mats and teacups and went to pray in the park.

Ubaidullah felt sad when he saw the news on the television. 'I remember my father saying how wrong it was when people praised a man to the skies for fifty years and then turned on him after he was gone.' He thinks that to destroy monuments built to the memory of the dead is one of the greatest sins.

'I thought we needed to be wise and careful,' said Muhammadjan Shukurov. 'We had become a nation but we didn't know what "nation" was. In the Soviet time we said "people" – the Tajik or Uzbek people of the Soviet Union – not "nation". We had never lived in a nation state. Suddenly we needed to understand the idea of "nation". We needed to have a "national interest". National interest? We didn't know what that was! People knew just their own interests, or the interests of their family or their village.'

Tajiks chose a new president for their new country on 24 November 1991. It was the first time ever that there had been a meaningful choice of candidate. The combined opposition put up a cinematographer from the Pamir, Davlat Khudanazarov, who took a disputed 30 per cent or so of the vote and lost. The old Communist Party candidate, Rahman Nabiev, with the state apparatus behind him, took 57 per cent and moved into the pinkish-grey stone Presidential Palace – the former Communist Party headquarters – on what had been Prospekt Lenina and was now Rudaki Avenue.

Nabiev's heavy face and white hair were well known. Born in Khujand, like every republican leader since the Second World War, he had served as the Tajik party chief from 1982 to 1985 under Brezhnev, before being swept away by the new broom of Gorbachev, ostensibly on grounds of ill-health. Nabiev had all the weight of his traditional power-base behind him. He also had the support of many people who feared a sudden shift into the political unknown, including some reformists. The large Uzbek minority – a quarter of the population – and the Slavs and Europeans were also broadly pro-Nabiev, who as a life-long communist seemed unlikely to turn into a nationalist promoting only Tajik interests.

Nabiev set out to lead a country in which many people were impatient for change. Almost all were poor and – most importantly – knew it. More than half the population was under sixteen years old. Nabiev was fifty-nine and had been called out of his enforced retirement to do the job, a man with a weak heart who smoked heavily and drank to excess. 'He used to get to the office at twelve and go home early – he didn't do much,' remembers a contemporary. A month after his election, the Soviet system he had known all his life came to an end. On 25 December 1991 Mikhail Gorbachev resigned, the Red Flag was hauled down for the last time over the Kremlin in Moscow, and the white, blue and red Russian flag run up in its place. There were no crowds, no ceremony, no cheers except from a few foreigners who happened to be walking through Red Square that evening.

Muhammadjan Shukurov described the next few months as a curious time in which nothing was different yet everything had changed. Independence first felt real to him when the foreign embassies began to open and he saw diplomatic cars with their special red number plates driving around town. The Iranians got licence plate number 001. Then six Americans turned up and made an embassy out of six rooms on the top floor of the blue-green modernist Oktyabrskaya Hotel (formerly kept for Party grandees) in the city centre. The Turks came next. But it really sank in that Tajikistan was a *country* when the Russians sent envoys.

Nabiev got off to an equable start. He laid a wreath at their memorial to commemorate the second anniversary of those who had been killed on 12 February 1990. Yet the banners held by some among the quiet crowd pointed poignantly to the fact that fundamental questions were yet to be resolved. 'How shall we live?' read one placard: 'What is to become of us?'

A month later, Nabiev began to move against his potential adversaries. The mayor of Dushanbe, Maqsud Ikramov, who had allowed the Lenin statue to be pulled down, was arrested on charges of corruption. The Interior Minister, Mamadayaz Navjavanov, was sacked on similar grounds. The sackings – particularly that of Navjavanov – set in play new political forces. When, on 27 March, the speaker of parliament, Safarali Kenjayev, made a televised speech about Navjavanov's alleged corruption – in itself not an especially controversial issue – he explicitly insulted Navjavanov's Pamiri origins. A small number of Pamiris responded by gathering outside the Presidential Palace on Shahidan Square to demand Navjavanov's reinstatement and the dismissal of Kenjayev. People's regional roots had quite openly become a political factor – and Kenjayev a symbol of an old guard jealously defending its power.

Tough, energetic and plain-speaking, Kenjayev had been in charge of the investigation into the shootings of 12 February 1990, the results of which had never come to light. He appeared to be set in the classical communist mould, but the man beneath the image was hard to typecast. The holder of a doctorate in jurisprudence, he later in life adopted a rumpled, scholarly air and the half-moon spectacles of an academic. He was the author of several non-fiction books and at least one detective novel, rather than the poetry more usually written by Tajik and Uzbek politicians.

Kenjayev's life illustrates the subtle complexities of Tajikistan. Unusually for a member of the ruling élite, he was not born to privilege, and was not from Khujand. His family came from the remote mountainous pocket of Yagnob north of Dushanbe, whence they moved down to near the capital. When Safarali was about ten, a poor mountain boy with a bad stammer, he went to live in the Turajanzada household, because his father was a *murid* of Ishan Turajan. 'He was like my brother,' says Turajanzada. 'I used to say to him, "we are like finger-tip and nail, inseparable". And I never thought of him as an enemy, despite everything that happened next.'

8

Kartoshka, kartushka – *war in Tajikistan*

'Beware of the enmity of men, for it sullies
The Purity of every drinking-place.
And do not stir up war even though thou reliest
Upon a firm support and a strong shoulder,
For the wise man will not drink deadly poison because
Of his confidence in a tested antidote that he has.'

ANTI-COMMUNISTS OF every kind joined the Pamiri demonstration on Shahidan Square in the last week of March 1992. People
called for the resignation of Kenjayev, for new elections, for greater
freedom of speech, and generally for political and economic power to
be shared out beyond the old élite. Hezb-e Nahzat-e Islami sent to
the mountains and to the fields of the Vakhsh valley for more supporters – and so many came that people called it a 'Gharmi' protest.

Led by their elders and mullas, hundreds of farmers left their jobs
on run-down *kolkhozes*, packed themselves into buses and headed for
the capital, in some cases several days' journey away. 'We came
because we thought this was the way to a better life,' said one demonstrator. 'We earned just pennies in the *kolkhoz*' – a cotton worker's
wage at this time was about thirty roubles a month: about twenty
cents – 'and we were desperate for flour, oil, and clothes for our children.' Some came because they believed that to do so was the duty of
a good Muslim: the rumour went around some villages that if a man
did not go, he would no longer be a Muslim at all, and would have to
divorce his wife. 'I loved my wife,' one demonstrator said. 'Of course
I went to the meeting.' The demonstrators stayed with friends in the

town because petrol was expensive, returning each day, despite the heavy spring rains, to Shahidan Square to pray, recite poems and listen to speeches. Hezb-e Nahzat-e Islami leaders addressed the crowds, as did Akbar Turajanzada. 'Awake! Awake!' a single voice would call into the tannoy. 'Awake from this deepest sleep!' came the response, resounding through Dushanbe. 'From India to Samarkand, to Iraq and Hamadan!'

It was *ramazan*, the month when practising Muslims abstain from food between dawn and dusk. Each evening the organisers cooked rice and lamb in kitchen tents. The smell of cooking rose through central, modern Dushanbe as crowds of poor country people sat around their fires and broke their fast together.

'I looked from our balcony,' remembers the son of an élite communist family living on the square. 'And I saw more and more of them. I had never seen such people before! All those old men with turbans. I could not imagine what they wanted in our city.' The Nabiev government, though uneasy, did nothing to disperse the crowd. The trolley-buses still passed down Rudaki, people went to work and life went on. 'How could we have broken up such demonstrations?' says one government official of that time. 'These were the fathers and sons of people we knew.'

Fifteen thousand demonstrators were in the square for morning prayers on *eid-e fetr*, the holiday at the end of *ramazan*. In a special broadcast address, President Nabiev called on the demonstrators to go home quietly. The crowds on Rudaki took no notice.

A witness gave this account of the scene a week later:

Every day beginning at 5 a.m. thousands of Muslims who have occupied the main square in front of the Presidential Palace begin chanting 'Out with the Parliament! Out with Nabiev! Long live the Islamic state!' Every day, too, processions of young and old men march on the TV and radio stations. The square has been transformed into a giant camp site with hundreds of tents, a temporary mosque and outdoor kitchen. Prayers take place five times a day. Morale is good among the campers, who say they will stay put until Tajikistan becomes a democratic state. One of the demonstrators . . . abandoned his job at a chicken co-operative farm when the mass demonstrations began. He said thanks to the generous contributions of all Muslims and funds donated by the fifteen hundred mosques of the republic, nobody is starving.

Leaders of the demonstration called repeatedly for the dissolution of parliament and a new constitution, and President Nabiev responded. He accused the leaders of Hezb-e Nahzat-e Islami of trying to overthrow the secular state for reasons of personal greed and claimed that, when they came to power, they would enforce the sort of 'Islamic' social rules in use in Iran. 'He was right, I think,' said one young woman who watched the crowds. 'Those men knew the state was weak. They wanted power, and so they used the old Gharmi men.' Hezb-e Nahzat-e Islami leaders and Turajanzada told the public time and again that they had no intention of forcing women back into the veil – that emblem of Islam that so dominated the public perception of revolutionary Iran.

In the middle of April 1992, the remnants of the Soviet order across the border in Afghanistan fell to pieces. Under an agreement with Washington after the USSR collapsed, Moscow had abruptly stopped sending money and weapons to the last communist Afghan president, Muhammad Najibullah. He grew weak. Government soldiers all over the country pulled off their uniform jackets and deserted him, especially after the sudden defection of an important general, Abdul Rashid Dustam, an Afghan Uzbek with forty thousand men and his own fief in the northern borderlands around Mazar-e Sharif. On 14 April the northern *mujahedin* led by Ahmad Shah Mas'ud, now in alliance with Dustam, came out of the mountains and camped at the gate of Kabul, only an hour's drive north of the city; other *mujahedin* factions, notably Hezb-e Islami, pressed in from the south.

Inside the capital, Najibullah took sanctuary in the basement of the United Nations building. Some of his ministers had already slipped out of the country. On 16 April his staff found the body of Ghulam Faruq Yaqubi, head of KhAD, the intelligence service modelled on the KGB, in a pool of blood beside his glass-topped desk, on which still stood his Soviet hot-line telephones and a model watch-tower.

The *mujahedin* moved into the leaderless capital on 25 April. Some swarmed to the top of the old Communist Party building, pulled down the Red Star and smashed it. The *mujahedin* formed an interim government, to be led by a cleric, Sebghatullah Mujaddedi. In Afghan embassies across the world, diplomats inked out 'Democratic' and inserted 'Islamic' before 'Republic of Afghanistan' on the first visas for the new country.

The idea of a poor, determined and brave people winning freedom, overthrowing a Goliath, starting life anew – surviving, at huge cost, the predations of two superpowers – caught the imagination of people across the world. For Tajiks, the *mujahedin* victory held an extra significance no one else could fully appreciate. 'Mas'ud was a Tajik: the most and only famous Tajik in the world! We needed a national hero so badly!' said a young journalist covering the story of the Dushanbe demonstration, which had now stayed solid for three weeks. 'Everyone at Shahidan knew Mas'ud was a Tajik like themselves, though of course not many knew anything else about him. By that time, a lot of people were shouting things they did not really understand. When they shouted "Nabiev! Ist'fa! Ist'fa! [Resign! Resign!]", some of them thought "Ist'fa" was somebody's name. We began to worry because there were so many people there, too many. They had come with good intentions, but the politicians were keeping them there.' The square overflowed, and thousands of people spilled down Rudaki Avenue.

Nabiev's inner circle took a decisive step. Two days after the *mujahedin* moved into Kabul, they sent to the countryside for counterdemonstrators to face down the crowd at Shahidan. Nabiev himself, according to men close to him, was drinking heavily at this time and had little grip on events. According to most accounts, it was Safarali Kenjayev who made many of the decisions, probably in conjunction with hidden advisers – but there were surely other ambitious men waiting in the wings.

The region chosen from which to draw the counter-rally was Kulab, the poorest and least developed part of the rural south. Tucked between the mountains and the Afghan border, Kulab had been relatively well-off at the start of the twentieth century. Its fields were fertile, its pistachio thickets productive and filled with pheasants, while the Amu provided a steady if modest income through trade.

The reed-thatched houses along the straight, broad streets of the town of Kulab were home to a diverse population of Tajiks, Uzbeks, Afghans, Kirgiz and Kashmiris. Twenty-two calligraphers worked in the tiny district of Sar-e Khassa alone, and the saddle-making guild of Baljuan drew students from Afghanistan and as far away as Karshi, one of the main cities of the old emirate of Bukhara. Later history and geography did not go Kulab's way. The early years of Soviet power left it shattered. In some districts, about half the population left in the exodus of the 1920s and 1930s. The region became a stock-breeding area about as remote from the centres of power as it was possible to be. There was no railway to Kulab and only two roads, one of which ran through the mountains.

'The phone call came from Dushanbe, asking us to come,' one Kulabi remembers. 'People thought, well, why not! Many of us had never seen Dushanbe and it sounded like fun. All we had to do was sit on the bus, and when we got to Dushanbe there would be free food. There was no more Soviet Union and we had no idea what would befall us tomorrow. So we went.' When muddled rumours ran around Kulab that the Gharmis at Shahidan Square were trying to seize power, whereupon they would take the Kulabis' daughters, many more people felt it was time to protect their families by going to Dushanbe. In the last week of April, a column of shabby buses arrived in the capital and disgorged hundreds of men outside the Parliament building on Azadi Square, less than a mile away from the rally at Shahidan Square.

A short, stocky man in his seventies, 'Grandpa' Sangak Safarov, took the helm at Azadi. He worked the crowd skilfully, scratching at their rawest fears and supplying a flattering solution. 'Fifty Kulabis' could restore order to Dushanbe, he boasted. Safarov was a wealthy ale-house owner who had come to Kulab as a deportee from the mountain town of Tavil Dara in the 1950s. In between, he had served twenty years in Soviet prisons for murder. According to friends, he read widely in jail and educated himself. He was not a pious man, nor a 'communist' – in one speech at Azadi, he cursed the communists for 'killing his fathers' – but a tough, self-made survivor. Safarov's message of general solidarity against 'hooligans' cut through any ideological complexities. Within days there were five or six thousand demonstrators crowded into Azadi. Most were from Kulab, but there were also some from Uzbek-majority areas, especially Hisar, only an hour's drive from Dushanbe.

Journalists covering the story were worried by the way Tajikistan was dividing not only poor southerners against the northern élite but poor southerners against one another. Some felt that a potentially lethal game of divide and rule was going on. It was particularly worrying that one convoy of Kulabis had been shot at on its way into Dushanbe by people whom Shahidan leaders maintained were not theirs. The journalists stuck together, shuttling to and fro along the short strip of Rudaki that lay between the squares; every day, the strip grew shorter. Some Azadi demonstrators shouted wildly that Turajanzada was a criminal, and should be put on trial. One government man initially in sympathy with the Shahidan group froze in horror when someone there yelled: 'Burn the communists' houses and let them suffocate in the smoke!' He was not alone in feeling that things had gone too far, and that people had begun to play dangerous parts.

President Nabiev lacked the most basic implement of state security: an army. Most former Soviet republics had made national armies out of the leftover Soviet army divisions on their territory – much as the Aeroflot fleet had been shared out according to which aircraft were on whose ground when the USSR collapsed. But Nabiev had declined to do this, because (he said) Tajikistan could not afford the cost even of the six thousand men or so of the 201st Motor Rifle Division, the part of the 40th Army that had been based in Qunduz during the Soviet occupation of Afghanistan and had withdrawn to Tajikistan afterwards. It was also felt that the officers, 96 per cent of whom were Slavs, were unlikely to fight under a Tajik flag.

Nabiev could not give orders to the 201st Division, or to the other, smaller ex-Soviet units left in Tajikistan – most importantly, the guards along the frontiers with Afghanistan and China – which were commanded nominally by the Commonwealth of Independent States, the loose partnership of former Soviet republics created in 1991. He could, however, request assistance from them. With tens of thousands of people on the streets in his capital, he sent to the garrison for help. The garrison could not act without orders from Moscow. Moscow gave no orders.

On 1 May, Nabiev's inner circle created its own 'National Guard' by handing out 1,700 or so Kalashnikov rifles at Azadi Square. Most of the guns went into civilian, untrained hands. The leaders of Shahidan expressed outrage and demanded that the guns be collected up again within three days. They were not. On 3 May, President Nabiev issued a decree ordering the Shahidan protestors to go home. Shahidan protestors ignored the order and spent the afternoon building barricades across the entrance to their square with buses and concrete traffic-control blocks. As dusk fell, some began to keep vigil. From time to time, one leader or another got up and shouted through the megaphone into the darkness, appealing to the 201st Division to stay neutral. Campfires burnt throughout the night.

As 4 May dawned, ten thousand or more people settled in for the day at the two squares as usual, cooking and talking, reciting prayers on one side, singing folk songs on the other. When helicopters flew over the city, many residents were so on edge that they believed 'the Russians had come' at last – but the helicopters only scattered leaflets:

> Tajikistan today is on the verge of a split and a catastrophe is approaching. The moment has now come when the fate of the Tajik people is being decided. Dear residents of Dushanbe, be vigilant and do not yield to provocation. It is your choice.

On the critical day of 5 May, President Nabiev proclaimed a State of Emergency. All political parties, rallies, and strikes were banned, and a dusk-to-dawn curfew was imposed in the capital, starting at 9 p.m. A few shots rang out in the afternoon and most residents were safely at home long before the curfew hour, many of them watching television. At about 6.30, Tajik television fell off air in the middle of a programme. When the television sets flickered back to life an hour and a half later, opposition leaders from Shahidan filled the screens, urging the public to ignore the State of Emergency. They had commandeered the television station, without great difficulty.

That night, the 'power' ministries – that is, those whose personnel had the right to carry arms – took sides. At 10 p.m. guardsmen at the Presidential Palace in the heart of Shahidan Square threw in their lot with the demonstrators around them. Then, at 2 a.m., a large number of Interior Ministry men – the police force – came over to the opposition, bringing with them their arsenal. The Security Ministry, still generally known as the KGB, stayed with the government. Significantly, even after independence almost all the senior officers were non-Tajiks. Had this not been the case, the outcome might have been different – one official said privately that there were 'more Islamic Party members than communists' among the Tajiks in the KGB of 1992.

Strengthened by the windfall of the Interior Ministry guns and armoured personnel carriers, opposition activists took the airport and headed for Azadi Square where the parliament building stood. Leaders of the rival demonstrations struck a deal, allowing the Kulabis to leave the square and return home and giving them an escort until they were beyond the Dushanbe city boundary. As there was heavy shooting at Azadi in the meantime and several men were killed, the Kulabis kept their guns to cover their withdrawal.

President Nabiev had disappeared into the relative safety of the Security Ministry building, which was guarded by the supposedly neutral 201st Division. By the night of 7 May, this was the only centre of power outside opposition hands. Yet no clear leader emerged on the opposition side. Someone appeared on television announcing that a 'Revolutionary Council' had been set up – five hours later, a second announcement cancelled the first.

The next morning, Colonel Vyacheslav Zabolotny, the Belorussian commander of the 201st Division, offered to negotiate a settlement between opposition leaders and the helpless Nabiev, who had sought refuge in the 201st Division garrison after an attack on the Security Ministry. 'Thousands of demonstrators waited, looking to us for leadership,' says a senior opposition figure, 'but still we failed to agree among ourselves. I thought any coalition made on Russian terms would end in disaster – how could the Russians possibly be neutral? – but others disagreed, and they prevailed.'

While the talks went on, first at the garrison and then at the old Communist Party *dacha* on Rudaki Avenue, a sour, frightened tension soaked through the capital. The demonstrations had created ill-feeling that was easily aggravated using the standard Soviet techniques of suggestion. 'They filmed the things the Kulabis had left behind them in Azadi, like scraps of food and bottles and sticks,' recalled a television viewer. 'They wrote "Museum of Kulab" on a board and showed it all, saying "Look how dirty these Kulabis made our city!" They showed a room in the basement of the Parliament building filled with condoms and bottles, and the television said: "This was where the Kulabis took our girls and raped them." In reality, those things came from a chemist's shop. It was all lies.' Even some imams taunted and insulted the Kulabi 'losers' and mocked the Uzbek minority at Friday prayers.

On 11 May, a coalition Government of National Reconciliation was announced. Nabiev was to stay on as president and most of the other main figures from the old government kept their positions. Opposition forces were to get a third of the cabinet posts. The crowds of demonstrators at Shahidan waited around for a while after the announcement, drinking last cups of tea and chatting, unsure what to make of it. Then, after fifty days of almost unbroken protest, they folded their tents, packed their few belongings, and returned to the remote villages from which they had come.

The Tajik Government of National Reconciliation represented by far the most radical political experiment by any state of the former Soviet Union. It faced enormous odds. The men in charge of the country – which was only six months old – had no reason to trust one another, and had no experience of managing public affairs beyond the Soviet system or underground organisations. The president was befuddled by drink and had been shown to be powerless. The parliament, made up mainly of old communists, refused to meet. There was still no army. The 201st Division, standing in place of an army, was commanded by the former colonial power. There was no calculable economy. The Tajik SSR had depended on Moscow for aid, and in 1990 – the last full year of the Union – had received 762 million roubles, which was reduced to only 25 million devalued roubles in 1991; in 1992, subsidies ended. The allocation of a third of government positions to the anti-communists applied only in the capital, leaving the opposition unrepresented in the countryside, not least in the southern and mountainous provinces in which it had real support. Worst of all, region had been set against region. Khujand declared at once that it would not take orders from the new government. Kulab followed suit. Dushanbe stood exposed as a rootless city with no tradition of government over the plains and valleys around it.

In the Vakhsh valley, the June harvest had just been gathered. Heaps of wheat lay drying in lanes bordered with pink mallow and roses. Daler (not his real name), aged about twenty, was on his way home to his village in the Rah-e Lenin *kolkhoz*, east of the valley, close to the town of Panj on the river Amu. Daler had just completed eighteen months of his military service in the polar desert of Franz-Josef Land deep inside the Arctic Circle, where the Soviet Union kept an observation station. When he was called up, it had been to the Soviet Army, but that was now the army of a foreign power – Russia. His service should have lasted two years, but Daler was released early after a telegram arrived from Tajikistan saying that his mother was very ill. This was the first inkling Daler had that there was something wrong at home.

There were few cars willing to go as far as Rah-e Lenin, but eventually Daler found a driver to take him home. There he discovered that his mother was safe and well: his father had sent the telegram, from a need to have his eldest son at his side in what he felt were ominous times. Rah-e Lenin, like most, was a mixed *kolkhoz*. Daler's father was a tractor mechanic, son of a migrant from the mountains – so the family was 'Gharmi', as were several others. His neighbours were Uzbeks. The two communities were well integrated. Daler spoke good Uzbek, and had sat side by side with Uzbeks at school. 'All my neighbours were Lakais and Turks, we always went to each other's weddings and cradle parties,' he says. A week after his home-coming, Daler married the girl his mother had chosen when he was still a baby.

Daler's father's worries were well founded. There were constant rumours of friction between local Gharmis, Kulabis and Uzbeks, some of whom had been up in Dushanbe at the rallies, and even talk of shootings – though it was impossible to judge which stories were true. Daler says that at one point, Kulabi men came and stole weapons from a local police station. 'Our people were afraid. They took up spades and hunting guns. I had to protect my family. I knew how to handle a gun – I had been in the army. We crossed the river into Afghanistan with some carpets, some cows and some horses and swapped them for better guns, Kalashnikovs. Guns were very cheap there.'

The purchase and distribution of weapons among the Gharmis was handled by the Hezb-e Nahzat-e Islami, which had a house in each village. The local financier was the man who had managed the *kolkhoz* for the past forty years, 'Kabud' ('Blue') Saifuddin, who held the Lenin Prize for record-breaking levels of cotton production and had grown rich on the profits. The combined self-defence forces of different *kolkhozes* blocked the road to Kulab with tractors and concrete slabs. 'We thought only to protect ourselves,' Daler says. Other Hezb-e Nahzat-e Islami forces, seeking to defend what successes they had had in Dushanbe, also built blockades along the two roads between the capital and Kulab.

Jafar (also not his real name) was on the Kulab side of the barricades. 'Of course, we took up arms to protect ourselves,' he also says. 'Every family put up a son to join Sangak Safarov's militia. From my family, I was that boy.' After security, the most pressing concern of ordinary Kulabis was food. With no reserves to fall back on, families were rendered destitute when the Dushanbe road was cut by the blockades. 'There was no soap, no flour, nothing,' says Jafar. 'The only way to get food was to to go on raiding parties. Families sent their sons to fight, not for the glory of Kulab, or for power, or for Sangak, but because their boys might come back with some potatoes. And then they could manage for another day.' Safarov opened two prisons and put the convicts in the front lines. 'He understood the criminal mind very well,' one fighter remembers. 'He knew how angry these men were and how they would fight if need be. Of course, it was much safer to be in such a force than out.'

Like the Hezb-e Nahzat-e Islami supporters, the Kulabis sold their securities, the gold of their women and the carpets from their walls, and crossed the Amu into Afghanistan to buy weapons. Guns were so cheap that the cost of a Kalashnikov rifle that June was only two small carpets. In theory, the river bank was tightly patrolled by the Russian-led border guards who had retained control over this sensitive international border in the same way as the 201st Division had stayed on in Dushanbe. In practice, people of every stripe crossed. Morale among the guards was low. Colonel Ravil Mullayanov, the commander of the Panj corps in the summer of 1992, said his officers received no salaries that year until one sent a plane especially to Moscow and brought back nine tons of banknotes in arrears. Mullayanov reported that sixty local men crossed the Amu in a single day in late May to buy guns. 'Now there is no Soviet Union,' he said, 'one has to ask whom one is protecting.'

'The Russians sold us their bullets,' Daler remembers 'and a few guns as well.' The bullets, naturally, fitted the weapons bought in Afghanistan, as all were of Soviet provenance. 'Then we went to the Russians and paid them to come with us in their tanks and shoot Sangak's men. We used to rent them for an hour or so, for about a million roubles. Sometimes more.' (A million roubles was worth about a thousand dollars: probably much smaller sums also changed hands.) The Kulabi militia did the same. 'The Russians would shoot at us for up to a week sometimes. Then they would turn around and shoot the Gharmis,' says Jafar. 'The more they changed sides, the higher they could drive the price.'

There was no news service, there were no telephones, and many of the roads were blocked, so neither Daler nor Jafar knew anything of what might be happening outside his own village. 'Dushanbe? We knew nothing of Qurghan Tappa, let alone Dushanbe!' Daler said. Similarly isolated home-grown vigilante groups were springing up in many parts of southern Tajikistan, and ordinary people everywhere had begun to do extraordinary things.

The need to survive narrowed the pool of trust in *kolkhozes* made up of scores of families of different origins, most of them deportees at one time or another of the forced migration, the *muhajarat-e ijbari*. In some places Uzbeks, for instance, stood alongside Arabs for fear of Gharmis, while in others they were shoulder to shoulder with Gharmis to save their village from Kulabis, depending on the make-up of the *kolkhoz*. 'We were all simple people,' says a journalist who took up arms. 'We had no idea what would become of us. It was easy to make us fear each other.' 'I had to side with my own people,' said a senior KGB officer – a Tajik (unusually), and a Gharmi. 'I was threatened all the time because I was born in the mountains, and I had to protect my children.'

A number of gruesome killings sent chain reactions rattling through terrified communities which lacked any of the apparatus of a working state – such as ambulances, police, or an army – to support them. In the city of Qurghan Tappa, for example, a sweet-maker nicknamed 'Tela', 'Gold', because he was reportedly rich, was found dead and allegedly skinned. 'Tela' was an Uzbek, with roots in the town of Urgut in Uzbekistan. Terrified Urgutis banded together in their own self-defence force. A nearby Tajik-speaking district heard that the Urgutis were on the warpath and 'had a list' of every Tajik household they were going to kill. Tajiks quickly drove local Uzbeks out of the village next to them. 'Tajiks came in the morning and told us "All you lot go, just leave here straight away",' one Uzbek woman remembers. She grabbed her children and ran.

Looters swarmed into the house she left behind. They yanked the carpet from the wall, and bundled kettles, teapots, piles of quilts, even the window frames, into a stolen tractor. 'Of course, everyone needed money. How else could we live?' one fighter said later. 'And, to be honest, some people got a high out of shooting. You'd go home after a raid with a kick like adrenalin, and then everything would fall flat. So you'd go again. I know because I was high as can be.'

Tens, then hundreds of families began to run from their villages as the mosaic of southern Tajikistan cracked and split. Intermarried families had to decide which way to go – that is, who it was safest to be. Uzbeks made for Uzbek-populated areas – west to Hisar, north to Khujand, and across the border to Uzbekistan. Some 'Gharmi' families headed for the mountain villages they had left in the *muhajarat-e ijbari*. Others piled into buses and lorries and headed up the road towards Dushanbe, past cotton-fields empty of people, past apricots and apples unpicked on the trees. Once in the city, they made for the houses of relatives who had no idea of how bad things were in the south until they saw them, or found a few feet of floor space in mosques or hotels. Fuel, bread and medicine were already running low in Dushanbe, and ran lower still as the population grew. Farmers were too afraid of roadside bandits to bring their crops to town. 'There was only one state bakery still working by July,' a resident remembers. 'Huge crowds were massed in the yard there. The bread truck couldn't move. Gunmen – from the government – climbed up on the roof and shot into the air to scatter the crowd.'

'We absolutely had to do something about Nabiev,' says a former member of his government. 'He did nothing to stop what was happening, and he didn't want anyone else to take his place.' Nabiev's coalition partners finally jettisoned him in early September. 'The flames of civil war are threatening the whole country,' read a statement by the parliament, broadcast on Dushanbe Radio on 2 September. 'It is felt that the President of Tajikistan is an irresponsible person without authority and is an alien in his own state.' The next day, Hezb-e Nahzat-e Islami issued its own statement: 'It has become obvious and clear to every sound-minded person that every day the president remains in power will be a tragedy and calamity for the republic.' Nabiev was by now more or less living in the garrison of the 201st Division in Dushanbe. Its commander, unusually, was a Tajik. Major General Muhriddin Ashurov, originally from Gharm, was in a helplessly compromised position. He admitted privately to friends that he did not know what to do, and so did nothing.

Two hours' drive to the south, war moved out of the villages and into Qurghan Tappa, the main city of the Vakhsh valley. It was 5 September. Sergey and Rita, long-time residents of Qurghan Tappa, never forgot the date because Rita went into labour that day. She could not get to the hospital as four or five thousand armed shepherds and farmers had closed in on the city and divided it, district by district, pulling farm machinery and concrete blocks across the lanes. Like most Slavs, Rita and Sergey lived in a flat with running water, but the mains had been hit, so Sergey and their young son had to scramble to the river with buckets. Dodging bullets and weaving through alleys, they managed to bring some water home, and Rita delivered her daughter successfully with the help of a neighbour.

Sergey felt that one still ought to do the responsible thing. He dashed out to the abandoned bank and, for safe-keeping, took charge of the cotton-harvest accounts held there. It felt like a practical step against the day when peace would surely return. 'We all thought that life would just go back to how it was, once the war was over,' says one fighter on the front line at Qurghan Tappa. 'A teacher thought he would go back to teaching. How could we see beyond the war? We could not have known that nothing would ever be the same again.'

Two days later, on 7 September, President Nabiev ventured from the garrison building in Dushanbe, saying he would formally announce his resignation – on condition he could do so in his mother-country of Khujand. He went to the airport. Gunmen cornered him in the VIP lounge and made him sign his resignation then and there. With shooting breaking out all over the airport, some of Nabiev's coalition partners managed to get him back to town. When they went to check that he was all right, at eleven o'clock that night, they found his car was gone. Nabiev had left by road as discreetly as he could – over the Anzab pass towards Khujand, hidden, apparently, in the boot. He never returned to Dushanbe.

It was after this that Tajikistan reached a point of no return and ragged, local fighting became war. According to military commanders and politicians on both sides, there was a great increase of weapons arriving in the country in the middle of September. These were not bought by village forces making local deals – they were direct supplies from foreign countries that felt they had pressing, important reasons of their own to become involved in Tajik affairs.

The forthright President of Uzbekistan, Islam Karimov, had taken a dim view of the Tajik political experiment from the outset. He had sneered openly at Nabiev's weakness in not stamping out the Shahidan demonstration while he had the chance. The Tajik problem was a 'time bomb', Karimov said just before Nabiev fell, afraid that Uzbekistan could follow her neighbours into chaos. In the early autumn of 1992 Karimov's police broke up the founding meeting of the Uzbek version of the Hezb-e Nahzat-e Islami, and began to arrest, harass or send into exile religious and civil rights campaigners. At the same time, according to numerous witnesses, Uzbekistan began to supply weapons to ethnically Uzbek parts of Tajikistan to create a buffer zone, primarily against the 'Islamic' Gharmis but also to stop Sangak Safarov's Kulabis from becoming too powerful.

'The Uzbeks set up an air bridge with Uzbek-populated areas around the border,' claims one very senior Tajik official. 'They sent Antonov 24s and Yak 40s [small, standard Soviet civilian planes] supposedly full of food, but of course they were full of weapons.' Foreign observers reported sightings of weapons arriving by road. 'Everything I had came from Uzbekistan,' Safarali Kenjayev confirmed later. The Uzbek government repeatedly denied supplying arms to Tajikstan, but few people in Tajikistan believed it. On the ground, local 'Tajik' Uzbeks paid the price, as their neighbours –

understanding no difference between 'Uzbeks' and 'Uzbekistan' – blamed them for fuelling the war.

Uzbek involvement was so blatant that at times many ordinary Tajiks looked no further than Tashkent. Many senior Gharmi commanders, however, felt that the subtler contribution of Moscow was more significant – one went so far as to say he believed that the majority of weapons used were provided by the Russians, in both *ad hoc* and organised distributions. In the crucial month of September, it appears that the Russian military became more consistent in its support of the 'anti-Gharmi' side, primarily because it was led by people familiar to them. 'We're with the Reds [the former 'communists'],' said one senior Russian official, 'at least for the moment.'

Not surprisingly, the number of leaders on this side proliferated. Some Uzbeks and Turkmens fell in behind a young half-Uzbek, half-Tajik officer with the 201st Division, Lieutenant Mahmud Khudaberdiev, who joined in the war by simply driving three or four tanks out of the Qurghan Tappa garrison with the help of a few friends.*

---

* Mahmud Khudaberdiev played an interesting role in the war and in subsequent politics. His father – so the story goes – was called the 'Black Commander' and fought against the *basmachi* in the 1920s. If this is the case, he must have been elderly when his son was born in the 1960s. Khudaberdiev was a professional soldier in so far as he fought with the 40th Army at Qunduz in Afghanistan during the Soviet occupation. On his return home, he remained in what became the Russian army until his defection in 1992, keeping up his contacts in northern Afghanistan the while. After the Tajik war, Khudaberdiev became very powerful around Qurghan Tappa, though he never won a post in Dushanbe – a position not unlike that of Abdul Rashid Dustam in Afghanistan in the early 1990s.

Khudaberdiev's administration at Qurghan Tappa was strikingly similar to Dustam's at Mazar-e Sharif – from the Soviet-style uniform of his troops and the moustaches adopted by his inner circle to his unusual attention to civic amenities – for example, long after the chlorination system in other parts of Tajikistan broke down, Khudaberdiev paid to have the piped water in Qurghan Tappa treated; as a result, Qurghan Tappa stayed free from typhoid during the outbreak of 1997, and Khudaberdiev was much admired locally. Like Dustam, Khudaberdiev spoke Persian (Tajik/Dari) with a heavy Uzbek accent – and many men around him were Uzbeks or Turkmens. He was not, however, an Uzbek 'nationalist' so much as an ambitious man who survived his times as well as he could with what he had.

Khudaberdiev was a sociable person and a sharp political analyst, always keen to discuss the twists and turns of the affairs of the day. In early 1996 he expanded his sphere of influence by sending his soldiers into the region around Hisar, west of Dushanbe. At that time, he appeared to be perhaps the most powerful man in Tajikistan – close to President Rahmanov, yet free to run his own concerns. Only a year later, however, he was on the run – caught out by the changing political scene. He had stood against elements of the peace deal signed in June 1997, which would have cost him both territory and power, and was denounced as an 'enemy' of the government. What Khudaberdiev called his 'fortress' of Qurghan Tappa fell very quickly – as has happened so often in Central Asia. He fled, according to the guards on duty that day, across the border into Uzbekistan.

Loosely allied groups like Safarov's in Kulab, Khudaberdiev's at Qurghan Tappa and Kenjayev's around Hisar adopted the general, collective name of 'Popular Front', though those involved did not necessarily trust or even know one another.

The provenance of arms supplied to the 'Gharmi' side was harder to pin down. Several field commanders say they received some weapons from Hezb-e Islami, the Afghan *mujahedin* group most closely backed by Pakistan, though probably these were not very many. According to Popular Front sources, Iranian guns and ammunition were also available in Tajikistan in the summer of 1992. Iran had long tried to extend its regional influence by backing different groups at different times in Afghanistan, and taking sides in Tajikistan might have been a natural extension of this policy. In addition, some Iranians felt they needed a presence in Tajikistan to offset Russian and Uzbek designs there. 'Gharmi' sources agree that they did have some help from Iran, though not, they say, until well after September. The Iranians were not, at that time, a well-known quantity in Tajikistan – a fact that is masked by the similarity of their language.

The supply of weapons in wars is notoriously hard to analyse. One thing is plain, however: in the autumn of 1992 a number of foreign countries, at least one of which had no experience of making foreign policy, and most of which lacked the most elementary knowledge of Tajik politics or even geography, were playing an active part in what had become a war.

War unrolled across the plains of southern Tajikistan through late September. In Qurghan Tappa, truck-mounted rocket launchers, troop carriers and tanks reeled crazily around town, skidding clumsily in untrained hands. The gas was cut, the lights went out. Fighters over-ran the hospital and stripped it bare, grabbing drugs and bandages to treat their wounded. Many Slav civilians – workers from the fertiliser and electrical-transformer factories, local government officers, doctors, plumbers and hairdressers – took cover in the city garrison, now all but reduced to just its Russian officers. Tajik and Uzbek families had no one to protect them. They sent their sons out to man the barricades of bed-frames and tractors they had built to guard their *mahallas* or neighbourhoods.

Defences gave way suddenly when the Popular Front finally took the city on the night of 27/28 September. 'My father-in-law woke us at three in the morning. He said, "It's time. Get out now",' says Nisa, then aged twenty-five and living in Qurghan Tappa. She asked no questions. 'I took my two little boys and the baby. We packed nothing, not even food. No clothes. We walked out of the city.' The Dushanbe road was closed by fighting so Nisa turned south, making for her father's house in the town of Shahr-e Tuz, about sixty-five miles away. 'It took us three days to get there. The children were crying for water and bread, but we had nothing. We walked, and sometimes we got lifts. All our neighbours went with us. Everybody headed south.'

The villages of the Vakhsh valley fell with Qurghan Tappa. Some had been trying to put together local peace deals. On 24 September, Said Abdullah Nuri had had a sheep slaughtered for Sangak Safarov and shared a meal with him – a gesture close to that of holding *ash-e ashti*, the Pilau of Peace which is the customary way to end disagreements (other sources remember this meal as taking place in late August). Popular Front tanks rolled into the village three days later. 'It was as though we had dropped into a war film,' Asadullah, Nuri's brother, says. 'One side attacking with tanks, and the people screaming and running away.' Asadullah gathered the family together – twelve adults and thirty-five children – squeezed them into cars and took the road south to Jilikul. Gunmen stripped the house behind them before burning it down. By 15 October Kolkhozabad and Jilikul had fallen, and the villagers headed further south.

The National Reconciliation Government in Dushanbe, powerless to stop the fighting to the south, tried desperately to maintain order in the city. The speaker of the parliament, Akbarshah Iskandarov, took on the role of acting president and cast about for help from the outside world, sending urgent appeals to President Yeltsin and the United Nations. Russia responded by despatching a small contingent – only about a thousand troops – to bolster Major General Ashurov's 201st Division. They were assigned to protect Russian citizens, many of them the wives and children of army officers, and to guard important strategic points like the airport and the television station.

The reinforcements did not otherwise protect the city. War came to Dushanbe on 24 October, when residents of the western suburbs awoke before dawn to the sound of heavy vehicles moving in from the direction of the town of Hisar, stronghold of the Popular Front near the Uzbek border. At five o'clock in the morning a column of Popular Front tanks, armoured cars and buses full of fighters burst through the city limit and charged down Rudaki. Gunmen shot their way into the presidential palace and swarmed into the parliament building.

One young woman remembers how she and her mother were picking over rice for lunch when fighting exploded in the city centre. 'We ran up to the top floor and I could see two groups shooting straight through our apartment block. My little brother was crying and my mother was so upset. The phone was still working and I managed to ring my father. He got hold of an armoured car and came to rescue us in it.' A shopkeeper remembers counting seven bodies in front of the presidential palace, and more in the walkways under Rudaki Avenue. United States diplomats evacuated their embassy.

That evening, Popular Front commanders took over the radio station and addressed the city on air. One voice was very familiar – it was that of Safarali Kenjayev, the *bête noire* of the anti-communist movement, who had disappeared from Dushanbe after the coming of the Government of National Reconciliation in May and had spent the summer as a Popular Front commander in Hisar. As the capital grew weaker Kenjayev seized his moment, and rode back to Dushanbe in the lead tank in order, as he put it, to 'save' the city. Safarali Kenjayev, the radio said, was now the President of Tajikistan.

Kenjayev's attempted *coup d'état* lasted one frenzied weekend. It might have lasted much longer had the 201st Division not intercepted a second Popular Front column marching in from the south. Forty-eight hours after the attack on Dushanbe, soldiers from the 201st Division ran Kenjayev and his men out of town. Returning to the west, the invaders re-encamped around Hisar. There, they closed the road and pulled up the only railway track running between Uzbekistan and Dushanbe, thus severing the last land route between the capital and the outside world.

Stranded trains loaded with food and fuel collected on the Hisar side – but nothing got through to Dushanbe. By the middle of October there was perhaps a month's supply of bread left in the capital, the population of which was swollen by close to a hundred thousand refugees. The head keeper at the zoo hid the most precious edible animals – a llama and two deer – away from hungry people and slaughtered the herd of donkeys one by one to feed the carnivores. All the animals starved to death anyway.

On the Dushanbe side, wagons also filled the sidings: they were full of people rather than freight. The incomers of Dushanbe – mainly Russians, but also Tatars, Germans and others – had gradually been selling up and leaving since 1989, unsure of what their future might be in the land some had called home for two generations. When the war began, uncertainty turned to terror. Most realised that they were leaving for good, and with all their possessions, down to their furniture, set out for the railway that their grandfathers had built. When the railway line was cut hundreds of these families were trapped at the station, unable to go on and unable to return to their flats, which they had sold. They moved into unheated goods wagons in the immobile trains. By night they slept on their packing cases. By day they tried to keep their children's spirits up, and made cold meals of the food they had packed for their journey to Russia.

In early November the Popular Front moved on the towns of the south-west, Qabadian and Shahr-e Tuz, both packed with 'Gharmi' refugees from the fighting around Qurghan Tappa and elsewhere. In Qabadian, many families had found sanctuary in the main mosque where they survived on water, onions and grains of wheat. When the soldiers came, those who could got away down the fifteen miles of road to Shahr-e Tuz – the southernmost town and the end of the line. After the Popular Front took Qabadian on 11 November, the defenders of Shahr-e Tuz – local men armed by Hezb-e Nahzat-e Islami – knew they probably had only hours left.

'That night, I was at our post on the bridge,' said one, Shahrukh, a teacher (not his real identity). 'We had five or six machine-guns from

Afghanistan, some of them broken, and no real artillery. An armoured car came over the bridge, fast – they began firing at us and five of our people were killed. I told the others to wait, and I went to check the side roads. I saw they had three lines of men coming in – men with black battledress and red headbands; I'm sure they were not local, they must have been from Uzbekistan – at any rate their leaders were. I knew we could not hold on.'

Shahrukh ran home to gather up his sleeping family. He had spent the summer trying to stop the tension in his home town from tipping into war. 'We had cooked so many *ash-e ashtis* – every day, a village made *ash-e ashti* – but at night, someone else would disappear.' Shahrukh lost one of his four brothers, then a second, then a third in this way, and was desperate to save his children, his wife, his father and his remaining brother. 'All over Shahr-e Tuz, soldiers were breaking into houses, stealing, raping girls. Local people did it too – not many tried to help their neighbours. People claimed they were Uzbeks, Arabs – anything to stay alive.'

Shahrukh and his family, along with tens of thousands of other 'Gharmis', made for the only place of safety left – the bank of the river Amu, about twenty miles away. Within days, 'Gharmi' families filled the raw stretch of desert around the village of Auvaj, once a ferry station, but since Soviet times a poor farming settlement populated by local Arabs. 'The Qabadian people had some flour and we had a bit,' says Shahrukh. 'I suppose we had enough for about fifteen days.'

With their side in the ascendant, the Popular Front and its supporters suddenly bid for peace. Under pressure from Russia and Uzbekistan the acting President in Dushanbe, Akbarshah Iskandarov, agreed to attend a special meeting in the old communist heartland of Khujand, at which a deal would be worked out and a new head of state chosen. 'Iskandarov should have held out – it was a terrible mistake to agree,' said a senior member of the Government of National Reconciliation. But Iskandarov's position was desperately weak. His capital was hungry and under threat of attack, the south of his country was engulfed in war.

On 16 November the Khujand meeting began under the guard of uniformed troops from Uzbekistan. The Russian presence was more discreet. Leaders of the Popular Front attended, including Sangak Safarov. The meeting chose the man whom they hoped would serve all the complex interests of the winning side: Imamali Rahmanov, an unknown, who was the manager of the Vladimir Illych Lenin state collective farm in Kulab. The choice of a Kulabi rather than an Uzbek was thought to suit the Russians, who were keen to limit Uzbek influence in Tajikistan. Rahmanov was endorsed by a special vote of parliament as its speaker – in effect, the President-in-waiting. 'It was a strange thing,' said a Kulabi field commander. 'We had not fought to became the rulers of Tajikistan – we had had no plan at all. And all of a sudden, there we were.'

Imamali Rahmanov could not enter the capital, which was still defended by the Government of National Reconciliation. He flew to Termez, in Uzbekistan, on 30 November for a meeting with defence and intelligence officials, mainly from Uzbekistan and Russia and also from Kazakhstan and Kirgizstan. According to several sources, Uzbekistan made it clear to Rahmanov that there was to be no coming to terms with the 'Islamists' who still hung on in the extreme south of Tajikistan, and whom Uzbekistan still considered a threat. All sources speak of extra weapons making the short journey from Termez across the Tajik border.

The burning of southern Tajikistan began. Newly reinforced after the Termez meeting, the Popular Front marched southwards, running the remaining 'Gharmis' before them and torching the houses they left behind. Early December, after nine months of sunshine and before the snow, is the driest time of the year, and mud-brick strengthened with straw caught easily. More than fifteen thousand houses went up in flames. Some families had scrawled on their walls THIS IS AN UZBEK HOUSE, DO NOT TOUCH. But the gunmen either could not read Tajik, or did not care. Besides, by now it was harder than ever to say who was in the Popular Front and where their local loyalties might lie. Before they poured the petrol, the gunmen took tin roofs, beams, doors and window frames. They filled the *ariqs* with wreckage. They destroyed irrigation systems, burnt orchards, and shot cows for food.

The 'Gharmis' camping by the Amu ran out of bread. More than fifteen days had passed and they had virtually no flour left. The women pulled up grasses to eke out what they had. There was almost no water, and children fell ill. Some women who gave birth buried their infants where they were born. The families lived under windbreaks made by draping cloths on sticks, or in holes they scraped in the ground and covered with reeds.

'We were crushed against the frontier,' Shahrukh says, 'and we realised that not a soul in the world knew what was happening to us. All the party leaders – Nuri and others – they were in Dushanbe: there was nobody with us. Each refugee gave a little money and we paid a Russian officer to take one of our men safely to Shahr-e Tuz, so that he could tell the United Nations or some other foreigner. The officer took the money, but our man never got through.'

On 1 December, at four o'clock in the afternoon, Sangak Safarov arrived at the camp by helicopter to negotiate with the refugees. 'He said that some buses would come for us the next day, and take people to Fakhrabad, from where they could return home. The first bus was to be for girls, then women, then elders, and so forth. They said that the young men would be taken to the stadium in Shahr-e Tuz to be "filtered". We asked, "What's that?", and they said "You'll see." They flew off. The next day, the buses came. About twenty families of Kirgiz got on, following their elders. And about three hundred women and children, including my wife and our four children. They set off. Fighters – I don't know whose – took them on the road. They killed the Kirgiz and threw them in a pit – about a hundred and fifty of them. On the other side they threw the dead Tajiks. My wife did not return. There was nothing I could do.'

This account is broadly confirmed by a Popular Front commander who was there. He says, however, that those who waylaid the buses and killed the passengers were not regular forces but fighters, possibly from Uzbekistan, who were not under orders from Safarov. He says that the plan to take the 'Gharmis' home to their villages was sincere, and that 'filtration' was intended to weed out the large number of armed men on the 'Gharmi' side. He also puts the number of dead much higher – at perhaps even a thousand. Like almost every incident in the Tajik war, the killings outside Auvaj have never been investigated.

A column of Popular Front gunmen closed in on the camp at Auvaj a few days later, around 7 December. 'Three or four troop carriers flying rags of Soviet flags lurched towards the camp so clumsily that one drove straight into some barbed wire,' remembers one of the very few witnesses to what happened in Auvaj – a journalist, Yuri Kushko. 'The gunmen moved in among the crowds, taking the Gharmis' cars and televisions. They put some men in trucks.' There is strong evidence, which includes photographs, that these men were driven away from the eyes of witnesses, put up against a wall and shot.

That evening, a group of Popular Front gunmen built a camp fire out on the plain and sat around it, hunched in their *chapans*, cooking a victory supper of rice and mutton. A few 'Gharmi' corpses lay on the ground around them. One had had the ears cut off, before being soaked in petrol and lit. Kushko recognised him as a local man he had been talking to that afternoon – killed because of a rumour that he had killed somebody's aunt. The small contingent of border guards at their post nearby were powerless to intervene, even if they had wished to. A total of three or four officers, all Slavs, and fewer than twenty men huddled in the freezing barracks, living on handfuls of macaroni and water and sleeping in their overcoats. It was impossible for them to leave or for supplies to be flown in to them – all flights had been banned after a rumour spread that Akbar Turajanzada would try to escape Tajikistan in a private helicopter. Climbing the garrison watch-tower, Kushko looked out over the mass of refugees on the river bank. Through binoculars he could see figures break away from the crowd and scramble into the Amu. More and more followed, until the river was full of heads.

On planks of wood lashed to oil barrels, on car doors and tractor cabs, balanced on tyres or swimming, tens of thousands of 'Gharmis' set off across the Amu over the next several days. There were scarcely any Tajik boats because of the Soviet prohibition on fishing in a military zone. Some lucky contingents were rescued by the Afghan government, whose helicopters landed and left with no interference from the watching Russian border guards, but the majority crossed on tyres and inner tubes. Women held their children tightly, but several infants were swept away and drowned. Some people remember apparently drunken gunmen taking pot-shots into the river full of swimming, paddling people.

On 10 December, a column of Popular Front and Uzbek army troops – one guileless soldier even told a journalist that he was from the Ferghana valley in Uzbekistan – marched on Dushanbe from Hisar. They overwhelmed the weak force of defenders in the capital, drove down Rudaki into the heart of the city, and captured the presidential palace for Imamali Rahmanov. The blockade of Dushanbe was lifted, and the first food supplies in forty days got through to the capital. Members of the Government of National Reconciliation, fearing for their lives, scrambled to get out of the city, heading mainly for their mountain villages.

At the end of December the Popular Front took the last pockets of the south around the town of Panj, and the forty thousand or so 'Gharmis' there followed the first wave at Auvaj. Some crossed in Afghan boats sent from the little port of Imam Saheb, at first out of charity, then in return for a cow, a motorbike, a television – whatever people had left. Some Popular Front fighters stood on the banks and watched them go. 'A present for Afghanistan,' one laughed.

By early January 1993 there was almost nothing left of the 'Gharmis' of southern Tajikistan. Their villages were razed, their farmland burnt black and unusable. In Dushanbe, the 'winning' side rounded up many people of mountain origin and put them to death. On more than one occasion, gunmen stopped a bus, ordered off all the men who appeared to be Gharmi or Pamiri, and shot them on the spot. Passengers were often asked to say a few words first so the executioners could identify their accents. His pronunciation of the word for 'potato' – *kartoshka* in a city accent, *kartushka* in the speech of some mountain districts – was enough to kill a man. It was not a scientific way to discern the difference between the two sides, but it was no less meaningful than any other.

The men who had launched the first political party in former Soviet Central Asia, the leaders of Hezb-e Nahzat-e Islami, had disappeared with the rest. Said Abdullah Nuri had fled to the mountain village of Sangvar, sent his possessions (including the books his father had kept safely through the Soviet time) to Afghanistan and then followed them through the crossing at Ishkashim to the Afghan side. The silvery Friday mosque on Rudaki Avenue stood empty. Akbar Turajanzada, by his own account, left the city for the mountains and – 'with snow up to our chests' – on 28 January 1993 crossed the border out of the country.

9

On both sides of the Amu

'All the wise and the great were bewildered thereby and
distraught at the vicissitudes of Fate; and every one spoke and
suggested a course of action according to his own intellect and
understanding.'

B RIGHT SUNSHINE POURED into Dushanbe from the middle of the
morning. It was the first day of spring – 21 March 1994. The war
had been over for a year, and the little capital stretching towards the
snowy mountains was brilliant in the reflected light. The branches of
trees, nobbly with leaf-buds, stood out sharply against the powder-
blue and cream façades of Rudaki Avenue. Small but vivid, the new
red, white and green tricolour of Tajikistan blew out from a distant
flagpole.

It was also New Year's Day, and families had been out since early
morning to enjoy the holiday of *nauruz*, a holiday Tajiks share with
most Afghans, Iranians, Kurds and others. *Nauruz* celebrations were
strictly limited in Soviet times, but since 1991 had enjoyed a renaissance. Small parties promenaded up and down Rudaki. Scholars from
the university, in topcoats and fedoras, stopped to shake hands.
Parents had spent the little they had to dress their daughters in bright
gold hats and their sons in new sashes, and took them for a clattering
turn on the swing-boats in Lenin Park. Under the outstretched arm
of the old revolutionary – still standing, like most of the Soviet-era
monuments in Dushanbe – women laid out spectacular rounds of
bread a yard high. The men roasted a whole sheep and stood it
upright, grass in its mouth, to the excitement of the watching chil-

182

dren. Someone climbed the lamp-posts and strung hammer-and-sickle fairy lights, leftovers from the past.

Except in high, mountainous places still waiting for the winter ice to break, all Tajikistan was celebrating *nauruz*. Women cooked *sumalak*, wheat porridge, in pots outdoors: an annual sign that the hungry months were over. In Hisar, west of Dushanbe, riders filled the plain beneath the old fort for a *nauruz* match of *buzkashi*, a sort of horseback-football with a goat carcass played on holidays all through the borderlands of the river Amu. Spectators packed the rim around the field, boys rushing away squealing when horseman careered up the slope to the edge. In Dushanbe people skirted silently the underpasses where the dead had been thrown: here in Hisar no one among the chatting and laughing crowds talked about what lay beneath the plain.

The Tajik war had ended in almost as much seclusion from the wider world as it had begun. There were no war trials or commissions of inquiry, no disarmament of fighting men. Without outside observers to open unmarked graves or count the dead, it was impossible to know with much accuracy how many had people been killed. Little by little, people pieced together scraps of reckoning. Residents of the Shahr-e Tuz and Qabadian districts made a rough guess at three thousand local dead. A Tajik who fled the Hisar region for Moscow listed deaths he had heard of for a Russian newspaper: 73 in Lahuti, including 20 children; 40 in Pakhtakar; 35 in Pakhtakar-e Payan; 170 in Chapayev; 28 in Leningrad; 15 in Shirkent; 130 in the town of Tursunzada. People in one part of Qurghan Tappa collected photographs of a hundred and seventy-five local dead and stuck them up as a home-made memorial. People in Khurug did likewise. The most energetic humanitarian agency to arrive during the war, the United Nations High Commissioner for Refugees, made an estimate of between twenty thousand and sixty thousand dead between June 1992 and February 1993. The figure stuck, and the Tajik war went down as probably the most deadly of all the conflicts to break out in the wake of the collapse of the Soviet Union.

Of a population of five and a half million, 486,000 people had left their homes, according to the UNHCR – that is, about one person in ten. Of these, ninety thousand had crossed to Afghanistan, where about sixty thousand remained. Some villages, mainly those built by the deportees of *muhajarat-e ijbari* in the 1950s, were completely deserted. The town of Vakhsh lost 93 per cent of its population. Parts of the Vakhsh valley were so thoroughly destroyed that whole villages had disappeared into the plain from which they were made, leaving lumps of ochre dust. In Qabadian, only their fresh scorch marks made these lumps look different from the ruins of the bek's fort, burnt by Bolsheviks in 1920. Many of the areas most badly hit at the end of the Soviet period were, mainly from reasons of geography, the same as those that had been razed at the beginning. The town of Qurghan Tappa lost 58 per cent of its population, almost precisely the proportion it had lost in the 1920s.

The war had been fought without armies, despite names like 'Popular Front'. Few people had died wearing a uniform. Very large numbers of deaths had been murders, sometimes of people well known to their killers. In some cases, whole families had died in a single attack. Neighbours of Shaikh Kamal of Kulab, aged seventy, said that when he was killed, so too were his sons Abdullah (43), Jabar (40), Zaer (38), Rahim (32), Said (30), Khaliq (23), Khurshid (16), and his grandson, six-year-old Majid. Although in some areas the war had altered local demography greatly because communities had run away, in many others the families of murdered and murderers were still neighbours.

It was this terrible intimacy that made the *nauruz* promenaders in Dushanbe and the crowds at the *buzkashi* match in Hisar keep their silence. Digging into what had happened might entail uncovering things it was better not to reveal, not only about one's neighbours but perhaps about oneself. Wives, mothers and elders cradled dreadful secrets about what their loved ones had done. Such was the fear in the marrow of the south that parents in one village near Hisar asked no questions about the whereabouts of their own children, who they said had been taken away from school by men claiming that they were needed to pick cotton. Not one of those eighty-four children was seen again. Much later, an old man in a nearby village who said that his son was killed that same day – 5 December 1992 – showed a visiting journalist the unmarked pits in the hills where, he alleged, three hundred or so corpses had been dumped. He said he had lost a total of sixty-three relatives.

Many Tajiks who could bear to talk about the war at all felt a sense of utter degradation. From being proud to be Tajik, some became miserably ashamed. 'We are a gentle, hospitable people,' one woman said. 'What can foreigners think of us Tajiks, when brother kills brother? I do not know what sort of people we have become.' Lacking a vocabulary to describe the intricacies of the war, the handful of foreign commentators who took an interest cast it in terms of 'ancient hatreds' 're-emerging' between 'clans'; or wheeled out the old chestnuts about Islamic 'fanaticism' that had done service ever since the *basmachi* wars.

Ubaidullah, stepson of Hindustani, was one of those who simply could not talk about what happened. When his son Abdullah's car was discovered empty, he had feared the worst. The corpse was found a few days later. Ubaidullah and his surviving sons made no enquiries. Abdullah had been a farmer and a civilian, and there could be no consoling or helpful explanation for his murder. The family quietly shouldered responsibility for Abdullah's young widow and four children.

Ubaidullah just about managed to keep his horticulture business going through 1993 and 1994, though it became more and more difficult to do so. The small municipal subsidy he had received had disappeared with the Soviet Union. It became impossible to find seeds or fertiliser, or to keep in touch with his contacts in the Baltics and other parts of the former USSR. And it was hard to imagine a day when people would again buy bunches of roses and carnations on their way home. Ubaidullah, his surviving children and his fifteen or so grandchildren had to eat. They dug up the nursery beds and planted wheat, but did not consider leaving Dushanbe. 'All my friends are here,' said Ubaidullah. 'The graves of my boys and my father and mother are here. I could go to my homeland, to Ferghana, but the old generation who knew me are all gone now. Where would I go?'

A walk down Rudaki Avenue showed how fast the familiar knitting of the Soviet world had unravelled. Men from the villages now sat in the painted ministry buildings once occupied by the old élite. 'Suddenly a driver could be a minister!' said one man who, frustrated by lack of opportunity all his short life, shot to power with Rahmanov. 'We had not known that we were taking part in a revolution, but we were – it was like the Russian revolution in a way!

After the Khujand meeting, everyone said "Those farm-boys won't be able to keep Dushanbe – they'll be out in six months" – but we did manage.'

The city they inherited was much changed. A poster for a Sylvester Stallone film (voice-over in Russian, sent from Moscow) was still gummed to the cinema – only two years old, it belonged to a faraway life in which there were people who could spare three hundred roubles (now the price of a little more than two rounds of bread) to spend for pleasure – or went out in the evenings at all.

After four o'clock these days Dushanbe belonged to poor *kolkhoz* boys from the ruined countryside who had followed their commanders into the city. Cocks of the walk in the capital they had not known they were fighting for, they took the names of cinema heroes – Rocky, Van Damme – and sashayed down Rudaki, half-cut on stolen vodka, pistols in their waistbands, bandoliers across their shoulders. They helped themselves to the spoils of war – money, cars, girls, apartments. There were no security forces to stop them: they were the security forces. Even in the daylight, the glance at a man's hands before looking at his face became a reflex action among those in Dushanbe who went outside. At night the streets were empty.

Barakat bazaar, on the west side of the avenue, showed an economy in revolution. The cost of a round of bread was a hundred and thirty roubles, up a thousand per cent in only a year – and rising faster than ever. Thirty eggs were unaffordable at five hundred roubles: the equivalent of about twenty pounds in London. Sugar was valuable contraband. Tea (which was imported) and even salt (Tajik) were short. Small necessities like buttons and thread were impossible to find – a bought toy was a thing of the past. Privatisation, discussed lengthily elsewhere in post-Soviet countries in conjunction with advisors from the World Bank and the International Monetary Fund, happened of its own accord. Country people with wheat and greens brought them into town and sold them, city people grew tomatoes and kept chickens on their balconies. Life went on.

Barrow-boys, young hawkers and beggars worked in the bazaar. Most of them would once have been at school. Some were orphans, some the sons of widows, now supporting their families generally by selling pistachio nuts and lemons. Some were girls. 'She's married! She's married!' A gang of boys selling cigarettes pulled forward a ragged girl with fairish hair and bright turquoise eyes. Mavluda, who was about thirteen, said that she had been given as a second wife a few weeks before as her mother could not afford to keep her. She had no idea how old her husband was, she said, looking down at nails chewed to the quick. His family had been unkind to her, and she had run away. Many children slept rough, generally at the airport or curled into outdoor bread ovens.

Those children who did keep going to school – only about a quarter of some classes – sat in unheated classrooms without books, paper or pencils (school supplies came from Russia or Uzbekistan). Sometimes they arrived to find there was no teacher. Without a working state there were no salaries, so teachers drove taxis and sold oddments in the bazaar to survive. Their occasional absences became permanent. Those – the majority – who were Slavs and Tatars, Germans, Jews or other non-local nationalities left the country, mainly for Russia. Many Uzbek teachers went to Uzbekistan.

Qarabalo hospital in Dushanbe, the largest in Tajikistan, was out of everything – medicines, syringes, blood pressure gauges, thermometers, tongue-depressors for looking down throats, bandages, ear-torches, washing powder, soap, food. There was no milk for the babies because so many cows – about half the herds in the country – had been slaughtered during the war. Patients were slow to recover because their relatives could bring them no more than a little bread and water. There was no longer any psychiatric care, such as it had been. Like the teachers, many of the doctors were Slavs, and like the teachers were leaving the country. There were few equally qualified local men and women to take their places.

The teachers and doctors were only those most conspicuous by their absence. Among the two hundred thousand Slavs and Europeans who had left Dushanbe by the spring of 1994 were fitters and menders of gas pipes, drains and telephones – all the modern things that the incomers had brought to the city, and which now began to go wrong. People complained of 'not being able to find a Russian' when a lift broke down. Archaeologists, botanists and zoologists left. So did most of the offbeat Soviet intellectuals who had set out for the south for one reason or another and settled there, like the Jewish scholar born in Berlin who came to Dushanbe to teach Latin and in her spare time perfected her command of the haiku. The priest of the

Catholic church said Mass one day, shut the doors, and disappeared. The Jews went to Israel. Most of the Germans moved to Germany, courtesy of the German government. Few felt quite at home in their ancestral lands, where local people called them 'Russians' – but at least they had passports and a future for their children.

Most of the rest of the non-local population planned to leave as soon as they could get the money for a ticket. Scholars split up their libraries and sold them off book by book. Old ladies, humiliated by necessity, swapped their grandmothers' silver icons for hard currency. A geologist's collection of amethysts and cats' eyes, garnets, rubies and *lal* – the ruby-like stone found in the Pamir mountains – was arranged in his sitting room because the museum was no longer safe from looters. Embarrassed, he named a pitiful price.

Slavs with nothing sat on kerbstones selling socks they had knitted with wool from their sweaters or, *in extremis*, stretching out their hands for the charity of the Tajiks. The great majority, even two and three generations on, still spoke no Tajik, but some learnt to bless the almsgivers in the Muslim manner.

It says much about the kindness of many ordinary Tajiks that they gave what they could to the Russians in their distress and, while some were pleased to move at last into the centre of Dushanbe, taking the apartments the leavers left behind, most people did so with no sense of victory gained. Very few blamed the Soviet system for having created a civic structure so fragile, unbalanced and reliant on non-Tajik expertise that less than a year of war left classrooms and wards empty of equipment, children on the streets, and homes without heat or light.

'I was so sorry that the Russians left,' said Ubaidullah, stepson of Hindustani. 'They knew how to do things and they helped us build a country. They were good people. Everyone is sorry now, but it is too late.'

The doors flapped askew in the silent Writers' Union building where journalists, poets and photographers had enthused over the future in the late 1980s, yet Dushanbe still retained some of the yeast of intellectual life that had made it different from other Soviet Asian capitals.

Muhammadjan Shukurov had stayed put during the worst days of 1992. As the postal service had broken down he was unable to write to his sons, all three of whom were in Moscow pursuing academic careers of their own in Muslim art, Byzantine studies and astrophysics, respectively ('The odd one out in our family,' says his father of the last, amused) – and bringing up their families. Muhammadjan Shukurov kept up his spirits by working on *Khorasan Inja Ast*, a scholarly volume about Persian culture, which he managed to publish after the war.

Muhyeddin Alempur was still in town. He cut a bold figure, with his flowing beard, denim jacket and camera bag, as he tried to rush along Rudaki, stopping to chat to countless friends, from academicians to the kitchen staff at the Hotel Tajikistan. Muhyeddin's television music show *Setaraha-e Sharq* had collapsed, but he had numerous other projects on the go. He had taken a step that was courageous even by his own standards, becoming the first Tajik reporter for the BBC, at a time when mistrust of foreigners and foreign radio stations was widespread in the former Soviet Union. He had also recently become one of the very first Tajiks to cross not just the Atlantic but North America. His radio travelogue took his listeners from coast to coast across the United States, opening a window on the world for them just when it was most needed.

Muhyeddin set up a tiny office high above Rudaki with a superb view across the city, and stuffed it full of photographs, tapes and manuscripts – written carefully on both sides, to save paper. He planned to take up video-photography, and talked of learning English, which he saw as the new language of the future. He already had one phrase – 'Ready in a minute! Ready in a minute!', copied from a Russian television advertisement for macaroni. The flat became a haven for all manner of intellectuals drawn by Muhyeddin's ability to cheer them up. 'Tajik honey. It's the best!' he proclaimed buoyantly, having saved enough to buy a tiny jar for his guests. He sliced lemons for their tea, and stirred potatoes in a pot. As he cooked, he sang snatches of songs, wrote his stories and played his tapes.

Muhyeddin and his guests never talked about their pre-war hopes for intellectual freedom or open government. Nor did they talk about the war. Politics had become a dirty word in Dushanbe. There was much to debate about the future of Tajikistan – what sort of history should be taught in schools, for example, how much Russian language should be maintained. But discussion of the longer-term shape of the country was shelved until the mountain of economic and social problems looked at least manageable.

Imamali Rahmanov settled into the pinkish-grey presidential palace on Rudaki. A tall, heavy figure, he appeared uneasy in his dark blue business suit and spoke very little in public. Rahmanov's sudden rise from the *kolkhoz* in Kulab had given him no time to prepare for the burden of office now upon his shoulders.

Born in 1952, Imamali Rahmanov had roots typical of the Tajik south. His family came originally from the mountain town of Nurak but were transferred to the plains to cut sugar-cane in a plantation developed in the 1940s.* A drought so severe that several deportee children died caused the Rahmanovs to move again, this time to the remote district of Danghara in Kulab, where Imamali was born. He was brought up as a farm boy and got his first job as an electrician in an oil plant in Qurghan Tappa. Called up for military service, nineteen-year-old Rahmanov went to sea as a rating in the Soviet Pacific fleet, about as far away from landlocked Tajikistan as is imaginable. On his return he married and began a conventionally large family (seven daughters and a son by the late 1990s). In 1987 Rahmanov became head of the Vladimir Illych Lenin *kolkhoz* in Danghara, a position of some local power that helped him become a parliamentary deputy. Here he remained until, so unexpectedly, becoming head of state.

Rahmanov was confirmed as the President of Tajikistan by elections on 6 November 1994 in which he ran against a rich, established politician of the old Khujandi élite, Abdumalik Abdullahjanov – who called the vote a fraud. President Yeltsin, however, at once sent Rahmanov a congratulatory telegram. Confirmed as Moscow's choice, Rahmanov received practical support in the form of financial aid – by some estimates, Tajikistan received twice as much help from Moscow under Rahmanov as it had as a Soviet republic. Russia also maintained and increased the 201st Division and the frontier units – roughly 25,000 men in all, under the aegis of the CIS. As before, these troops were commanded by Moscow, not Dushanbe.

---

* The same sugar-plantation that Turajanzada's grandparents worked on.

These arrangements meant that Russia, the disintegration of the USSR notwithstanding, remained in power along the Amu, the strategic baseline along the border of Afghanistan that it had held, at least in parts, since 1865. Tajikistan's foreign frontiers – with Afghanistan and China – were therefore controlled by another power and its ability to conduct foreign relations circumscribed. 'We must not forget that Tajikistan is the border of Russia itself,' President Yeltsin said. President Rahmanov was in charge of internal policy, however, including the multitude of problems left by the war, as the leader of a sovereign state. The status of Tajikistan moved from that of in effect a colony to that of something like a protectorate, and the president's position was not unlike that of the amirs of Bukhara in the years between the Tsarist conquest and Soviet rule.

Rahmanov set about building a presidency with the strengths he had. As a *kolkhoz* man, he knew the bones of his country better than most members of the urban élite could. His relative youth and lack of political baggage was also in a sense an advantage. He gathered about him the men – mainly country people like himself – who had fought hardest in the war that had brought him to power. (Popular Front commanders thinned out. Sangak Safarov was murdered. So – much later – was Safarali Kenjayev.)

With the support of this circle and the prop of, if not command over, the Russian Army, Rahmanov faced the most immediate of his problems – what to do about the significant numbers of people both inside and outside the country who did not accept his government and were still determined to fight for power in Dushanbe.

Of the tens of thousands of people who crossed the freezing river Amu in the mid winter of 1992/3, about thirty thousand did not stay long in Afghanistan. They set out eastwards along the Afghan bank of the Amu and re-crossed into Tajikistan high in the mountains – a snowbound journey that killed so many that local people renamed one valley the Valley of Death, after finding the bodies in the thaw.

The remaining refugees stayed on the harsh, sandy plains of northern Afghanistan. Some were taken in by Afghans, housed in mosques and schools. When they heard of the mass crossings, one Kabul family who had fled Qurghan Tappa in the 1930s at once made the journey to the Amu, where they found a great-niece whom they took home. Shahrukh, the teacher who had fought to the end in Shahr-e Tuz, lost three of his brothers and given up his wife and children for dead, met an uncle of his wife's who had crossed by the same route three generations before. It was the one less-dark spot in an otherwise unremittingly bleak time. Few Afghans, however, were in a position to give much help even to distant relatives.

About half the refugees went to a large camp made by the UNHCR at Sakhi, just outside the city of Mazar-e Sharif. Of these about forty thousand were repatriated by the UNHCR, who escorted them home to their ruined villages in 1993. Those who judged that the time was not yet right to return were mainly the 'Gharmis' who were most afraid of reprisals, such as known fighters and their families. These people made what lives they could in Afghanistan. Some of those living in Sakhi found odd jobs in Mazar-e Sharif to supplement their UN handouts. The line of Tajiks pleading for alms along the desert road to the city became a familiar sight, their European-style shirts and trousers growing more tattered by the month. Some of the men knew that road all too well. As Soviet soldiers, they had driven along it from the border a decade before.

The leaders of the demonstrations in Shahidan Square, scattered by their flight from Tajikistan, in exile quickly resumed their alliance in opposition to the new Dushanbe government. Akbar Turajanzada, after a complex journey through Kirgizstan, Russia and Azerbaijan, reappeared in Iran, where he lived as a guest of the government in Teheran. From there he kept in touch with Hezb-e Nahzat-e Islami leaders who went to Pakistan and especially to Afghanistan, where they had much influence in the migrant community and opened alternative refugee camps along the border with Tajikistan. North Afghanistan was the obvious choice of location for an opposition headquarters. Hezb-e Nahzat-e Islami took a large house in the border town of Talaqan, courtesy of the Afghan government, and Said Abdullah Nuri moved in as the head of an anti-government movement intending to return, one day, to Dushanbe. The movement eventually became known as UTO, or United Tajik Opposition.

Nuri was a well-chosen leader. In his grey, clerical robes and

Central Asian black-and-white hat, he had a grave, modest appearance and seemed rather older than his forty-five years. His humble origins, his scholarly and pious pursuits and, above all, his time in the prison camp in Siberia, brought him respect and credibility. Nuri lived quietly at Talaqan. From there he travelled around the refugee camps, leading prayers at refugee mosques and establishing himself as the man who would lead his people home. This would be done, he announced, through *jihad*, or holy war, against the Russian-backed Rahmanov government in Dushanbe.

'The mullas spoke to each of us and asked us to join the *jihad*,' says Shahrukh of Shahr-e Tuz. 'I had lost my family, my home and my country. I did not believe in war and I refused.' 'I joined the *jihad* at once,' said another young refugee. 'I believed desperately in Islam. I believed in Nuri. My whole life had been destroyed and I hated the communists. They bled us for seventy years. They made us grateful to have nothing, and then left us.'

Over mainly mountain routes the Islamic Movement Army – the foot-soldiers of the UTO – re-crossed the Amu back into Tajikistan. At first, such raids were extremely hard work. 'We had absolutely no military experience,' one commander says. 'We had to learn as we went.' It was difficult to judge when weather would turn, what supplies to carry, and what awaited them on the far side. Many had very little knowledge of the lie of the land. Gradually, life became easier. The paths they used, the supply lines and bases, were the same ones used by the *basmachi* in the 1920s. The mountain towns of Gharm and Tavil Dara – where the *basmachi* had fought their last battle of note – became the first and strongest opposition camps. Remote and inaccessible to Russian tanks, the mountain areas were also home to people who had been sometimes horribly punished when Popular Front troops drove home their victory among the mountain people through the spring of 1993. Some local families willingly joined the *jihad*, giving up valuable cows, wheat and fodder as well as their sons; others were pressed to the cause at gunpoint.

By mid 1993, at least some of the supplies used by these fighters were probably coming from Iran. One foreign observer said he saw UTO fighters unload guns and boxes of ammunition from Iranian aircraft at Qunduz. Propaganda materials were also produced in Iran, including 'Nuri' windscreen stickers and posters and *Message of the*

Migrant magazine, whose first edition carried a reprinted article by
Mortezar Mutahari, one of the chief ideologues of the Iranian
Revolution of 1979. This does not mean that most people in the
UTO had any interest in pan-Islamic or pan-Persian hegemony.
They simply wanted to win their war, and accepted what help they
could get in the way of weapons, boots or warm clothing.

While the young men went to fight, the great majority of Tajik
migrants in Afghanistan did what they could to make their lives tolerable. The biggest camp after the UNHCR-run camp near Mazar-e
Sharif was further east, at Bagh-e Sherkat in Qunduz. Well-armed,
alert Islamic Movement Army guards in dull mustard-coloured fatigues
and balaclavas patrolled the perimeter and main buildings. Inside,
Hezb-e Nahzat-e Islami had built a sort of microcosm of the Tajikistan
they were fighting for. There were thirty mosques with madrasas
attached to them in which refugee children received a formal religious
education. The alphabet they used was Arabic, though the handwritten camp newspaper was in Cyrillic for the benefit of Soviet-educated adults.

A small boy standing outside the communal bakery piped up a salu-
tation to Nuri in a high-pitched sing-song:

Hail, man of God, we praise you for your brave generosity!
We praise you for your wise nature, your learning, your deeds!
You broke the chains from the minds of the people.
Praise to the breaking and the destroying of that chain!
Ustad Nuri, you are illuminated by the light of God;
You are a true follower of the Prophet.

Your way is a way of real learning and belief!
Your way is the will of God.
Your purpose is the victory of holy Islam.
He who says he is your enemy is an enemy of the faith.
Ustad Nuri, you are illuminated by the light of God;
You are a true follower of the Prophet.

The guide patted his head. The small crowd that had gathered to
watch burst into applause.

Life in Bagh-e Sherkat was tough. The plains of Qunduz are
notoriously inhospitable, dry and barren but with marshes full of

malaria-carrying mosquitoes, bitter winters and scorching summers: precisely the same conditions the refugees' parents had contended with when they were moved to the Vakhsh valley – only a few miles away on the other side of the Amu – during the *mujaharat-e ijbari*. Many children died of pneumonia. A small number of medicines and other supplies were donated by Iran and by charities in Saudi Arabia, but these were often of poor quality and the supply soon dried up.

The refugees of Bagh-e Sherkat longed to go home, and many would have re-crossed the Amu any day had they felt it was safe to do so. Nearly all the news they had from home was bad, filtered as it was through UTO leaders whom they had no choice but to follow. Asked if he considered himself to be 'in the opposition', a tall, thin elder replied: 'I was out in the fields. When I returned home I saw a wall of fire. It was my village burning. I ran towards it and met my neighbours running the other way. They said "Run! Run! Your family is dead already." I turned and ran with them. I am a Muslim and I crossed the river. If that is what "opposition" means, then I am in the opposition.'

The opposition radio station 'Voice of Free Tajikistan' began broadcasting from Talaqan. Using a rousing mixture of music, prayers, news and messages of hope, it played an important part in keeping the migrant community together. As well as news of partisan victories against Rahmanov – the 'puppet of the Kremlin' – 'Free Tajikistan' broadcast imaginative specials and, at one point, a 'Mujahed of the Year' competition. Listeners on the Tajik side tuned in covertly to the haunting poetry written and read by refugee women. For most people, it was the only way they could get any sense of what the lives of their missing relatives – if they were still alive – might be like.

In the middle of Bagh-e Sherkat, camp leaders had built a cultural centre: a large single room with the green, white and red flag of the opposition pinned across one wall, mats on the floor, and a generator-powered video-player on which to show the trilogy of films they had made about the *jihad*. The men crowded in to watch as the screen filled with scenes from the exodus of 1992 – heads bobbing in the water, women weeping for their children – recorded should the refugees ever forget who drove them from their homes. In another, *Men of the Front*, strong-looking armed partisans rowed across lakes, pitched camp on beautiful mountain sides and knelt in rows to pray. A stirring commentary praised the fighters of the Islamic Movement Army who would one day defeat the enemy. All the commanders were homesick. 'We want peace,' one said, 'and we will fight forever until we get it. We have found our roots now, we are Muslims. And we will return with our heads held high.'

Exploratory peace talks between the Tajik government and the opposition opened in Moscow two weeks after *nauruz* in 1994, under the aegis of the United Nations. The opposition set out its main demand: a share of power in Dushanbe amounting to about a third of official positions – that is, the proportion it had won through the demonstrations of 1992. The government, with the power of Russia behind it, refused. Talks reconvened in Teheran, a venue more sympathetic to the opposition. There, the two sides agreed on a ceasefire that, though instantly and constantly breached, enabled the UN to introduce observers to monitor it – the first outsiders to keep any official record of what was going on in the battlefields of the mountains. Then came talks in Islamabad, in Pakistan. Then came Almaty, capital of Kazakhstan: Ramiro Piriz Ballon, the UN special envoy assigned to broker the deal, spoke of his hopes that a breakthrough was imminent when talks opened there in May 1995.

Akbar Turajanzada took centre-stage at Almaty as chief negotiator for the opposition, while Nuri stayed out of the public eye in Afghanistan. Turajanzada seemed born for the role. Eloquent and passionate, he appealed for what seemed like the impossible – a more or less unconditional return to legal politics by the side that had been comprehensively defeated in the war. His hotel suite had a flavour of the *glasnost* era, with journalists and allies from the Democratic Party – most of whom had fled to Moscow during the war – pottering in and out, drinking tea and discussing the next steps. Exile had had the advantage of adding, of necessity, a kind of worldliness to the opposition leaders.

The leader on the government side, Mahmadsaid Ubaidullayev, was an old ally of Rahmanov and a tough opponent. 'We have total support inside Tajikistan,' he said, relaxing in a tracksuit in his hotel after a session in Almaty. He turned down the volume of a television cop show and reached for a sheaf of papers. 'See, this is a petition in our support. There are hundreds of names here. They come from all the *kolkhozes*.' A number of side issues could be discussed, he said, but the return to power of the opposition was simply not negotiable.

The UN despaired. 'They are making fools of us,' said one attendant diplomat privately. 'They agree to talk because they like to meet each other and discuss tactics.' 'They've agreed on *nothing*,' said another, after an exhausting ten-day session. 'The only thing they see eye to eye on is the menu. They have a big meeting and decide to have *pilau* for lunch. And that is all.' The talks broke up without agreement. In the mountains the war went on: the politicians reached stalemate.

The list of foreign advisors present in Almaty showed the web of countries that by now had made Tajikistan their business. Russian, Iranian, Afghan and Pakistani faces were ranged around the polished tables of the old parliament building, behind the circle of Tajiks. One of the most important outside powers was not present, however. Uzbekistan, always secretive about its part in the civil war, largely bowed out of Tajik affairs once its objective was achieved. It did nothing to support the Kulabi government which – in so far as it had helped defeat the 'other side' – it had helped to bring to power, but instead tried to isolate itself from Tajikstan, even cutting all air links with its turbulent neighbour, in the hope of keeping Tajik instability out of Uzbek territory. In the autumn of 1995, with all eyes on the deadlocked Tajik peace talks, the political centre of gravity of Central Asia shifted to Uzbekistan – heralded by a small, almost unnoticed happening in the heart of the capital, Tashkent.

IO

A year in Tashkent

'. . . when the extent of their territories became broad and vast and important events fell out, it became essential to ascertain the activities of their enemies, and it was also necessary to transport goods from the West to the East and from the Far East to the West.'

To cross the border from Tajikistan to Uzbekistan in the middle 1990s was to cross from one state of mind into another. This was especially so at the dust-dry desert crossing at Termez. On the Tajik side stood a few ruins that had once been some farmhouses, a Soviet army watch-tower, long since abandoned, and a few pillboxes set in the bank of the Amu, their lids flapping off to reveal rusted gun barrels poking into the air, aimed crazily at nothing. The border guards were a bunch of boys – none had a uniform, most wore plastic flip-flops, all carried guns too large for their narrow shoulders. They smiled cheerfully, admired a pack of playing cards they had found, looking at each card in turn, before waving the car on towards Uzbekistan.

A hundred yards away, at the Uzbek frontier, their counterparts had boots, badges, uniforms. Their post was made of brick and there was a stout metal barricade across the width of the road. They had a field telephone on which they received orders and checked who was permitted to cross (almost nobody) and who forbidden. Once on the Uzbek side, travellers could proceed without fear of the banditry that comes with war, although the plains were just as lonely as on the Tajik side and the few people who live there were equally poor. Uzbekistan, at this time, lived inside the bubble of peace, where orders are followed and the authorities have authority. Politics was not a 'festival of personalities', as one diplomat described those of Tajikistan. Power rested, at least ostensibly, in the hands of one man: President Islam Karimov.

Stocky, grey-haired, and middle-aged, Karimov made the preservation of the bubble of peace, with himself at its centre, the guiding star of his presidency. 'Stability is the basis for everything,' he once said, setting out his stall for the world. 'If there were more Karimovs out here in this region – people whom [the Americans] call dictators but who are in fact the very bastions that stand in the way of fundamentalism – you would not have had that explosion in New York City at the World Trade Centre [in 1993].'

Karimov ruled with the means he had: impunity, a large intelligence service, and – most importantly – a population so innocent of knowledge about the outside world or even, in some respects, Uzbekistan that they lacked a frame of reference in which to set their lives. The rubber-stamp parliament met twice a year to – sometimes literally – recite poems in Karimov's honour. After a brief flurry of political activity in the early 1990s, all opposition leaders had disappeared into prison or exile. All the opposition movements that had emerged in Uzbekistan in the late 1980s and early 1990s were suppressed from 1992 – the time when the war in Tajikistan began – onwards. Police broke up the founding meeting of the Islam Tiklanish Partiasa, the mirror party to the Tajik Hezb-e Nahzat-e Islami in 1992. Its leader, Abdullah Uta, was detained in December of that year but has never been charged or stood trial. Leaders of the two city-based nationalist-democratic parties, Birlik (Unity) and Erk (Freedom), soon followed the Islamic leaders into prison or exile.

The 'loyal opposition' parties set up to give Uzbekistan the image of being an 'emerging democracy' were so much Karimov's creations that members of one, Adalat (Justice), actually went to sleep during their founding conference in 1995. Nearly all foreign newspapers were banned, including those from Russia, and every word spoken or printed by any local journalist was checked by the censor – virtually no one in Uzbekistan, therefore, had the faintest idea about Uzbek intervention in Tajikistan. Telephones were monitored as a matter of routine, and bugs were set in the house-walls of anyone suspected of unconventional thought.

Islam Karimov's control over the lives of his people was direct and intimate. He was a keen tennis player, and when he ordered the mayors of Uzbekistan to play an annual tournament, portly dignitaries all over the country dutifully struggled into tracksuits. Tennis was declared to be the national game of Uzbekistan. Karimov ordered that a world-class President's Cup event be held in Tashkent, and the organisers scrambled to renovate rooms in the Hotel Uzbekistan to accommodate the international stars invited to compete. Out in the villages, the elders referred to Karimov as *padshah*, just as they had the amir of Bukhara and Stalin.

For all he ruled with old tools, however, Karimov was much more than a cardboard tyrant. He was clever – his spoken Russian far outclassed that of any other Central Asian president (and of many Russians) – and he had the gift of magnetic and passionate eloquence. He could be choleric, and was reputed to subject his ministers to scalding humiliation, but he could also charm. Karimov was hard-working, not atrophied by vodka like many Soviet-era politicians, and did not go in much for showy mansions and fancy cars. Unlike most of his contemporaries in power in other former Soviet republics, he appeared to care about his country and to want to make something of it.

Islam Abdughanievich Karimov was born in humble circumstances in Samarkand in 1938, just at the end of the Stalinist purges. Like many in Samarkand, where the Persian tradition is strong, the family was of mixed Uzbek and Tajik blood. Karimov's early life is obfuscated by legend. Official sources say only that the family was poor and lived on bread and tea, with *pilau* once a week; some versions have it that he was sent away to boarding school on the charity of the state. A class photograph from 1947 shows the future president as a ragged boy at the end of a line of other ragged boys.

Karimov was born at the right time. Part of the first generation to reap the rewards of the Soviet experiment, he pulled himself out of poverty through a secular education and graduated from Tashkent Polytechnic as an engineer. While working at the Ilyushin aircraft factory established at Tashkent during the Second World War, he studied economics. He came of age just around the time when local people were beginning to climb on to the higher rungs of the Party apparatus. As was proper for a young internationalist, Karimov's first marriage was to a Slav. His second – and lasting – marriage was to a half-Tatar, half-Belorussian, Tatyana.

Karimov rose swiftly and joined the State Planning Committee, the springboard to his appointment as Finance Minister and eventually as First Secretary of the Uzbek Communist Party Central Committee. His transition to head of the independent state followed naturally. In 1991 Karimov set up his presidential offices in the old Communist Party headquarters, built on the exact spot – a mound on the east bank of the river Anhar – on which General Chernayev had positioned his artillery in the June of 1865, and so begun the conquest that gave Tsar Alexander II his base in Central Asia, and Tashkent the standing and authority it had enjoyed ever since.

The Tashkent of 1995 was still the biggest city in Central Asia, with a population of about two million, and an air of cautious optimism. Slowly, little by little, its glass was rising. Uzbek cotton, the bedrock of the economy, was now being sold on the world market, and Uzbekistan became the fourth largest cotton exporter in the world. Trade with foreign countries, though still at a modest level, brought novelties to the bazaars. Rich people tried bananas for the first time, and took home their shopping in the new plastic carrier bags. The Tashkentland funfair opened – at an elaborate party held at midnight because the presidential entourage was delayed – as did small branches of the Turkish supermarkets Ardus and Demir. A handful of people began to use e-mail at a computer centre run by a charity from the United States.

Attracted by the unexploited resources, the imagined open markets and the promised stability of Uzbekistan, a few big-name companies set up in Tashkent. The US mining company Newmont blazed the way with a project to strip gold from the leavings of a Soviet-built mine in the Qizil Qum desert. British American Tobacco opened, with a view to selling cheap cigarettes locally and for export. Coca-Cola made Tashkent its base in the hot, thirsty lands of the former Soviet south, headed locally by Karimov's Uzbek-American son-in-law, Mansur Maqsudi, scion of an émigré Ferghanachi family that had originally fled the Soviet Union three generations before and become factory-owners in Kabul before moving on to the United States.

Elsewhere, the world of the old USSR seemed to have gone mad. Quite apart from the wars in Tajikistan, Azerbaijan, Georgia and

Chechnya – all explained to the Uzbek public as simply the work of wicked men lusting for power – other former Soviet economies crashed, the poor begged in the streets, the new rich flew their children to Swiss boarding schools, 'mafiosi' paid two hundred dollars apiece to get into Moscow nightclubs where Uzi-toting bouncers made them check their weapons in the cloakrooms. In Tashkent, where children still played safely in the streets and a foreign car was so rare that pedestrians stopped to watch it, many people thanked their lucky stars that they lived where they did. 'Developed countries would be envious of our achievement,' said President Karimov, smiling, as he took the first gold brick from its mould at a re-vamped Soviet-built foundry at Uchkuduk, in the heart of the desert. 'Very few countries are so rich in minerals as we are. Soon we will be self-sufficient in oil and petrol, and in grain! We have secured our tomorrow!'

The first step in the long, slow test of the Karimov doctrine came in the late summer of 1995, when a handful of men presented themselves at the United Nations building in Tashkent. Their black-and-white hats and soft high boots marked them immediately as out-of-towners, and they stood awkwardly in the shining lobby waiting for help.

They had made the journey from their home in the Ferghana valley with, they said, some shocking news: Abduvali Mirzayev, the imam of the Friday mosque in Andijan – the biggest in Ferghana – had vanished. With his assistant, Ramazanbek Matkarimov, he had left Andijan for Tashkent, whence he was due to fly to Moscow for a conference on religious affairs. The two had arrived on 29 August at Tashkent airport, where they checked in to board an Uzbek Airways flight to Russia. Friends who were to meet them in Moscow had reported that they never arrived.

The group from Ferghana, mainly elders, had come to the capital to try to stir international interest, and to beg President Karimov to find their imam. Three hundred and seventeen Muslims 'great and humble' had signed the petition they carried, but no one would agree to see them. The United Nations officer for human rights thought the case 'too political' for her remit. Officials at the Presidential Palace turned them away. The elders stood about for a while in the street, then tried again. On the third day they returned to Andijan.

The Ferghana valley is divided from Tashkent by a long ridge of mountains which until the Russian conquest formed the border of the khanate of Kokand. It was in these red, ore-laden mountains that Hindustani hid his family in the ominous year of 1936. Almost sixty years later, opaque pillars of smoke from a Soviet-built foundry stood like columns over the town of Angren, where he had worked covertly as a mulla. Beyond Angren the mountain road twists ever higher until, over the Kamchik pass at 2,268 metres, the land opens up and it runs smoothly down into the Ferghana valley. The first town one comes to is Kokand, near where Hindustani was born, followed by a skein of others of which Andijan, the easternmost town of Uzbekistan, is the last.

Thousands upon thousands of men answered the midday call to prayer in Andijan on the first Friday after the petitioners travelled to Tashkent. In ones and twos and groups they walked across the main square to the Friday mosque, followed by boys in their best white shirts, each holding a holy book. The Andijan mosque – one of the biggest in all Central Asia – was soon packed to bursting. Men stood in every inch of the courtyard, craning round trees to see, and hushing one another. Three hundred or so women and girls converged on their own courtyard to the right. They were veiled from head to foot – something scarcely ever seen in Tashkent. Once within the precinct, they hung up their outer clothing and sat round trestle tables set with tea. Many were in tears.

From over the dividing wall the women could hear the sound of Abduvali's deputy leading prayers. 'There is one truth: it is unbreakable,' he intoned. 'Even though generations may try, they will fail. The truth is steadfast. Through history many people have perished, but truth will remain. Whatever happens, the faithful will worship.' Abduvali's followers did not say so explicitly, but it was clear that they believed he had been abducted by agents of the SNB – the post-Soviet name for the political police. Some, especially the young, were angry. Far more were, quite simply, horribly afraid of what his disappearance might presage.

After prayers the congregation filtered out into the bazaar, where cassettes of Abduvali's sermons were set out near the rows of plastic sandals, pens, and sachets of hair-dye brought by truck across

Kirgizstan from China, on the far side of the Tien Shan. A row of elders sailed past on heavy Chinese bicycles. As the crow flies, Andijan is as close to Kashgar as it is to Tashkent.

Abduvali Mirzayev had been foremost among the new generation of Uzbek imams who stood apart from the establishment, nearly all of whom came from the Ferghana valley. As a young man he had been close to Said Abdullah Nuri and others at the house of Hindustani in Dushanbe, and he had walked a delicate line ever since. He preached passionately about the need for truth and justice, always keeping within religious precepts. While he did not speak out against President Karimov, neither did he plaster his mosque with portraits of the leader. According to his friends, he never joined any sort of religious revival party, maintaining that politics and faith must always be kept separate – 'Otherwise,' he had said, 'our religion will become spoilt and corrupted. We would become puppets.'

'The government says it is worried about what happened in Tajikistan, but I don't think the same would happen here,' said a follower of Abduvali. 'It's more likely they are just afraid of *anyone* who is popular. Abduvali was perhaps the last of the great imams. Many people in Ferghana are worried. They are afraid and insulted. But nothing is inevitable. What will happen now in Ferghana depends on what Tashkent decides to do.'

In the small hours of 3 September 1995, five days after Abduvali Mirzayev disappeared from Tashkent airport, an army of tall men wearing black turbans and carrying white flags captured the city of Herat in western Afghanistan, near the Iranian border. Called the Taleban, or students, they imposed on the city a set of social rules so striking that they – briefly – caught the attention of the outside world. These rules – derived, the Taleban said, from the word of God as revealed in the Quran – limited what women could do outside the home, stipulated what women and men might wear, abolished pursuits the Taleban leadership thought frivolous, and banned images of living things.

Life in Herat changed in a day. Female students about to take their finals were unable to do so. Girls stopped going to school. Women could not set foot outside the house unless they were wearing the all-enveloping *burqa*. Armed men smashed the horse-statues around the fountain in the main square, festooned the trees with confiscated cassette-tape, and banned the watching of television. 'We sent the children to hide the *dutar* and *rubab* [stringed instruments],' remembers a musician, 'but the Taleban found them in the garden and broke them too.'

The Taleban had begun to emerge as a military force in Afghanistan in 1994. Backed by Pakistan, they had gradually become the strongest force in southern Afghanistan, which was predominantly Pashtun, as were the Taleban leaders. The support given to such religious groups by Pakistan is acknowledged by senior figures in the Pakistani military. General Mirza Aslam Beg, Chief of Staff of the Pakistani Army from 1988 to 1990, described how Islamabad and Washington encouraged the formation of 'a chain of madrasas' in Pakistan that would be 'soldier nurseries' to 'make the Soviets bleed'.* In the early 1990s, at least some of the men who became leaders of the Taleban were field commanders around Qandahar, but the name only became known in a wider sphere after they captured the southern district of Spin Boldak, near the Pakistani border, in October 1994. The movement took on some of the character and function of Hezb-e Islami as its leader, a Pashtun, Gulbuddin Hekmatyar, began to lose power during the wars for Kabul in the mid 1990s. A turning-point came in 1995, when Mulla Umar declared himself Amir-e Muminin (Amir of the Faithful) and held aloft one of the holiest relics in Afghanistan, the cloak of the Prophet, as a signal of his authority. The march on Herat began shortly afterwards. The fall of the city cut off Kabul on its western side. At the same time, as Herat is Persian-speaking, it gave the Taleban their first city outside their Pashtun-majority southern heartlands.

Although it was the movement's first spectacular success, the capture of Herat soon showed the weakness of the Taleban. The Qandahari soldiers who took over the city never blended in. They spoke Pashtun rather than Persian, the language of the city, and caused resentment by taking over top official posts, and making decisions – such as altering the syllabus at the university – without consulting

* Aslam Beg's own antecedents lie in Andijan, making him – at several removes – a 'Ferghanachi'.

local people. Some Heratis disliked such practices as that of throwing petitions to the Taleban governor through the windows of the citadel. Many Heratis became 'Taleban' but few had the conviction of the Qandaharis – some privately flew kites behind the wall of Herat fort, to cite one small example. Even a year after taking the city, the Taleban had not moved their families from Qandahar and their air was very much that of an occupying army, the officers of which were rotated through the various provinces.

The Taleban campaign to take over Afghanistan was conducted in the name of Islam and of peace – the idea being that Afghans would unite under one leadership. Events have since moved on, but at the time many outsiders – including commentators in the US – were not against the idea. There is considerable evidence to support the claim that Pakistan gave increasing amounts of military support to the Taleban during its campaign. Among the Taleban forces were also some foreign volunteers who had come to Afghanistan during the 1980s to fight the Soviet Army and, along with the *mujahedin*, had received support from the United States and its allies. The most famous of these was the Saudi-born dissident Usama bin Laden.

Seen from Soviet-educated Tashkent, the Taleban appeared sinister and incomprehensible – from the kohl around their eyes (used to cut glare) to their dark clothes to their invisible leader – Mulla Umar, who was never photographed because to do so would be to depict a living form. From the city-Uzbek point of view the laws they brought to Afghanistan seemed to belong to the days of the emirate of Bukhara – the 'dark past' in which, Central Asians had been taught, time had 'stood still' for hundreds of years.

Along with this instinctive response to the image of the Taleban went what seemed like compelling political reasons for taking a hostile stand towards this new, unknown force. The Uzbek author-ities feared that the social codes the Taleban espoused might attract people casting about for some notion of truth in ideologically con-fused times – perhaps people like those who followed Said Abdullah Nuri or Abduvali Mirzayev – and so lead to a direct challenge to the Soviet-era leadership. Moreover, the Uzbek leadership, still feeling its way in foreign affairs, was generally suspicious of anything to do with

Pakistan, which had played such an active part in the war against the Soviet occupation of Afghanistan.

Uzbekistan had in place a rudimentary foreign policy to ward off the possibility of any group it considered unfriendly becoming too powerful in Afghanistan. Ever since the early 1990s it had, along with Russia, tried to maintain a buffer zone in northern Afghanistan by supporting the Afghan commander who controlled Mazar-e Sharif and Hairatan – the areas abutting Uzbekistan. This commander's name was Abdul Rashid, but he was known universally as 'General Dustam'.

Dustam's journey to his seat of power in Mazar-e Sharif began on the harsh, dry plains of Jauzjan in north-west Afghanistan, border-lands populated largely by Uzbeks like himself, many of them migrants who had crossed the Amu to escape the Soviet Union in the 1920s and 1930s. The Uzbeks were khans, or lords, in these, their own lands, but had never gained political or intellectual standing in Kabul or in Afghanistan at large. Even to read a newspaper, an Uzbek had to learn Persian or Pashtu, the languages of literate Afghanistan. Illiterate Uzbeks – the great majority – were famous as fighters and horsemen, symbolised by their skill at *buzkashi*, a sport Dustam later played though he never became a star. 'We were the horse-boys to the Pashtuns,' as one Uzbek put it. 'Always soldiers, never officers. Until there was Dustam.'

Dustam was born in 1954, the eldest son of the second wife of a poor farmer, Abdul Rahim, in the village of Khuja Do Ko near the town of Sheberghan. He left school at about thirteen, after the sixth grade, to work on the farm with his father and brothers. New pros-pects appeared when the Soviet Union greatly increased aid to northern Afghanistan under Muhammad Daud Khan, President of Afghanistan from 1973 to 1978. Dustam and some friends left their village for Sheberghan and found work at the new oil and gas factory.

The Soviet invasion of December 1979 brought further opportu-nities, and Dustam's two full brothers took new, Soviet-inclined paths in life. Abdul Qader went to Baku in Azerbaijan to study engineering. Rustam went into KhAD, the Afghan security service modelled on and coached by the Soviet KGB. Dustam also joined KhAD, as a soldier, and was sent to Uzbekistan for intelligence training. Back in Sheberghan, he set up his own militia of three hundred young Uzbek farmers, dressed in KhAD uniform but answerable to him. As his forces grew, they became indispensable to Muhammad Najibullah, the last Soviet-backed President of the Kabul government, as the guardians of the route from the Friendship Bridge across the Amu, through which came not only weapons and ammunition but sugar, wheat, school-books and all the commodities that flowed from the USSR to Kabul.

Dustam had briefly come into sight of the eyes of the world when he suddenly switched sides against the failing Najibullah in 1992, after quarelling with him mainly about money – a move so unex-pected that some of his soldiers literally did not believe it and stayed on at their posts. He marched his men into Kabul alongside his former enemies, Ahmad Shah Mas'ud's *mujahedin*. But he quickly fell out with the *mujahedin* leaders – who, he thought, grabbed all the best jobs for themselves when they formed their government – and returned to the plains of the north-west, where he created his own fief in partnership with a powerful family whose province, Fariab, adjoined Dustam's territories. General Dustam made a niche for himself in Afghan politics as a secular leader, a champion of minor-ities, and a man with whom former Soviet states could do business.

Uzbekistan piped gas and sent wheat and electricity across the Amu to the Uzbeks in Mazar-e Sharif; it also, according to General Dustam's men, sent weapons and ammunition. With Mazar-e Sharif and the plains around as a barricade, the southern border of Uzbekistan felt protected from hostile forces – real or imaginary. 'He sees everything in terms of *walls*,' said one man close to Karimov. 'He thinks, let's keep out the Afghans, let's keep out the Tajiks. Let's build a fort around ourselves.'

Abduvali Mirzayev's followers spent the autumn travelling to and fro between Andijan and Tashkent. They searched for a Russian woman who had apparently been on duty at the airport the day that the imam disappeared. On their first visit, they claimed, she told them that she had seen two plain-clothes men with Abduvali, and had asked them why they were holding up the queue at the boarding gate. On a later visit, they said, they found no one at Uzbek Airways with any recollection of such a woman. They petitioned the presi-dential palace and the ministries in vain. They warned that the crowds coming to Friday prayers were growing ever larger. No official in Tashkent said anything. The forty-day anniversary of Abduvali's disappearance came and went.

In Andijan there were rumours of arrests, and the anxiety that had begun at the Friday mosque began to seep around the city, spreading to devout Muslims who had nothing to do with Abduvali. Some began to pray at home, rather than attend public prayers and risk being noted as pious by SNB agents in the congregation. A few people, determined not to be mastered by fear, agreed to meet foreign journalists, to expose what they believed to be state-sponsored kidnap and intimidation of the devout. They used false names, codes and passwords, arranged their meetings in subways and on lonely highways at night. Each time the pick-up was at a different point; each time a different silent driver careered around the alleys to shake off any tail. 'It is ridiculous that we have to behave in this way,' one man said, embarrassed. 'This is 1995, not 1937!'

An anonymous man palmed a cassette in a bazaar. The unnamed voice on the tape was addressing what was clearly a packed meeting:

We believe in God and in President Karimov! We know that our constitution protects citizens of Uzbekistan!

But now we know that the constitution is just for show. We know that the reason our brothers have disappeared is because they are believers. We are tired of these spies who dog us. The young are with us, and the old. We have asked Tashkent to let us hold a demonstration.

If they do not answer, we will hold it anyway. Thousands of us will stand. We will hold banners and hold up photographs of our brothers! We demand that those responsible for this evil act be brought to justice.

'We have a one per cent chance of success,' said a young man waiting wearily for an answer to the application. The application was turned down.

The Muftiat of Uzbekistan ran its affairs from the Barak Khan madrasa, the pretty, medieval complex of buildings in the heart of old Tashkent. Its main mosque, Tela Shaikh, the Golden Shaikh, was the

Friday mosque for the capital, and its library housed one of the earliest and most precious books in the Muslim world – a giant Quran written on gazelle skin for the Caliph Usman in the mid seventh century and, the story goes, splashed by his blood when his enemies stabbed him to death. The Quran followed the fortunes of the Caliphate from Medina to Baghdad and later Damascus before arriving in Samarkand – removed there by the armies of Amir Timur in 1485 along with numerous other treasures from conquered lands. Four hundred years later, Russian soldiers under General Kaufmann in their turn took it to St Petersburg, where it stayed until Lenin ordered it to be returned to Central Asia. By 1995 the manuscript had lost about half its original 706 folios – a few stolen in the disorder following each imperial collapse.

The Muftiat had, since independence, played an ambiguous role. An energetic young Ferghana cleric had risen to power on the tide of change that came in with Gorbachev, sweeping aside the discredited founding dynasty of Babakhanovs who had kept the post through three generations. Muhammad Sadeq Muhammad Yusuf, called Mama, opened mosques and madrasas with vigour. He was a friend and mentor of Akbar Turajonzada, with whom he had studied in Jordan, and was cut of similar cloth. After Turajonzada fled Tajikistan into exile, Karimov sacked Mama. Mama vanished, to reappear in Saudi Arabia and later Libya. Long since out of sight, Mama still commanded much respect in Uzbekistan.

The Mufti of 1995, Hajji Abdullah Mukhtar, dressed in a grey robe and white turban, sat at the head of a long table. He made his position quite clear.

'We are the head of five thousand mosques: in the Soviet times there were only seventy,' he said. 'Our president has done much for Islam. Did he not hold up a Quran at a session of the Supreme Soviet and say "My name is Islam"? These imams you speak of, they are unlettered people, self-taught. Like a quack who sets himself up and says "I am a doctor." Would you trust such a man? We have seen their work in Ferghana. They stopped children from going to school and learning science and technology. They are disruptive and against stability.

'We met Abduvali once in Mecca and said, "Come to us! Whoever is the Mufti you must recognise us as in charge." But he was obstinate. There is not a shred of evidence that the state has taken him. His

people have been here, and I told them so.' Asked why Abduvali's supporters would make up such a story, he said that perhaps they were
mistaken and, in any case, it was not Muftiat business.*

That autumn, the Muftiat began a campaign to tighten its grip over
the mosques of Uzbekistan. It decreed that every imam in the country
must sit an exam – much of which comprised questions about state
policy. Those who failed it, or refused to take it, lost their jobs.

Winter comes to Tashkent with the smell of burning leaves. Children
who have spent the summer playing are hard at work with their
mothers, sweeping the leaves into the *ariqs*. Orange bonfires flicker
against the sky at dusk, dark, bundled shapes before them. On a cold
day in December, the police shut down the Friday mosque in Andijan.
They glued a notice to its massive chained doors: 'By order. This
building is now undergoing restoration. It will re-open as a museum
by popular demand.' The tapes of Abduvali's sermons had disappeared
from the bazaar. Local people said that the police had begun to raid
houses, picking up young men and planting drugs on them. Some
believers had been taken to police stations and forced to shave off their
beards. The campaign to find Abduvali and bring his kidnappers to
justice had failed. 'We are forbidden to leave Andijan,' one man said.
'They watch us all the time. We have been silenced.'

With the disappearance of Abduvali, there remained only one
high-profile imam in Uzbekistan who thought along independent
lines. Abedkhan Nazarov had been on the plane to Moscow – Uzbek
Airways Flight 668 – that Abduvali was supposed to have boarded.
Abedkhan spoke out against the matter at Friday prayers. Abedkhan
was no provincial outsider: he was a senior Muftiat man, the imam of
the Takhtabai mosque, one of the biggest in Tashkent.

Across the border in Tajikistan, in the mountains bordering
Afghanistan, Said Abdullah Nuri's opposition fighters – the Islamic

---

* In February 1996 the government put out a statement. It said that Abduvali Mirzayev and
Ramazanbek Matkarimov had flown from Andijan to Tashkent by Flight 100 to transfer to Flight 668
to Moscow. They had checked in, gone through the customs and security checks, passed into the departure hall, boarded, and taken off. Their boarding-pass numbers were 73 and 74. There were witnesses to
corroborate all this. The case was closed.

Movement Army – went from strength to strength. The pretty high-land town of Gharm, self-sufficient enough in the pre-Soviet period to import modern firearms and even white sugar over the mountains from Ferghana, was in government hands only in as much as President Rahmanov's men held the ribbon of houses along the valley floor. The mountains around were home to guerrillas, supplied by local farmers who, both willingly and under duress, supported them with wheat and, sometimes, livestock.

According to a weary Security Ministry officer, the opposition were growing bolder all the time in their raids on government posts and convoys. 'Oh, they call themselves Islamic fighters, but really they are bandits. They hide behind Islam,' he said, leaning across the large desk that was one of the few signs left of the Russian century. The most powerful local commander was, he said, Mirza Khuja Nezamov, a former gym teacher who had been a lieutenant-colonel in the police until the civil war came and he changed his uniform. Mirza Khuja was forty-five, the owner of two or three houses and father of a dozen children. His influence in Gharm ran deep. 'They attack at night, generally. It is difficult to fight them because they work at night and move constantly. Now he is out there.' He nodded towards the mountain wall outside. There was nothing stirring.

There were several Nezamovs, and little that Dushanbe could do in Gharm, Sangvar, Tavil Dara or any of the other mountain towns that formed a chain back to the supply base on the Afghan border. The national army of Tajikistan, finally and hastily put together in 1993, consisted almost entirely of teenagers pulled out of the bazaars and off buses by the press-gang. Those who could not afford to buy their way out were sent to the front, sometimes begging or stealing petrol and bread for the journey on the way.

Frostbite and malnutrition claimed many casualties. 'I am going home to Khujand,' said a boy, shyly showing his blackened right hand. He was eighteen but looked much younger, trailing round a Dushanbe hospital in a Soviet-issue dressing gown. 'This war is being fought by the sons of the poor,' said an angry Tajik Army officer. 'Where are the Popular Front commanders now? Sitting in their nice houses.' The tanks of President Rahmanov's main weapon, CIS forces, were as ineffective as their forerunners had been on the south side of the same mountains in Afghanistan in the 1980s. And as in

Afghanistan, they resorted to bombing villages, killing civilians, and destroying the highland roads. Mountain people went hungry because they could not get their goods to market. Under the old *kolkhoz* system, villages had been encouraged to concentrate on a single crop – now that the roads were impassable and exchange impossible, some villages survived only on apples, some only on apricots. In the warm weather, the situation was grave enough – and there was no food to store for the coming winter.

Government and opposition leaders began a new round of talks in Ashgabat, the capital of Turkmenistan. It was two thousand miles from the mountains, and felt like it.

As the snow began in the winter of 1995/6, Dushanbe seemed to edge towards social collapse. Gaps began to appear in the lines of trees along the avenues. Those who had firewood locked it up. Uzbekistan demanded hard currency for the electricity it supplied to Tajikistan; the Tajiks could not pay, and the Uzbeks cut them off. The worst epidemic of diphtheria seen anywhere since the Second World War swept through the country, spreading quickly through villages where families huddled together hugger-mugger for warmth, sharing teacups and blankets.

'Now we sit in the kitchen, my wife and I,' said a retired government official. 'If there is electricity we listen to the radio. If not, we sit in silent darkness. Sometimes we get a little gas, because we live in a government building. If it comes, we cook whatever we have found in the bazaar, but we have to be quick because we don't know how long the gas will last. We don't know *when* it's coming, either.' It was not what he expected after a lifetime of service in the KGB.

People were murdered for trivial amounts of money and sometimes even just for bread during this particularly cold and depressing winter. Even the exuberant Muhyeddin Alempur, beacon among intellectuals, seemed low. He still bounded about town, he still played his music tapes and welcomed guests, but his beard had begun to turn grey. 'If someone decides to get me,' he once said quietly, 'there is nothing anyone can do to help me.' The light fades early towards the turn of the year. Muhyeddin insisted that everyone should leave the office by five o'clock, and travel only with people they knew. His body was found in the early morning of 13 December 1995. He had been shot through the heart late the night before and left near the river Dushanbe. He had last been seen waiting for his bus home.

The small town was stunned. Every poet and *savant*, every man of letters, came to the office to pay their respects, their breath like smoke even indoors. They were not just chilled, they were frightened to the bone. 'With Muhyeddin alive, one felt decency was possible,' said Pierre-François Pirlot, head of the UNHCR and doyen of the foreign community, at a packed memorial service. Like almost all the others, Muhyeddin Alempur's murder was never solved. Awkward policemen clumped around the apartment, poked at his tape collection, offered their sympathy, and left.

The new year of 1996 came in much as the old had gone out. On 21 January gunmen burst into the house of Fatullah Khan Sharifzada, the Mufti of all Tajikistan. They shot him dead, along with his wife, his son and other relatives. A few days later, leaders of the local Uzbek community in Hisar and Qurghan Tappa staged a sudden uprising. On the first day of *ramazan*, opposition fighters shot and killed between twenty and twenty-five young government soldiers who had been escorting a military supply convoy along the Gharm road. Heaped together in the back of a truck, they looked as though they were asleep in their underwear – their valuable outer clothes had been stripped and taken. Local children, their eyes huge, their feet bare in the snow, grabbed tins of meat from under the smouldering remains of the convoy and stuffed the charred onions into their ragged shirts to take home to their mothers.

The United States put out a shocked statement of condemnation. The United Nations called urgently for peace talks. Tajikistan looked suddenly, perilously, close to terrible violence.

On a raw April morning in 1996, the faithful of Takhtabai mosque in old Tashkent slithered through the snow to prayers to find militia posted at the wooden gates muttering into walkie-talkies and policemen even inside the mosque. A new imam, sent by the Muftiat, was taking Friday prayers for the first time. He was a replacement for Abedkhan Nazarov who, having failed to turn up for the loyalty exam set by the Muftiat, had lost his job. Windowless, unmarked police wagons were standing by in case of trouble. It was – almost –

an open show of force in a city where the hidden hint was usually enough. Out of sight of the militia, a few of the congregation spoke. 'Abedkhan? I don't know him,' said one woman, blank-eyed. Her friend was braver. 'They have taken our imam. This new man – we don't know him, he's not ours.' Many people, she said, had not come to prayers that day. Some of the congregation had been bussed in.

Prayers went quietly. The congregation filed home.

The scene around Takhtabai illustrated the helplessness of the Uzbek poor. The parish was in the middle of a slum clearance scheme, and the mosque perched, like a fort on a cliff, above a gulf of yellow mud that had been a street a few weeks before. The streets that remained had been neglected for years – the wooden doors were smashed, the walls of mud had burst to show their internal straw and criss-crossed wooden laths – the building methods of five hundred years ago still in use in modern times. The Takhtabai families had been promised new, modern flats with running water and electricity. Most looked forward to these enthusiastically, but were not sure where they might be, or if they had been built yet.

'We are very pleased about the demolition,' said an elderly couple drinking tea in a three-walled house. The fourth, the street wall, had been sliced away a few days before. When they stepped outside, they had to be careful not to fall into a twenty-foot-deep gully. They ate and slept in the open air while the snow drove in against the faded roses of their wallpaper.

Abedkhan Nazarov had gone to ground. That night, after the usual elaborate drive around the city, his intimates walked single file up the staircase in a Soviet-built apartment block. All the left feet trod softly together, then the right feet, as though the six people were one.

A thin, light-eyed man in his late thirties, Abedkhan sat on the floor next to a cloth spread with fruit, salted kernels and sugared peanuts. Followers padded to and fro, setting out tea. Their leader was pale, and had been ill – it was for this reason, he said, that he had not turned up to the Muftiat's exam. He hardly ate.

'I respected Abduvali of Andijan,' he said. 'But I did not follow his way. After he was taken, I spoke out. I said that this was work of wicked men. Even in the days of the Soviet empire, when they attacked our religion and denied the very existence of God, they never kidnapped religious scholars. After the sermon, I was summoned to the authorities and they accused me of being against the state. I am not against the state, I am not against the President.'

Abedkhan had come far in life. The son of a cotton worker in Namangan, in the Ferghana valley, he had received his early religious education from his father Sabetkhan and his mother Muharramkhan-aya, herself a respected preacher among women. At twenty-two, he won a place at the prestigious Muftiat-controlled Imam Bukhari madrasa in Tashkent, where he was a contemporary but not a friend of Akbar Turajanzada of Tajikistan. He spoke Uzbek and literary Arabic, and understood some Persian. His appointment, at only twenty-seven, as deputy imam of Tela Shaikh, the Friday mosque of all Tashkent, marked him as a man to watch in the Muftiat, even before he became imam of his own mosque, Takhtabai. But, he said, he ran into difficulties.

'I did not praise the government in sermons, and this they chose to find unacceptable. They said I mixed religion with politics, but actually it is they who do that, by forcing imams to serve the purposes of the state. I stand against corruption, against bullying and coercion. And that is why ordinary people come to hear my sermons. Eighty per cent of them are young and the Muftiat cannot draw crowds like that. My cassettes sell fast in the bazaar! They even sell abroad. That is why the government is afraid. It is afraid of the people.'

Abedkhan's rift with the Muftiat had widened in 1995 after he received what his followers describe as a present of religious books from Saudi Arabia. Such gifts were very common at that time, often donated by 'Ferghanachi', émigré families with their roots in Ferghana, who had settled in Saudi Arabia. Summoned by the Tashkent city prosecutor, Nazarov was roundly abused, accused of spying for the Saudi intelligence service, of meddling in politics with a view to setting up an 'Islamic state'. His sermon condemning the disappearance of Abduvali Mirzayev was the last straw. Since his expulsion from Takhtabai, Abedkhan had gone very far indeed, in Uzbek terms, in publicising his case. His people used telephones, faxes and even press releases to try to tell international bodies, like the UN, what was going on.

Abedkhan Nazarov and his group were far from naïve. When Muftiat officials first went to Takhtabai to introduce his replacement to the congregation in February, someone had lodged a video camera ready in the rafters. The film captured an extraordinary scene of defiance.

'All the trouble comes from this mosque!' called the Mufti official, Yusufkhan, caught on film in a sea of protesting worshippers. 'You've asked for this and you've got it! Accept the imam or I close you down.' Against a chorus of 'Prove it! Prove it!' the *muezzin* reached to grab the microphone and began to sing the call to prayer. Militia waded in. Fighting spilt out into the muddy alleyway in front of Takhtabai. Some of Abedkhan's people were detained, including the *muezzin* and the deputy imam, Taher Ibrahimov, who, his friends say, was beaten up before having hashish planted in his pockets; he was then ordered to leave the country.

'Uzbekistan is a mess, and I do not know where we should go from here.' Abedkhan nodded at some new guests who were padding into the apartment. 'We should not be like Iran, nor Saudi Arabia nor Afghanistan. Nor Turkey. No country is a model for us. Syria and Egypt are both examples of disastrous collision between the mosque and the state. Our government is pushing things the same way. Every day they arrest some man with a beard, or a woman in a veil . . . As for me, I shall remain true to myself. We have been very open up to now. But the government is forcing our congregation to choose: either to go with the Muftiat, or to hide. If some new underground movement starts, I shall not be able to answer for it.'

Abedkhan was vulnerable. Despite all the security precautions, the legions of militia and secret servicemen of Tashkent could easily have picked him up any day.

In the spring of 1996 President Karimov's strategy for Uzbekistan took on new shape and colour. He had always been the Central Asian president most defiant of the former colonial power. Russian troops of the old Soviet Army had left Uzbek territory in 1994, when Uzbekistan became the only Central Asian state to control its own borders. Now, Karimov began a series of blistering attacks on what he saw as post-Soviet Russian imperialism. The catalyst was a new economic union proposed by Russia and Belarus in April 1995 that might pave the way to a closer integration of CIS states under the leadership of Moscow. 'We have been invited to join this thing. But I say NO!' thundered Karimov to an audience of diplomats and journalists. 'It is absolutely unacceptable to us. Under what flag, what anthem should we live?' With tears in his eyes, he went on to list the crimes of the Soviet era, including the 'genocide' of Uzbeks. 'We would be the underdog of any such union. We would vegetate in the background of the world economy . . .'

His plan was that the new Uzbekistan should have a strong relationship with the United States in order to provide a counterweight to Russia. Meanwhile, outside investment from friendly states was encouraged. President Demirel of Turkey, an old ally of Washington, visited Tashkent in May. Turkish investment in Uzbekistan, he said, was now second only to that of the USA, at about a thousand million dollars. No sooner had the red Turkish bunting been taken down than red umbrellas filled Tashkent, handed out by Coca-Cola to celebrate the opening of its second bottling plant – due to turn out 15,000 bottles an hour.

Deputies were fulsome in their praise for the new strategy, which would help to secure ever greater stability for the country. 'Our President's views are discussed all over the world,' said one. 'He is like an emperor of Uzbekistan. He leads us as a star in the sky.'

The reward, when it came, was good. President Karimov's office had long been angling for an official invitation to the United States, and in late June the final arrangements were made. President Karimov flew to Washington a week later. (Immediately before the visit the Uzbek government released ten political prisoners. This was announced by fax to the US embassy, and nowhere else. The Ministry of Justice later denied that any releases had taken place.) Karimov met the Secretary of State, Warren Christopher, and the Defence Secretary, William Perry. As he walked up the steps of the White House to meet Bill Clinton, face to face, President to President, Islam Karimov's stock had never been higher. They talked for much longer than was usual, Karimov's aides reported with quiet satisfaction. It seemed to set the seal of US approval on Uzbek policy.

Shortly after Karimov's return home, his government took a step so confident that many people could hardly believe it: they agreed to an OSCE* proposal to have a conference on human rights in Tashkent. There had been such conferences before – toothless affairs, mostly, at which earnest foreigners preached the values of free speech, democracy and human rights for a couple of days and then went away again. The speakers rarely took questions, and most such affairs were essentially junkets.

This conference was to be different. On the list of speakers were both Abedkhan Nazarov, former imam of Takhtabai mosque, and Abduquddus, eldest son of Abduvali of Andijan – a young man determined to speak out about the disappearance of his father. It was all but unthinkable that such figures should be permitted a public platform in the very heart of Tashkent. Most of the handful of people who took an interest in such things simply did not believe it would really happen. Others – a tiny number – thought they detected signs of a political thawing brought on by Karimov's successful trip to the United States. After his return to Tashkent, for instance, the President had ordered the press several times to be 'free'.

On 11 September 1995 the conference opened in the grey Soviet-built Palace of People's Friendship in Tashkent. The scene outside was astonishing. Chatting in the sunshine on the long flight of steps stood huddles of people who had not appeared in public for years – people whose houses had been fire-bombed, people who had been put away for reading the wrong newspapers, country people down from Ferghana. Passers-by stopped and gaped at famous figures who had fled the country years before, laughing under the very noses of the police. No one knew how long all this would last – was it just a sop to the foreigners, people wondered, or did it really herald something new? In the sunshine outside the conference hall watermelon sellers did good business, chopping fruit into wedges for thirsty delegates. As one seller reached over to choose a melon, the walkie-talkie in his pocket winked in the sunshine.

Inside the hall, unlikely people began to take the floor. One was a long-standing establishment figure – once a Communist Party grandee – who had dared to run against Karimov for the presidency. 'This is my first statement for five years,' he said. 'I will not dwell upon the past and the wrongs done to my family. I want to talk about

* Organisation for Security and Co-operation in Europe

the press, and a special feature of Uzbek mentality. I am against the idea that because we are a young, inexperienced country it means the press should not be critical. It is sad. It is worse than in the USSR. The communists published half-truths and half-lies, but at least they published, for example, figures. What are the figures on, say, wages now? Is this good enough for our people? We have achieved very little in seven years. As for this meeting – generally OSCE meetings are fruitless, and I wonder if this will be different. When we feel the wind of change, we all ask, can we believe it? What will the future hold?'

That night, some delegates and their friends held a small party in a private apartment. Champagne glasses clinked to the 'Tashkent Spring' that might or might nor be on the way, amid laughter and talk of what the day might mean.

The next day the Ferghana contingent had its say. Dressed in a robe of golden cloth, Abduquddus Mirzayev of Andijan, son of the man whose disappearance a year before had set so much in train, stood up in the quiet grey hall to address the assembly of diplomats, ministers and assorted foreigners:

'Right up to the last moment, I wasn't sure if this conference would really happen, or if the imam Abedkhan would really be here. Have a look at him.' Heads turned towards the back of the hall, where Abedkhan Nazarov of Takhtabai stood, pale and quiet in his grey robe. 'You may never see him again. There is no guarantee that tomorrow he will not be found with drugs and guns in his pockets. I am flabbergasted that this conference is taking place at all, and that he is here, because in this country, any militiaman can pick up anyone, at any time, for any reason. Those are not my words: they are the words of a militiaman in Andijan. I hope above all that this conference is serious, that it really means the government has had a change of heart . . .'

Several speeches later, Abedkhan Nazarov rose to his feet. He faced the room full of delegates, smart in their suits, plump briefcases at their feet. They had come from Scandinavia, from eastern Europe, from America. Most of them grasped only very dimly who he was, or what he stood for.

He turned and appealed to the room, speaking quietly: 'You must understand that here Islam is a burning issue. I spoke out once and I have suffered for my words. Now, I would like to ask you, our guests, what do you think of what is happening here in Uzbekistan?'

If there had ever been any possibility that Uzbekistan had genuinely intended to tread a more accommodating line with potential dissidents, it receded when political police arrived at the house of one of the main speakers two or three hours after the foreign delegates went home on 14 September. It was laid to rest completely two weeks later.

In Afghanistan on 26 September 1996, residents of Kabul switched on the evening radio news and heard this proclamation:

> In the name of God, the Compassionate, the Merciful
>
> Announcement of the High Council of the Taleban
> Islamic Movement
>
> All faithful compatriots and in particular the esteemed citizens
> of Kabul are assured that the powerful and peace-loving forces
> of the Taleban Islamic Movement have ensured total security in
> all near and far areas of Kabul city and its surroundings, and that
> the situation has returned to normal.

The Taleban victory in Kabul had been so swift that many residents were barely aware of what was happening. With Taleban troops just outside the capital in the early afternoon, Ahmad Shah Mas'ud had called his commanders down from the mountains and ordered a general withdrawal in order, he said, to prevent a civilian bloodbath. 'I thought, this is it,' remembered one man close to the government. 'We had only one exit, the road to the north. The bulk of the troops went north, leaving a delaying force to retreat slowly. At around eight I got in a Toyota Landcruiser and left. There was a huge column of us. We were robbed on the way: it was total chaos. Perhaps half a million people left Kabul that night.'

Taleban soldiers drove to the United Nations building, where Muhammad Najibullah, the last Soviet-backed President of Afghanistan, had been living under UN protection since his fall from power in 1992. They took him out and killed him, and his brother. When

Kabul residents woke on the morning of 27 September, the two bodies had been strung from a traffic-control post in a city square.

With the fall of Kabul and the murder of Najibullah, events in Central Asia reached a watershed.

II

What happened in Mazar-e Sharif

'. . . But when his luck turned and the side-wind of adversity
extinguished the fire of prosperity, the water of success was
muddied with the dust of disappointment and the guides of his
counsels and deliberations avoided the pathway of righteousness
and strayed from the station of rectitude.'

THE TALEBAN HIT the headlines all over the world, as reporters
from international television stations and news agencies flew in
for the biggest Afghan story since the *mujahedin* took Kabul in 1992.
Images of fighters in black turbans rolling around Kabul in tanks gar-
landed with pink tinsel and of Najibullah's hanging corpse filled
screens and pages all over the world. Ordinary people of countries on
the doorstep of Afghanistan – Uzbekistan and Tajikistan – with
rather less idea of who the Taleban were than, say, informed viewers
in France, were shocked and uneasy. When the Taleban vowed to
press northwards from Kabul until they reached the river Amu – that
is, the northern frontier of Afghanistan – that uneasiness grew.

The fall of Kabul altered the political shape of Afghanistan within
twenty-four hours. As it streamed out of the city, the routed government divided into two parts. The convoy carrying President
Burhanuddin Rabbani sped north. It stopped forty miles or so short
of the border with Tajikistan in the small town of Talaqan and set up
offices in a compound next door to the one the Rabbani government
had lent to Said Abdullah Nuri, leader of the Tajik opposition. The
head of the military, Ahmad Shah Mas'ud, moved his weapons into
the Panjshir valley just above Kabul – his base throughout the Soviet
occupation – and blew up the entrance behind him. The way to the

north was open, and the Taleban set off after their enemies up the Salang highway.

Mazar-e Sharif shot to world fame as the last city in Afghanistan outside Taleban hands.

General Dustam had just returned home to Mazar-e Sharif from a visit to Tashkent when the news came from Kabul. He found himself at the centre of concentrated international attention at once. Pakistani, Turkish and Iranian emissaries presented themselves at his fort, Qalah-e Jangi. The Uzbeks and Russians were less overt, but equally present. Each power had a separate interest in influencing what Dustam would do next – fight the Taleban in alliance with the fallen Rabbani government, as some Iranians and perhaps some Russians would have it, or alone, as the Uzbeks might prefer, or make a pact with the Taleban and 'go down in history as the peace-maker of Afghanistan', as pro-Taleban Pakistanis put it. The envoys dug to find Dustam's weaknesses ('His flaw is greed,' one said; 'that is good enough for us'). 'This is a worrying time for us – we cannot trust any of these people,' said one of Dustam's intimates. 'But it may also be a time of opportunity.'

Journalists paced outside, waiting for word from the man on whom – or so it appeared in those few days – the future of Afghanistan, even all Central Asia, depended. The doors of Qalah-e Jangi stayed shut. Dustam sent out no statement. He appeared for a few seconds, large and smiling, only to be whisked away in his steel-plated black Cadillac.

The autumn days stayed warm and sunny and the mood in Mazar-e Sharif was buoyant. The city had known several years of peace since the Soviet withdrawal, and had prospered and grown to accommodate a quarter of a million or so people, spreading out in settlements around the beautiful tiled façades of the shrine – the *mazar* – of the Caliph Ali. Set on the road between Herat and Termez, Mazar-e Sharif was a natural trading-post. Electronic goods were bought in from Dubai, trucked across the Iranian border and sent for resale in Tashkent, while Chinese radios, rice and dress material, Indian tea, local carpets and fruit, all swelled merchant coffers. Books and most medicines were easier to find and cheaper than they were in Tashkent. Houses in the centre had electricity in the evenings, many had telephones – and the bazaar had a satellite dish for those who wanted to make international calls.

Mazar-e Sharif had a film studio, Asia Films – a fledgling airline, Balkh Air, in the process of buying a Boeing – a television company, several sports clubs, and a rising generation of the young élite who were polyglot, computer-literate and confident. Balkh University in the centre of the city opened as usual for the new academic year, its roll swollen by students newly arrived from Kabul. Six thousand were registered, more than a third of them girls, in what had become the last major university in Afghanistan to admit women.

'Best city in Afghanistan, Mazar-e Sharif,' said a cheerful trader, selling pop music tapes outside the shrine. 'The Taleban wouldn't dare come here, and if they do, we'll soon see them off.' Like many people, he had complained in his time that Dustam's Uzbeks squandered what should have been civic money; but now the city needed its strongman, and was glad of him.

Dustam's round, crop-headed face looked down from huge posters all over town. The coterie of men that made up his organisation, Junbesh-e Melli Islami (The National Islamic Movement), resembled the posters – they too wore battledress and neat moustaches – were all generals, even Abdul Malik, Dustam's right-hand man and spokesman on foreign affairs, who wore a business suit. The Junbesh army was said to number fifty thousand of the best trained and equipped men in Afghanistan – a flat-land force, it counted its strength in its forts and many tanks.

On 1 October, four days after the fall of Kabul, Dustam sent troops southwards to block the Salang Pass, the high point on the road that runs between Kabul and Mazar-e Sharif, to make a gate across the entrance to his territories. The first sprinkling of snow fell from the bright sky that day and Dustam's fighters posed confidently against the dramatic mountain backdrop, their turquoise turbans as bright as the sky, the rocket-launchers at their backs smart and new-looking. The bones of old wrecked tanks, remnants of Soviet-era battles for this strategically important point just above the capital, lay scattered around. 'The heights are ours,' said General Ruzi, one of Dustam's most trusted commanders. 'Our men are disciplined and have warm clothing. We can last the winter if need be.' General Ruzi pointed down the valley at the invisible Taleban, who by now had worked their way up from Kabul to the highway town of Jabal us-Seraj, about fifty miles north of the capital. 'They are down there. We don't want to fight them: they are not our enemies. But if we are attacked, we are ready.'

On the same day, two thousand miles away in Moscow, the head of President Yeltsin's security council, Alexander Lebed, raised the stakes with an almost apocalyptic speech. The Taleban, he told journalists, 'would not stop' at the Amu but would press on into former Soviet territory. 'Their plans include making regions of Uzbekistan – including Bukhara, one of Islam's holy places – part of the Afghan state. They will join with detachments of the Tajik opposition leader Said [Abdullah] Nuri, who shares the same faith. They will then sweep away our border posts.' Lebed, an Afghan war veteran then tipped to succeed Yeltsin as President, drew on every fearful prejudice ordinary Christian Russians held about Muslims and 'southerners'. The war of independence in Chechnya – which Russia had just lost – would, he said, would be nothing in comparison.

President Karimov of Uzbekistan attended a crisis summit with other Central Asian leaders in Almaty, the capital of Kazakhstan. While making clear that he thought Lebed's speech was excitable hyperbole, he also said that Uzbekistan would stand behind their man. Dustam, he said, defended 'a very important sector which in essence defends the north of Afghanistan from the arrival of the Taleban. If we really want to prevent a further escalation of the war . . . then we must do everything possible so that Mr Dustam can hold on to the Salang.'

Dustam emerged from Qalah-e Jangi and travelled south to the village of Khenjan. There, on common ground, he met his old enemy Ahmad Shah Mas'ud, embraced him and signed a treaty. According to one of his commanders, a hundred new Russian tanks had already arrived across the Friendship Bridge, but such figures were impossible to verify. Dustam returned to the north. Outside Qalah-e Jangi, Uzbek elders sat in the sunshine, reciting verses of the Quran. It was a Friday, 11 October. They had come, they said, to offer their sons for the defence of the north. Dustam heard their various petitions and went around the group talking and smiling.

'I am for peace,' he said. 'All problems should be solved through negotiations, so there will not be again war and bloodshed. There is no fighting between me and the Taleban. But if Mas'ud comes under military pressure, I will support him.' What became known as the Northern Alliance had begun. Dustam climbed into the black Cadillac and was driven away.

The march back to Kabul began. On Saturday, 12 October, men in the town of Jabal us-Seraj rose up against the Taleban. The next day, the only sign of the Taleban left in the town was the body of a boy soldier on the wayside. With Jabal us-Seraj fell a string of other towns and villages along the road to Kabul, and by evening the black, green and white flag of the fallen Rabbani government flew here and there in dusty, deserted streets and bazaars boarded up against what had been a brief battle. The first tank flying a white Taleban flag stood an hour or so's drive south of Jabal us-Seraj. 'We are the new front line,' said the Taleban beside it. They thought they were perhaps ten miles from the outskirts of Kabul, though they were probably more like twenty.

Mas'ud's commanders came down from the Panjshir valley, swept out rooms and set up radios to make a headquarters in Jabal us-Seraj for their campaign. Hundreds of local men milled about in the gardens, praying, chatting and waiting to be issued with rifles. Mas'ud moved to and fro between the headquarters, an observatory – the 'Star House' – and Panjshir. The helicopters flew low against Taleban attack, skimming over Panjshiri villages where pumpkins stored for the winter on the flat roofs made bright orange squares. Neat, green kitchen gardens sloped away – one of the skills that remains in Afghanistan but has receded in Tajikistan, on the north side of the same mountain, is that of terraced farming. Every inch of Panjshir was used for food. 'It's like old times,' said a former *mujahed* cheerfully walking the last mile back to Jabal us-Seraj one moonless evening. He scrambled over the rocks, the way lit by a pen torch. 'When Dustam sends his people, we'll go into Kabul.'

At twelve o'clock on the morning of 17 October the first trucks carrying General Dustam's Uzbeks rolled down the hill into Jabal us-Seraj from the north. By half-past twelve, a convoy of twenty tanks and other vehicles was moving through town, flying the flag of the Junbesh. Soldiers sitting on top waved their guns and shouted. 'There are twenty-five thousand of us! We're going all the way to Pakistan!

Tonight you'll have a road to Kabul.' There were not twenty-five thousand of them, but there were several hundred. Relieved and excited crowds of men milled around Jabal us-Seraj, many of them armed. Two had rockets strapped to their bicycles.

Despite the good humour of Mas'ud's men, Jabal us-Seraj and the towns and villages were suffering from their presence. As well as front-line fighting nearby, Taleban air raids had become a daily event. Most casualties were civilian, and the little hospital overflowed. One patient, Najibullah Rahman, aged twenty-two, had been trying to put out a fire at his mother's house, caused by a rocket, when someone shot another rocket at his legs from a distance of fourteen metres. Rahman had been a driver for Mas'ud's side in his time, and a driver for the Taleban – like everyone else, he needed to survive, and had absolutely no desire for war. When a dust-storm bowled through Jabal us-Seraj one night, men, their nerves on edge, shook their fists and screamed at the sky. On the worst day of air raids Hajji Nuri, a civilian elder of Kalakan village, lost all his seven children and his wife, who had been making bread when their house received a direct hit. She died beside the spilt flour. One daughter, aged about six, lay dead in her pink dress and bead necklace, without a scratch on her. 'This war', he said, weeping, 'has nothing to do with religion.' He held out some walnuts from his tree, compelled to kindness and hospitality despite the death, moments before, of everyone he loved.

The new troops with their new weapons climbed onto a ridge of high ground facing Bagram, an important airbase thirty miles or so north of Kabul. The airport fell at eight o'clock on the following evening. Northern Alliance troops advanced down the Kabul road to the last height before the capital.

Back in Mazar-e Sharif, General Dustam's advisers organised a series of public rallies against the Taleban. Thousands of people gathered at the football pitch in his home town of Sheberghan, chanting slogans against the Taleban and against Pakistan, whom everyone believed was supporting the movement. At the same time, Dustam kept his options open.

On 4 November, Dustam called a special evening meeting at his Sheberghan residence. He said he had something important to announce. He was, he said, going to open new negotiations with the Interior Minister of Pakistan. 'Tomorrow, Nasrullah Babur will come here,' he said, smiling, 'and we will sit together and find a way forwards.'

That evening General Dustam went to distribute some gold as largesse at a wedding party before sitting down to supper. The table was set with roast sheep, kebab, chickens, sheeps' trotters in jelly, and *pilau*. The white-and-gold dining room chairs had been brought in from Turkey. The curtains were swagged in the European manner. The General looked oddly humble with his crew-cut and brown, village Uzbek shirt open at the neck. 'I like food,' he said. He talked about his four daughters and three sons, and how he enjoyed life. A servant darted forward with tomato ketchup and the General dipped in the sheep's tongue he was holding. 'Which is better, Mazar-e Sharif or a town in the Middle Ages?'

Dustam never did talk to Nasrullah Babur. Next morning, the news came on the 22-inch televisions at Sheberghan palace before breakfast: the government of Pakistan had fallen. The Prime Minister, Benazir Bhutto, had been sacked for mismanagement. Her ministers' phones were cut off. They were forbidden to leave the country. President Faruq Leghari had put Pakistan under a caretaker administration, and Nasrullah Babur was nowhere to be seen. General Dustam had left the palace in the early hours.

With anti-Taleban troops at the gate of Kabul and diplomatic mistrust at its height, the long-stalled peace process in Tajikistan began to move at last. Intermediaries brokered a meeting between President Rahmanov and Said Abdullah Nuri, to be held in Afghanistan at a destination that was to be kept secret until the last moment. Pressure for the meeting came from Russia and Iran. Initially at odds over Tajikistan, these two found a confluence of interests in Afghanistan. If they were to support the Northern Alliance against the Taleban successfully, it was imperative that the Tajik war be wound up. The Rabbani administration also urgently wanted peace in Tajikistan. Having lost all its international borders except those with Central Asia when it lost Kabul, it needed friendly northern neighbours, if only so that supplies could be delivered to the areas it still controlled and its people travel to the outside world.

Negotiations got off to an unexpected start. On 8 December Said Abdullah Nuri left for the meeting from Iran, where he had been for consultations. In Afghan airspace over Herat, however, the Taleban forced down the United Nations plane in which he was flying. Nuri went on his way only after the flight had been diverted to Qandahar, the seat of the Taleban, where he had talks with the Mulla Umar, their unseen young leader. Rahmanov, meanwhile, made his way from Dushanbe, crossing the border into Afghanistan near Panj.

The meeting, at Khusdeh, outside Talaqan, was concluded fairly swiftly. Ahmad Shah Mas'ud held private talks with both Rahmanov and Nuri, who signed an agreement to a cease-fire at midnight on 12 December, the dismantling of military posts in parts of the mountains, and the release of some prisoners. The two leaders also initialled a draft document on power-sharing in Dushanbe – explicitly, the setting up of a Commission on National Reconciliation under the chairmanship of the opposition: in other words, the return of the exiled opposition to Tajikistan – to pave the way for a formal declaration of peace, to be announced in the summer of 1997. This initialled document was to be signed publicly and formally first in Teheran and then Moscow, capitals of the countries that were to be the peace-makers of Tajikistan.

The Tajik opposition in Talaqan began to pack up. Posters advertising 'Voice of Free Tajikistan' listings were still stuck on the walls in Nuri's headquarters, but broadcasts tailed off. The numbers of Tajiks in the town thinned out. Many had already crossed the Amu back into Tajikistan to see how the land lay. Those who were left enthused about going home some day soon.

Weary of summers spent fighting when supplies of weapons and food were erratic, homesick for their villages, disillusioned with the political leadership, sceptical about the endless peace talks held in flashy hotels to which they were not invited, the people who actually fought the war had had enough. Most of all, they were weary of wintering in snowbound villages at vertiginous heights at home or on the freezing plains of Afghanistan. The commanders on the ground, facing yet another such winter, had actually anticipated Nuri and Rahmanov's agreement with a local pact of their own that – they said – Nuri had not ordered and knew nothing about until afterwards.

This local pact, signed in Gharm on 19 September, came a full week before the fall of Kabul.

The months that followed the Khusdeh agreement were among the most tense and fraught with violence Dushanbe had seen since 1992. The war had dragged on for so long that numerous factions had appeared within factions and, with peace on the horizon, there was a sudden rush among them to get what they could while there was time. In just a few weeks in Dushanbe, more than forty people – most of them UN staff – were kidnapped, six men were murdered in a single night, someone threw a hand-grenade at President Rahmanov – which hit and slightly wounded him – and there was an upswell of insurrection in some Uzbek-populated areas that had done well out of the civil war and were afraid of losing ground to the opposition fighters who might soon be coming home. Despite these and many other serious difficulties, the peace process stayed roughly on course and the way was laid – slowly, painfully, violently – for the return to Tajikistan not only of the fighters but, after five years in exile, of Akbar Turajanzada and Said Abdullah Nuri.

The armies of Afghanistan wintered in relative quiet and recommenced fighting with the warm weather in the spring of 1997. Northern Alliance troops were still at the gates of Kabul. They had not been beaten back, but there was neither strength nor unity enough among their leaders or supporters for them to go forward. Dustam's men disappeared from the Kabul front, some saying they did not want to get drawn into a war while Mas'ud left his 'best men' in Panjshir. The Northern Alliance did not break down, however. General Dustam's inner circle decided to throw a party that would rally morale and show everyone how strong Mazar-e Sharif and its leaders were. The occasion was the fifth anniversary of the coming to power in Kabul of the *mujahedin* – or, in Dustam's terms, of the formation of Junbesh.

In the last week of April 1997, Mazar-e Sharif got ready for a tremendous military march-past, and three days of musical celebration of the kind that was not allowed in Taleban territory. Soldiers built plywood castles and mounted them on floats. Men sat in the spring sunshine polishing their tanks. They spread them with carpets and decorated them with huge portraits of their leaders – mainly Dustam but with a few others thrown in. Those walking in the parade had been issued with smart new sashes, turbans and plimsolls.

Drums began to sound early on the morning of 28 April, and the crowds rushed to get a good view over the widest avenue near the shrine of Caliph Ali. Men and boys climbed on to rooftops and clung in trees. Fighters stuck roses in their guns and lined the route to watch the parade. The infantry marched past with machine-guns and bazookas hoisted on their shoulders. A company of cavalry trotted along with rifles under their arms to represent the tribal traditions of the plains. Then came rows of newly painted tanks. Military aircraft screamed overhead.

General Dustam's little sons, like miniature generals, drove past in an open car, bolt upright and saluting stiffly. Their father stood in a raised stand with assorted dignitaries. At his right hand, as ever, was his spokesman on Foreign Affairs, Abdul Malik; unusually, he had changed his business suit for a turban and *chapan* and his face was as still as stone – otherwise, he looked much as usual. Dustam addressed the crowd through loudspeakers.

Greetings! Congratulations on our national anniversary. Five years have passed since the victory of the Islamic State and of Junbesh!

In these years we have achieved much. We have peace in our territory, despite the plans of our enemies and our many hardships. Junbesh is an Islamic faction: it keeps unity among different nationalities. Despite the propaganda of our enemies, we have stayed together throughout allied territory.

We are reconstructing the north. We are building schools, hospitals and shrines and roads, and restoring historical sites. We have electricity. We will have gas. We have two thousand phone lines. We respect women, they work and study in peace here.

Junbesh is a very powerful faction and the world knows it. Our alliance has many victories and many supporters and many brave soldiers. We have lost brave martyrs like Rasul [Abdul Malik's brother] and many others. We will never forget them. Thank you all for your sacrifices.

Our enemies have not completed their work! We should

miss no opportunity to act against them. We should know our enemies. They are called the Taleban! The Taleban are backed by outsiders. They want to capture our country and take away our freedom. So we need to pull together, to save our honour, our freedom, our religion.

We must be ready against the attacks of the enemy; if we do nothing, we will be destroyed.

Bands played at the sports ground that evening. The curfew was lifted. Families sat on the grass and ate picnics. As evening wore on, packs of youths, overexcited by the unaccustomed holiday and the lateness of the hour, took their place. They crowded up to the musicians. Junbesh police knocked them back with their rifle butts. The night grew wild.

The party lasted three days. Everyone agreed it had sent all the right messages. It had shown Mazar-e Sharif to be a fortress, lit from within by good leadership and guarded without by the latest military hardware. The party would be remembered for a long time to come.

Three weeks later General Dustam's regime collapsed, very fast and from the inside. His right-hand man, General Malik, defected on 19 May, breaking the pact his family had had with Dustam for many years. The news was so incredible that Malik had to telephone journalists himself and have his voice recorded and played on the radio before some of Dustam's generals believed it. According to people close to Malik as well as to his enemies, he had done a deal with the Taleban, for what one aide termed 'a lot less than two million dollars'. In his statement, Malik called Dustam a bad Muslim and an obstacle to peace in Afghanistan. He also accused him of being behind the murder of his elder brother Rasul, who had been killed in unclear circumstances in July 1997. Malik took with him his remaining brothers and other key commanders, including General Ruzi, who had been in charge at the Salang Pass. Many foot-soldiers, some of whom had not been paid for five months, also switched over.

In Malik's home province of Fariab, fighters shot at the Dustam posters before ripping them down, then set out for Sheberghan. There they found Dustam's palace deserted. They pulled down the swagged curtains, stole the gold-and-white Turkish furniture and Sony televisions.

'It took only six hours for us to collapse,' said one man who was with Dustam until the end, 'from the time we heard how many and who were defecting until we were on our way.' Dustam and his inner circle flew by helicopter from Sherberghan to Qalah-e Jangi, salvaged a few bits and pieces and headed in a convoy of trucks towards the border with their old ally, Uzbekistan. On the road, local gunmen stole what they could from their former leaders, down to the shoes of some. Some escaping generals climbed into Balkh Air's new Boeing, and flew it over the Amu; most of the company drove across the Friendship Bridge into Termez. (Ahmad Shah Mas'ud did send another helicopter to help, but it arrived too late. 'That was our story,' says one Dustam man: 'We need help at eleven o'clock, Mas'ud helps us at three o'clock. And the same the other way round.')

The Uzbeks waiting for Dustam in Termez were not friendly, not even polite. Terrified as ever at having their foreign policy made evident, they kept him waiting on the tarmac of the airport while a suitable third country of refuge was found. Turkey agreed. Late that night, General Dustam and fourteen of his closest men flew to Ankara.

Malik and his men turned for the frightened and leaderless capital of Mazar-e Sharif and passed swiftly down the undefended road. Malik was in the lead tank of the column that rolled across the city boundary and into the empty streets on 24 May. There was very little resistance. Those of Dustam's troops who still had weapons surrendered them. Malik's younger brother Gul Muhammad walked into Dustam's office and ripped up the black, red and green Junbesh flag. With the defectors came the first truck-loads of Taleban troops, invited into Mazar-e Sharif by Malik as his new allies.

The Taleban or their allies were now in power in every city of substance in Afghanistan, and on Sunday 25 May Pakistan became the first country to recognise them as the government of Afghanistan. At dawn on Monday, Taleban leaders and Malik went to the shrine of Caliph Ali together, and the Taleban issued a set of edicts on how local people should behave from now on, as they had done in Herat and in Kabul.

The next day, twenty-five-year-old Farid set out for work. Like many young men in Mazar-e Sharif, he chose to wear a European-style shirt and trousers rather than long, baggy clothes in the Afghan manner. The Taleban prohibition on European-style clothes had only been in force for a day, and he had not yet changed. He watched another huge convoy of Taleban vehicles roll into town from the west side. 'A Taleb pointed at me and said: "Look at his clothes!" I was scared, so I went home to change. Then, in the afternoon, I went with a friend to buy turbans. I thought, this is it now, it's all over: we have a Taleban government.' Farid went to a friend's house, and while they were all talking he heard shooting. It was not clear where the sound was coming from, but Farid judged that it was probably more sensible to go home than to stay, and he and his friend set off towards the centre of town.

They found a full-scale gun battle going on. 'By the time I got to the shrine, there were already dead Taleban lying in the road outside it, and the hotel was in flames. We ran to take cover in the bazaar, which was empty except for some fruit and vegetable sellers lying on the ground. I tried to help them but they were already dead. Bullets flew across the bazaar, so we carried on, street by street, towards my house. I lifted up someone who had been shot and I got covered with blood. When we got to the Balkh junction, there was so much fighting that we crawled along, as I had been taught in the army.' Eventually, Farid and his friend found shelter at someone's house.

By the time they got home at eleven o'clock the next morning, the Taleban were running for their lives out of Mazar-e Sharif. Some threw away their turbans and begged sanctuary from local families; others ran into the shrine, hoping that they might be safe, according to Farid, who had returned to town on his second attempt to get home. 'Fighters ran after them. I saw Taleban bodies laid out in the gutter. There were a lot, such a lot. People covered the bodies with straw against the smell, and because Muslim law tells us to cover the dead.'

Malik's soldiers had turned against their new allies when the Taleban tried to disarm them and take away their vehicles – acting as though they were masters, not guests, in Mazar-e Sharif. Phil Goodwin, reporting for the BBC, watched one incident of the kind that helped turn the whole city against the Taleban.

I saw it unfold on a street in the east. Several Taleban soldiers were gunned down trying to disarm rebel soldiers near a mosque. One of General Dustam's former commanders came to calm the situation. Taleban soldiers soaked with blood from carrying their dying colleagues into ambulances were persuaded by him not to attack. They left the area. It seemed like co-operation and good sense had prevailed, but one small group of Taleban came back shortly afterwards looking for revenge, and drove down the street towards the mosque in a single pick-up truck. It was a suicide mission, and they were shot dead. In a short space of time the situation degenerated into mayhem. Hundreds of Taleban soldiers came into the east of the city thinking they could easily resolve the situation. That was their biggest mistake. They were outnumbered in a city they did not know, outgunned and inexperienced. I saw them saunter down hostile deserted streets without taking cover, and then suddenly come under fire from windows and doorways. As some of them fell dead and wounded, the others stood still and fired about randomly. They were split into groups, and instead of fighting together, they ran into the labyrinth of small streets, scared young men blindly following older soldiers carrying only one or two magazines of bullets each. Disorganised and disorientated, they were slaughtered.

The Taleban were gone, but Mazar-e Sharif was not the city it had been. Local people never trusted or respected Malik, who, they felt, had tried to sell them. In the power vacuum left by Dustam, crime and chaos thrived. The currency fell and kept falling. Civic pride degenerated. Malik, in search of a regional backer, was courted by Iran, and in the very unsteady months of his leadership made a bolt-hole of the Iranian border city of Mashhad. Sources close to Malik said the family moved a hundred and five members – mainly women and children – 5.68 kilos of gold, thirty-five valuable carpets and a good car to Mashhad for safe-keeping. Tashkent did not try to make a partner of Malik in the way it had of Dustam, and Malik did not look to Tashkent. In this way Tashkent's policy in Afghanistan came to an abrupt stop. There was no more buffer zone, such as it had been, for Uzbekistan. There were no Russian troops, as there had been in Tajikistan. The Uzbeks were on their own. 'Let them defend themselves with what they have,' mocked the Russian nationalist Vladimir Zhirinovsky in 1998, '– their aubergines, their melons and their embroidered hats.' This was not the official Russian line, but expressed what a lot of Russians thought privately.

In June, the government in Tashkent made Termez a 'closed' city again, as it had been during the Soviet war in Afghanistan. This was not announced, since like virtually every policy in Uzbekistan it was a secret; but people arriving at Tashkent airport to fly to Termez found there were no planes, and read this as a clue. Nobody from outside Termez was supposed to enter the city limits, and officials walked into the offices of some foreign aid programmes and asked people to leave. The concrete blocks the Uzbek army had heaved on to the Friendship Bridge after General Dustam's defeat – in the apparent belief that any enemies, or refugees, who might come hurtling after him would be discouraged by such barricades – remained in place.

Recruits were drafted in from all over Uzbekistan to reinforce the short stretch of the river Amu that was the border with Afghanistan. They dug slit trenches in the bald banks of the river, and lined up tanks to face the water – to face Afghanistan. At midnight, when the temperature had dropped enough to make the heat tolerable, conscripts would leave their barracks for the city telephone station. 'Tashkent! Andijan! Karshi!' the operator shouted, adjusting her headscarf as she wrote the next numbers very slowly on small, economical strips of yellowed paper, and conscripts from the silent group would come forward to the lines she had connected to their home towns. The conscripts were young, eighteen or nineteen. Their broad brown army belts winched in folds of excess uniform, their heavy boots were not yet broken in. One by one, they thanked the operator and walked softly back into the hot, black night, thick with the song of crickets.

Uzbekistan's troubles did not come singly in the high summer of 1997. Not only had Karimov no substitute for Dustam in Afghanistan, but serious economic problems that had been building up throughout the preceding year suddenly came to the surface. The cotton harvest of 1996 had been very poor, but because of the time it took for export revenues to come in this became apparent only in 1997. The gap between the official rate of the currency (the *sum*) and the black-market rate had widened from about twenty per cent to more than a hundred – meaning that everybody changed their money in the bazaar rather than the bank. President Karimov had brought in rules to stop businesses converting their *sum* into dollars, hoping thereby to bolster the currency, but in practice, hundreds of foreign companies packed up and left the country. Since they no longer had to keep on the right side of Karimov, some executives spoke openly of the bribes they had had to pay to do business in Uzbekistan in the first place. Foreign investment fizzled to almost nothing.

Karimov told his people that they did not need such fair-weather traders anyway. 'We have many tomatoes in Uzbekistan. We should be making our own tomato sauce!' he said, with conviction. But matters could not be solved so simply. On the busy black market, the *sum* dropped so much that people had to use carrier-bags for the money to pay the telephone bill. In the towns, the price of food reached worrying new heights. In the *kolkhozes*, life was very much worse. Foreign diplomats spoke with wonder about the patience of ordinary Uzbeks, and about how much longer it would be before some sort of opposition to Karimov re-emerged.

The Muftiat worked its way steadily through the mosques of the nation, sacking and replacing imams it thought might be disloyal to the regime. The imam of Andijan, Abduvali Mirzayev, did not reappear. The former imam of Takhtabai mosque in Tashkent, Abedkhan Nazarov, lived quietly in the capital, where his supporters organised a series of small rallies – just enough to keep the authorities on edge. The secret police had them under constant surveillance and arrested some people, mainly women and the poor, but each side avoided an outright collision with the other.

While all this was going on, to add to the unease of the Uzbek government the peace process across the border in Tajikistan was moving into its final phase. The outlines of the settlement were clear. The opposition, led by Said Abdullah Nuri, was going to take a third of official positions all over the country – though Imamali Rahmanov would remain as President – and Nuri himself would be the head of the all-faction National Reconciliation Commission designed to think up policies and bridge differences. Opposition fighters were all to come home, and some were to live, fully armed, in their own garrison in the heart of the capital, to protect Nuri and other leaders.

The potential for all this to go horribly wrong was clear, and every step of the way was fraught with tortuous difficulties. There were obvious problems – like what jobs Akbar Turajanzada and many others were going to have, and what was to be done with released prisoners-of-war. There were also umpteen problems of detail about how agreed intentions were to be carried into practice. A row broke out over what colour the new opposition base in Dushanbe, the Hotel Vakhsh, was to be painted (it had to be done twice, once red, once green), there were rows about who would pay for the petrol to bring home the fighters, and about where they would live. Surplus US army food was offered for their welcome-home kits, as is not unknown in such settlements, but the sealed tin-foil packs of microwave-ready chicken and mushroom stew, crackers and chewing-gum did not go down well, while the run on welcome-home quilts and pots drove up prices in the bazaar.

Issues that might have been bagatelle in a richer country, or one with more foreign aid (fewer than fifty aid workers were in Tajikistan at any one time), were rocks on which the whole process might founder. 'Even the bread is dangerous here,' said one resident, after an outbreak of typhoid fever, carried by the decayed water system, made almost all city food hazardous.

In July 1997, the Tajik opposition began to cross the river Amu from Afghanistan on their way home. First came the civilian refugees. On 17 July the first two hundred and fifty from the Bagh-e Sherkat camp at Qunduz chugged across the river by barge and walked up the bank into Panj-e Payan. There they rested briefly, sheltering the babies from the scorching sun, before being bussed back to the Vakhsh valley. A hundred more followed and another hundred, until Bagh-e Sherkat was empty. Some came with nothing, some with the doors and windows of their houses, the flocks they had managed to raise, and – in one case – a vintage German Morgan car, dating from the Second World War.

A second contingent of refugees, from the remains of Sakhi camp, near Mazar-e Sharif, followed by train from Termez (the Uzbeks opened the border to let them cross, on condition that the Tajiks were locked inside the train). Shahrukh, who had lost his whole family except for his father and one brother as his home town of Shahr-e Tuz fell in 1992, set off towards more than he had imagined. Listening to the radio one day before he left the camp, he had heard on a programme about war-broken families the voice of his wife, for whom he had grieved for five years. Shahrukh got off the train to find that not only his wife but their four children were safe and well. It turned out that a local man on the side intending to kill them had recognised his wife as a neighbour's daughter, and spared their lives.

Within a few weeks, dead parts of the ruined Vakhsh valley began to come back to life. The returnees, many of whom had become much more self-reliant and practical in Afghanistan, mixed mud and built new houses on the stumps of the old. They dug narrow irrigation canals and planted neat rows of vegetables. Not all the refugees returned. A thousand or so, mainly boys, who had gone from the camps to Pakistan to study in madrasas – paid for by Saudi money – had stayed on there, mainly in Peshawar. Others went to the port of Karachi. They made for the refugee quarter of Suhrab Godh, in the north of the city, to find a cross-section of the century living side by side. There were thousands of Afghans who had fled the Soviet invasion, and thousands of others who had fled the Taleban. There were Ferghanachi, still keeping alive the traditions of Namangan and Andijan, and elders of Qurgan Tappa who had fled across the Amu as children in the 1920s on rafts made of planks and cow-gut. The incomers from 1992, who had crossed on planks and inner-tubes, settled next door to them and found what work they could at the local bazaar of al-Asif, planning, as every generation has, to go home as soon as they could.

On 5 September, after several weeks of mayhem in which various commanders struggled for top position in Dushanbe, trucks full of opposition fighters came rolling down the mountain into the capital from Gharm. Some laughed and waved, as village children rushed to watch, others brandished their weapons, shouting 'Allah-u Akbar', mainly for the cameras. With a final flourish of prayers they stopped outside the building chosen as their city garrison. At a time when every little symbol spoke volumes, their leaders ran up the green and white flag of the opposition next to, not instead of, the national tricolour.

On 11 September, delayed by a number of bus-bombs that closed the airport road, a small party gathered at Dushanbe airport. The

United Nations special envoy for Tajikistan, Gerd Merrem, stiff in his bullet-proof vest, climbed out of his armour-plated car and waited. On the left stood an armed guard of government soldiers, eyeing the armed guard of opposition men on the right. There was almost total silence. Then, at twelve o'clock, an Iranian aeroplane appeared. Bodyguards leapt out as soon as it landed, spinning round to check for trouble. Behind them, a small figure in a grey clerical robe stepped out. Most people at the airport had never seen Said Abdullah Nuri before, but there was no doubting who he was. Nuri and the other opposition leaders swept away in a cavalcade of white Volgas. 'I couldn't sleep that night,' said Nuri later. 'I was so excited to be home.'

Four days later, an extraordinary sight appeared over Central Asia. Five hundred United States parachutes floated gently through the clear sky on to a plain outside Chimkent, near the Kazakh–Uzbek border. The paratroopers had flown eight thousand miles from Fort Bragg in California, refuelling three times in mid air – the first time such a feat had ever been attempted. It was an exercise 'to test the possible' to mark the start of a new military co-operation deal between the United States, Uzbekistan, Kazakhstan and Kirgizstan. 'Uzbekistan doesn't have much for us economically,' one diplomat put it, 'but politically? Yes . . . it might be useful one day. I mean, look where it is – we need a friend in this region. And Karimov, he's willing – he's got away from the Russians more or less – but who are his new allies? Not Iran, not Tajikistan, not Afghanistan.' And that is how General John Sheehan, Commander-in-Chief of the Atlantic Command, became the first US soldier to parachute on to former Soviet soil.

12

The Glinka Street plot

'. . . wherever there was a king, or a ruler, or the governor of a city that offered him resistance, him he annihilated together with his family and followers, kinsmen and strangers . . .'

A T 10.40 ON the morning of 16 February 1999, a car bomb went off in central Tashkent outside the Interior Ministry on Yusuf Khas Hajib Street. Three others followed, two at Independence Square, near and at the Cabinet of Ministers building, in which all the senior ministers in Uzbekistan had assembled for a meeting with President Karimov. The last, at 11.20, was at the National Bank of Uzbekistan branch for Foreign Economic Activity.

Sixteen passers-by were killed and 128 injured in bombings that also blew apart Uzbekistan's image of rock-like stability. No officials were hurt. President Karimov's motorcade had been on its way to the Cabinet of Ministers building, but stopped short, just outside the square, after the first bomb went off.

In a quiet, residential street in south Tashkent, forty minutes later, a much louder detonation blew up a private house with such force that people ran outside to see what they thought had been a plane crash. Police said later that a thousand kilos of explosives had gone up at Number 22 Abdullah Qahar, a street known widely by its Soviet-era name of Glinka.

President Karimov at once addressed his people on television from the bomb-site at Independence Square, saying that the attacks were an attempt on his life – committed by 'Islamic extremists', added the

Interior Minister the next day. Over the next days and weeks, security officers of various kinds arrested great numbers of people – hundreds, possibly thousands – not only in Uzbekistan but in Kazakhstan, Kirgizstan, Turkmenistan, Ukraine and Istanbul, involved in what appeared to be an immensely elaborate plot.

It says something about post-colonial Uzbekistan that some Tashkent residents had thought at first that the bombers must have been Russians because, they assumed, only Russians could have the organisational or technical ability to make bombs and synchronise their detonation. 'It can't be us, it can't be *Muslims* – we wouldn't be able,' said one woman, unconsciously repeating the assumption of a hundred years. But this theory evaporated in the face of the official version, believed implicitly by most people – except those who thought privately that some circle within the government had been at least complicit in planting the bombs, to create the illusion of an 'Islamic' threat – or perhaps as a result of some invisible power struggle within the establishment. Truth and mirage had been twined together for so long, before, during and after the Soviet years, that no possibility was unthinkable.

In June the trial began of twenty-two men, fourteen of them from the Ferghana valley, accused not only of trying to assassinate President Karimov but of plotting to overturn the constitution of Uzbekistan in order to bring about an 'Islamic' state – hence the attack on government buildings. Number 22 Glinka Street was said to have been the headquarters of the gang, at which they had stored their home-made explosives and which they blew up, by accident or design, after the bombings went wrong.

The trial marked a culmination of events in Uzbekistan that had been unfolding for almost five years. Ever since the disappearance of Abduvali Mirzayev in 1995, the security forces had pursued a steady campaign against religious expression of all kinds by means which ranged from the taking down of loudspeakers from mosques to the detention of literally thousands of young men in the town of Namangan, in the Ferghana valley, after the murder of a local policeman. Such arrests took place quietly, often at night, as police went from house to house, removing the pious – a method far more frightening than any head-to-head collision. Nothing was announced, and it was rarely clear to relatives how long their young men might disappear for: perhaps an hour, perhaps much longer, or even – perhaps – for ever. Charges changed like chameleons. A man picked up for parking his car in the street at night might find himself charged with possession of a bullet or, most commonly, of a small amount of hashish. Trials of 'Islamic' thieves and even murderers had become not uncommon – but these were nothing on the scale of Glinka Street.

The trial was the zenith of the hunt for 'the enemy' within Uzbekistan, who now appeared as the enemy not just of officialdom but of the ordinary Uzbek, who needs must look to the President – the *padshah* – for protection. 'I am ready to rip off the heads of two hundred people, to sacrifice their lives, in order to save peace and calm in the republic,' Karimov had said after the bombings. 'If a child of mine chose such a path, I myself would rip off his head.'

To show the importance of Glinka, it was to be a 'public' trial, in that authorised local people, foreign journalists, diplomats and the representative of the US campaigning organisation Human Rights Watch, were to be allowed in.

In the days and weeks ahead, the Glinka Street trial came to dominate life in Tashkent in a way no political event had since independence, even to the blocking-off of traffic around the courthouse and the hours of coverage relayed on the television each night like a living detective story (one without alternative suspects), sometimes in the form of reportage, sometimes as documentaries dramatised with maps, sinister music and the sound of ticking 'count-down' clocks. Everyone in the generally sleepy city had been shocked by the bombings and by the sad processions of *chapan*-wearing men carrying their shrouded dead that threaded around the city the next day. Taxi drivers who usually talked to outsiders about little but the price of flour and cooking oil had something to say about the case.

Not everything that was interesting about the trial took place inside the courtroom. There were aspects that revealed themselves on the streets of Tashkent, in the bazaars and mosques of the countryside, in a chain of events leading back to the early days of the Soviet Union. Each episode of the trial showed something of what had become of the Uzbeks, how the government governed, and what ordinary people could expect from life.

The Glinka Street trial opened on 2 June 1999 at the Supreme Court, which stands by the river Anhar in central Tashkent. Around nine o'clock the permitted onlookers settled into their places on two rows of benches in a small, white courtroom panelled in chocolate brown to shoulder height, rather like a school-room. Those who had lost relatives in the bombings propped photographs of the dead on their laps.

In two large metal cages to the left of the judge's dais sat twenty-two pale, tired-looking young men. Other than their pallor and the puffiness round their eyes, there was nothing to mark them out as unusual. They were clean-shaven and neat, and some wore ironed shirts. Some gazed at the floor, others glanced up with no special interest at the spectators who were, in all probability, going to watch them be condemned to death. Each man had a thick orange book at his side in which were printed the statements they had all made during the investigation. This practice, like the layout of the court-room and the restraining of prisoners in cages, followed lines little changed since the 1930s. All those accused had admitted their guilt, as was usual. The task of the court was to establish the truth of their confessions though their reiteration – no material evidence, statements from forensic experts or other corroboration would be admitted – and then pass sentence.

The court rose while the chief prosecutor read a long list of spectacular charges, mainly to do with banditry, religious extremism, possession of contraband, and Article 159 – conspiracy to overthrow the constitution of Uzbekistan. As was customary, the prosecution lawyers then each asked the judge for a specific sentence to be handed down at the end of the trial. In the case of the alleged ringleaders of the group this was death, as expected; in the case of others who had supposedly been accessories – by, for example, acting as drivers, or supplying money through robberies – it was between fourteen and twenty years in prison. The judge might decide, having heard all the legal contributions, to hand down harsher or more lenient sentences than those requested: so even though the men in the cages had all confessed, the actual outcome of the trial would not be certain until the last hour.

The first figure to come to prominence among the accused was Zainuddin Askarov, a thin, excited man of twenty-seven or twenty-eight from Namangan. In a taut, high-pitched voice, he 'confessed' to the gang's plans for what would happen after the bombs had disposed of the government.

'We were going to announce on television and radio that all Muslims should stay indoors,' he began at speed. 'Then we were going to let off canisters of sleeping-gas all over Uzbekistan. Those in the streets would fall asleep for three to four hours. Then we would kill all the Russians and take power. We would release all the political prisoners, including the mullas, and the government would go on trial according to the shari'a. Then we would declare an Islamic government.' Askarov, wagging his finger, spoke louder and faster as his statement progressed over almost two hours. He did not once resort to the orange text-book. He said that he had personally played no part in the bombings, as he had been in Turkey at the time.

This sensational confession was broadcast on television on the third day of the trial. Nothing in the commentary on the broadcast suggested any doubt that the confession was reliable, and the same went for most comment in the street. Most people, with nothing to measure all this against, were shocked at the wickedness of Askarov's plan. They did not consider it preposterous or see it as being at odds with what, in other ways, seemed a well-timed and fairly well-executed plan. The more knowing cast Askarov not as a hysteric or someone from whom a false confession had been extracted but in the classic Soviet role of Big Mouth: the canary who sings for the secret police in return for a shorter sentence, while the 'real criminal' sits quietly in the background.

As the trial got going inside the courtroom, the relatives of the accused sat outside. An elder with a white turban and silvery-grey robe had brought twenty members of his family down from the Ferghana valley. 'I saw on the television news last night that the trial had begun, so we came to Tashkent straight away,' he said. They had brought quilts and bundles of bread in case their son was one of the accused and they needed to stay for the duration. This, they had just found out, was the case. It is normal Uzbek practice not to inform the family when a member goes on trial, though if the family is well-connected, with a member in, say, the SNB, they may get a tip-off.

The families were not allowed into the courtroom, or to see the accused in prison. In some cases detention had taken place many months before the bombings. If death or long prison sentences were to be handed down, they therefore had, without then knowing it, already seen their children for the last time. Each morning at eight o'clock, when the line of armoured wagons drove in to the court from the prison, a few mothers, in tears, rushed to wave at them 'in case he can see me.'

'My son is in there because he is a Muslim and prays five times a day,' said another elder, sitting on a quilt under the trees along the Anhar. 'There is no justice here.' 'I do not know if my husband is guilty or not but I know there will be no justice,' said a young woman sitting with a group of her sisters. She asked a policeman sitting in the sunshine for news from inside the court. 'What trial? There's no trial here,' he told her. From time to time the police shooed the families on, but each day they returned.

On 4 June, in the afternoon of the third day, came the moment the knowing had been waiting for: the confession of the man alleged to be the ringleader, the man behind the scenes, the brains, the man who was said to have thought up the plan and trained the personnel. Bahram Abdullayev – 'the amir' – was at once noticeable for his quiet, educated voice and reserved manner. Tall, thin and dark, he looked like a student in his striped grey shirt. It was 'a shame', as one Tashkent journalist put it – most journalists took the confessions at face value – that such a 'nice boy' had fallen in with criminals.

Abdullayev's confession set out the core of the plot, that the conspirators had held secret meetings through 1997 and 1998 in Istanbul, Baku and Kabul to put together an elaborate assassination. Those who would actually carry out the attack had been trained in Chechnya, Afghanistan and Tajikistan, while others spread 'religious propaganda' in order to ready the people. Some of the money required was collected from robberies carried out by a gang in Andijan, the rest donated by Uzbek opposition figures who, though in exile since the brief groundswell of political debate in the early 1990s, had never given up hope of seizing Karimov's crown – not for 'political' reasons, because they sought the national good, but for reasons of personal greed. This postulation chimed perfectly with the general belief held in Uzbekistan (and elsewhere in the former Soviet Union) that there was no other reason for entering politics – although the current leadership was considered to do its best for the people. Chief among these financiers was supposedly Muhammad Saleh, head of the nationalist, secular political party Erk which before the collapse of the Soviet Union had organised rallies around such issues as ill-treatment of Uzbek conscripts in the Soviet Army, who now lived in political asylum in Norway.

In the general confusion that would follow the assassination of the President, went the story, there would be a double military assault on Uzbekistan – a sort of pincer movement – led by disaffected exiles from the Ferghana valley. Jumabai Khujayev, called 'Namangani' after his home town, had left the valley in 1992 and gone to fight in the Tajik civil war on the 'Islamic' side. After the fall of Shahr-e Tuz in southern Tajikistan, at which he lost a large number of men, Namangani crossed the Amu with the rest and ended as a commander in the Tajik opposition. Namangani, the court heard, would support the coup by marching his men back over the mountains into Uzbekistan, where they would meet a supporting army from Afghanistan which would cross the Amu at Termez and march up to Tashkent from the south. This army would supposedly be led by another Ferghana exile, Taher Yuldash, who had, aged twenty four, become powerful in the Namangan of 1991 by handing out food to the poor and introducing what he called 'Islamic' rules in some districts. Yuldash had then dropped out of sight, to re-emerge in Taleban-held Kabul. The combined 'armies' of these two men, 'at least five thousand fighters', would take control of the country, whereupon Muhammad Saleh, as chief financier, would be declared President and thus achieve his heart's desire.

While the details of this amazing plan were supposedly being worked out, Bahram Abdullayev, the young 'amir' speaking so quietly from the dock, was arrested, in October 1998, while on a visit to Turkmenistan. Lacking his leadership the group, he said, dashed ahead with the Glinka Street plot, which went off at half-cock and failed to kill anyone except people who happened to be walking by. This early imprisonment of Abdullayev seemed significant, suggesting as it did that the intelligence services must have had some inkling of the alleged plot. If this were so, and they had yet, during the four months of Abdullayev's imprisonment before 16 February, failed to glean enough information from him to enable them to prevent the bombings, it suggested that Abdullayev was a man of rare fortitude, that he was genuinely in the dark – or, perhaps, that the intelligence services *did* know but were unable or unwilling to short-circuit the supposed plot.

The court broke for the weekend.

On Monday, 7 June, the trial reconvened. The temperature outside was creeping towards the forties; inside it was much hotter. Some of the accused looked even more tired than they had three days before, and had deep purple lines under their eyes. The time had come for the supplementary players from Glinka Street to stand up in turn and give evidence. The purpose of their confessions was to add the meat to the bones of an already established plot.

Delshad Kamalov, aged forty-one, neat in a pale blue shirt, rattled through his confession in a high, strained voice. He was, he said, part of a sub-group of plotters who, from their safe house in Kazakhstan, provided transport and other facilities to the bombers. 'They told me', he said, 'that they had got a car and guns and explosives and driven it to the Cabinet of Ministers. They shouted "Allah-u Akbar" and set off the bomb. They escaped by taxi and then killed the taxi driver and buried him by the road. I was told to go to the Iranian embassy in Kazakhstan, and that they would give me passports. I brought my Polaroid photos there and it took just forty minutes to get visas.' The row of lawyers, several of them plump Uzbek ladies, their hair done up in buns – the Russian hairstyle that symbolised the old Soviet image of the progressive, non-'Islamic' woman – asked no questions. One appeared to have nodded off only ten minutes into the confession.

Kamalov stumbled from time to time, but in a speech lasting more than an hour never had recourse to the orange book – 'the script', as a watching diplomat called it. His place was taken by six other men, one after another, each of whom confessed to playing a bit part and added a layer of detail to the story. There was a garage-worker from Namangan who spoke confidently, his head up, of his role as a go-between; a clean-cut young man in the SNB who had been approached for insider information on the meeting at the Cabinet of Ministers; a tractor-driver; a middle-aged man who owned a tailors' business opposite the Friday mosque in Andijan; a student on the edge of tears. Then came a baker, a chubby young man with rumpled hair who, bound by unbreakable rules of hospitality, had given *pilau* and a bed at his house on the border with Kazakhstan to an old friend who turned up out of the blue, and did not understand what he had done until the police came to arrest him. He was facing a sentence of fourteen years.

The afternoon wore on, the accused slumped slightly, a humble posture necessitated by the narrow, backless forms on which they sat. From time to time, one or another glanced up at a speaker. Some yawned. Some thumbed through the orange book. If these twenty-two assorted men had been strangers before, the investigation and the trial had made a group of them, binding them with loops of evidence that might trail off to Afghanistan or Kazakhstan but always trailed back again, fastening them together with recitations of detail. After weeks and months of going through the story again and again, after days of sitting side by side in cages, waiting for each to incriminate the next, the men looked as though they had lived no other life – as though there had never been a time when they had not known each other, a time when they had woken each morning in a house, not a cell, a time when they were not on trial in this sweltering room.

After lunch, an unemployed truck-driver from Andijan stood up to confess. At forty-four Qasimbek Zakirov was one of the oldest in the group, and he looked ten years older. He said he had been a driver for Abduvali Mirzayev, and when his boss disappeared at Tashkent airport he had been afraid of being arrested, and so crossed the border to live in Kirgizstan, only forty-five minutes away. Many of Mirzayev's supporters had done this, or gone to Kazakhstan, believing that the Uzbek police could not harass them there. In this way Abduvali's followers had kept together without, necessarily, any intention of doing so.

Zakirov, holding the bars of his cage, tripped awkwardly over the names of the people he incriminated as he ploughed through his long statement. Swaying and mopping his face with his handkerchief, he described how he had travelled to Afghanistan to help organise the plot. He had, he said, been given help by the Taleban, who had taken him to Mazar-e Sharif – the weakened city that had finally fallen to them in 1998 – and to visit a 'training camp' – presumably one connected to Usama bin Laden, or perhaps to some Pakistani group. He had just got to the point of confessing to having trained in a 'camp' himself when his voice trailed away. Prompted by the judge, Zakirov started up again. He ended with a flourish: 'The burden of guilt upon me is unbearable. Even my family cannot accept me, even my children. I beg the President for forgiveness: I confess everything.'

The families of the men incriminating themeselves and one another inside the courtroom did not go away, but continued to camp under the trees by the river Anhar. As the foreign observers passed by on their way out at lunch breaks and in the evenings, the families rushed to ask for news of their sons – how had they seemed when they spoke, did they show signs of having been beaten, what had they confessed to.

Many of the Glinka families had already paid terribly for the supposed acts of their sons. Some had lost their jobs as a matter of course, and had had second and third sons picked up for 'possession of drugs', so that there were no breadwinners left in some families. Several recounted far worse. 'We had not seen my brother for months,' one woman said. 'When the police came looking for him, they arrested my younger brother and both their families. They took our father and held him for fifteen days. When they let him out they put him, my mother and all the children under house arrest for thirty days. They could not go out for food, and the cow died. They survived on the bread the neighbours threw over the wall, but my father was weak and he died.' The woman began to cry, and sat down on a bench. 'They took us, three sisters, to an underground prison and separated us. They told me, if you don't tell us where your brother is we will arrest your husband for possession of drugs. They said that my children – they are six and nine – would grow up in the orphanage. That same night, at 2.30 in the morning, they took my husband.'

'I don't care who sees this now,' said her husband, who had been quiet up to then. He showed the scars on his wrists from where, he said, his hands had been tied. 'They picked me up, saying that they had found four machine-guns at my sisters' house. They beat me and hung me up by my feet for five and a half hours. They gave me elec-tric shocks and beat the soles of my feet. The police get drunk at night and then they do these things. They gave some people injec-tions of something. They held me for eight days.'

The Uzbek police had behaved in accordance with their own rules ever since independence and to some extent before it. They supple-mented their wages with low-level extortion from motorists, and fre-quently used the old Soviet-era devices of finding tiny amounts of hashish in car dashboards or single bullets 'in the sofa'. As the cam-paign against religious people grew, however, they seemed to be given an ever freer rein, and to behave more and more violently. By 1999, the idea of someone going in time of trouble to the police – always far-fetched – had become absurd.

The large police presence in Uzbekistan probably did deter some criminals. At the same time, it did not make the country as safe as the term 'police state' generally suggests. Security in Tashkent was so poor that four cars loaded with explosives were – it seemed – able to drive right up to the most important government buildings moments before the President arrived, and the police did not catch a single one of the men they saw jumping out of the cars and running away just before the bombs went off. This seemed so extraordinary as to prompt speculation that the bombings had been at least in part an inside job. Advocates of this theory pointed to cor-roboration in the fact that workmen filled in the bomb-craters before the US experts who were invited to assist in the inquiry had had a chance to look at them – though it could also be argued that it simply did not occur to the investigative authorities that the craters might be important, the restoration of appearances being seen as the more immediate task.

A row of policemen chatted quietly in the heat at the security bar-ricade between the families and the courthouse. An unmarked car pulled up – a car that should never have got beyond the first safety cordon, let alone to the very gate of the most important political trial ever known in Uzbekistan. It was an ordinary Zhiguli, as unremark-able as the cars that had driven up to the Cabinet of Ministers build-ing on 16 February. A young man dressed in black jumped out of the driver's seat and hurried away. One policeman looked a little troubled and gazed at the car for a while. After some minutes, perhaps five, he strolled over to talk to a second man, in the passenger seat, before returning to his friends. The car did not move, nor did it blow up.

The heat grew, the guests stuck to the benches, one of the plain-clothes men sitting among the foreigners nodded off. Some of the observers stopped returning for the afternoon sessions. A ripple of expectation ran through the benches when a 'witness' was called on 9 June, but he turned out to be yet another exhausted-looking man from Namangan – seemingly very young, with a shaven head and eager manner – who said he had been a student of Abduvali Mirzayev's and confessed to being part of the same alleged conspiracy. He was due to stand trial later on and was only a 'witness' in as much as he, a fellow suspect, added more detail.

The witness confessed to acquiring sulphur, aluminium and selitra (a fertiliser) and making from them a total of two tons of explosives, a skill he said he had learnt in Chechnya. Like most of the accused, he had apparently met all the key members over and over again in a variety of different places, first to lay the ground for their plan by undergoing military training and disseminating seditious religious literature and then to make the actual bombs. Every half-hour the armed guard in front of the cages turned smartly on its heels and changed, settling into the observers' benches.

On one level the evidence given to the court seemed impossible to believe, mainly because there was too much of it, too glibly told. The various stories confirmed one another too often, too easily, with no space for loose ends. The way the accused spoke also seemed unnaturally pat. Several in referring to one another used the family name followed by the first name, as is the norm on documents. In a country where surnames are barely used it seemed odd to say 'I met Abdullayev, Bahram' (for instance) about someone one really knew well. Then there were a few little slips. Why would a man who by his own account had spent two or three months in Afghanistan confuse the words 'Kabul' and 'Afghanistan'?

Then there was the fact that many of the admissions seemed to involve things that were not crimes but had carried the stain of criminality in Soviet times. People confessed to 'making maps' or 'travelling abroad' – like the *basmachi* of the 1920s and so many other Soviet-era criminals, they had become tainted by contact with foreigners (Turks, Afghans) who wished harm to the homeland. It seemed apt that one man confessed to importing a 'video against Stalin', another to bringing in 1,600 religious books ('1.5 tons of religious books' in another version) – without, judging by the evidence, knowing what they were called or who wrote them. Other charges seemed oddly inapposite – like the theft of 'gold-embroidered clothing' from a house, and the killing of a dog – both crimes for which other people were already in prison.

Some evidence seemed too far-fetched to credit. Apart from the sleeping-gas plan, the court heard of a side-plot to kidnap the President's daughter ('Ooh!' the court had murmured) in order to hold her to ransom in exchange for Abduvali Mirzayev. This plan, the court heard, was abandoned when the gang realised that they had nowhere suitable to put her. In other ways, the plotters seemed too naïve – especially for men who had at least visited the outside world and had some contact with people there. Did they really believe that two dissident armies numbering five thousand men, well-equipped enough for serious journeys across mountains and deserts, well-armed enough to overpower whatever resistance the fallen government might scramble together, would be able to march into Tashkent, take the presidential offices, make of them the seat of a new, just society in which lawyers of the shari'a would turn out the ladies with their buns, every wrong would be righted, and the poor and humble man at last live decently? Perhaps they did. In the feverishly hot courthouse, where the labyrinth of evidence led the mind in helpless circles, it was possible for even an outsider to believe anything – some spectators began to wonder whether some of the invisible characters who appeared and disappeared in the confessions existed at all.

On the other hand, the bombings had really taken place, and someone was responsible. If the evidence pouring out of the mouths of the twenty-two men was purely fictional, produced by the pressure of interrogation and of the police desire for a quick 'result', another set of guilty people was walking free. It seemed unlikely that the authorities would knowingly let this happen – unless some hidden grouping within the corridors of power had really planted the bombs themselves, which seemed an unnecessarily violent way to create the appearance of an 'Islamic threat'. The small slips and red herrings could be explicable as the result of adding embroidery to basically true accounts. The peculiar delivery might be caused by the pressures of rote-learning statements sometimes well over an hour long.

More fundamentally, where was the purpose in inventing a story that suggested that the government was so feeble the death of the President would put an end to it, that no one would rally on behalf of the fallen – that the twenty thousand men of the national army were so apathetic as to stand aside and allow the 'Islamic' fighters to cross the Amu and to enter Ferghana? It was possibly unwise, after all, to plant in the public mind the idea that President Karimov's castle might be weaker than it looked – so weak, in fact, that like General Dustam's it could collapse like so much matchwood? At times the trial seemed preposterous, at times plausible, often within the course of a single session. A long confession could lull the listener into a sort of mesmerised acceptance: a sudden jab of the unbelievable jolted one awake. Sometimes it seemed as though at least some of the young men in the cages might be guilty – and at the same time their confessions be pure fabrication.

On 9 June, having heard all the evidence, the court adjourned. It was due to reconvene in a week's time, when each man accused would have a chance to give what are called his 'final words', a statement of his choosing which generally involves an appeal for clemency. One potent element of the Uzbek justice system is that right up to the last minute the judge can reduce or commute a sentence: so, although the case against them was established, the fate of the accused was still uncertain.

The Glinka Street trial was by far the most conspicuous, but it was not the only trial of its kind going on that summer. In the smaller courts of Tashkent and in provincial courts in several other cities, in the Ferghana valley and in Khorezm, in the south-west, numerous men were on trial for a variety of 'Islamic' plots. One was of a group which had supposedly plotted to blow up the Chirvak dam above Tashkent and flood the city, thereby 'attempting to establish an Islamic state'.

There were few outside observers at these other trials, mainly because they were not publicised – although they were not secret either

– but also because the handful of interested observers concentrated on Glinka Street. From time to time, however, scraps of news seeped out. At one, in Tashkent, a young prisoner had read his statement in the usual way, and then shouted 'Everything I just told you is a lie! They held a gas mask over my face for ten days until I agreed to say it.'

A new ground for arrest was the crime of 'belonging to a religious organisation', and several people were on trial for association with a group called Hezb-e Tahrir, the Freedom Party, one new to Uzbekistan that was rapidly acquiring a following. The avowed aim of Hezb-e Tahrir, as set out in leaflets scattered by unseen hands in the bazaars, was the restitution of the Caliphate, the commonwealth of Muslim peoples that had existed in some form or other until the collapse of the Ottoman empire. The Caliphate lived on as an ideal among some Muslims struggling through lives of suffering, for whom it signified a restoration of dignity and a recognition of Muslim achievement. Movements based on this vision grew mainly in Arabic-speaking countries under foreign occupation – they never featured in Afghanistan or much in Iran – and Hezb-e Tahrir was originally established by a Palestinian cleric in the early 1950s. Popular among Palestinian refugees, it spread to Jordan, Lebanon, Syria, Iraq and Turkey as a transnational movement open to Arab and non-Arab, men and women alike.

The Uzbek version of Hezb-e Tahrir met needs being felt more and more achingly in Uzbekistan. Its clear vision, its feeling of solidarity, its simple rules attracted the poor *kolkhoz* boy and the educated student alike, who saw it as a beacon of hope in an unfair and insecure world. Its members – most of them male – met quietly at one another's houses once or twice a week, said prayers, and tried to live modestly. As members, men could feel an inner dignity and self-respect that provided some solace against the daily humiliations of poverty, the police and the *kolkhoz* bosses. For some people there was the additional advantage that the party endorsed practices many Uzbeks followed anyway, such as polygamy, which under secular law (such as it was) were illegal. One needed no qualification to join – not even enough Arabic to read the Quran. One was only required to be 'ready' in case one were called upon by the amir, or group leader, to perform some task.

Members did not have to interpret or understand the scriptures in any depth – one typical sixteen-year-old enthusiast earnestly told his aunt to remove the ducks from the pastoral scene painted on her living-room wall because they were animate beings. Despite the dismay this sort of behaviour caused in some households, many parents were delighted that their sons had found a path in life that would bring them closer to God and keep them out of trouble, and did not involve drinking or taking drugs. Members disapproved of alcohol and went only to 'white' weddings, at which there was no drink and no dancing, and the men and women guests sat separately. They refused to attend the extravagant weddings of local grandees, on the grounds that they were corrupt.

Hundreds of people suspected of being in Hezb-e Tahrir were rounded up, apparently in an effort to stamp out the party before it could take root. Despite this, Hezb-e Tahrir leaflets still circulated around Tashkent and other parts of the country. According to rumour, 'two hundred thousand' new leaflets were scattered in the city bazaars in a single day. It was impossible to know where they were coming from, because Hezb-e Tahrir needed neither mosques nor known leaders. It was also impossible, and perhaps not very important, to know how much connection there might be between the Uzbek party and other branches. Some observers maintained that the whole construct was not really a 'party' at all but merely a figment, invented and disseminated, using powers of suggestion, by the SNB – it was certainly not unknown for this to be done, generally in order to increase political control or to provide a pretext for mass arrests, and in the looking-glass world of Uzbekistan at that time the idea was not outlandish.

In sum, Hezb-e Tahrir was just the sort of headless organisation that Abedkhan Nazarov, the former imam of Takhtabai mosque, had said might spread if the popular imams like himself were suppressed and the mosques closed down. After two years in semi-hiding, he appeared to have left the country. He was last seen on 5 March 1998. After the bombings, his photograph appeared on the 'Most Wanted' lists stuck up at the airport and in other public places, on the grounds that he had 'taught them all'. Many people connected to him, including his wife, Munira, were arrested.

Still more people were arrested for being 'connected' with the exiles from the Ferghana valley – 'Namangani' and Yuldash. That summer a new term to describe them and their families appeared –

'Islamic Movement of Uzbekistan', IMU. When some IMU men surfaced around the mountain town of Batken in Kirgizstan, near the Uzbek border, and took hostage two geologists from Japan, many ordinary Uzbeks were shocked, terrified, and ready to believe that these men were 'fanatics', almost supernaturally powerful, and well capable of marching on the capital.

A great number of the arrests followed the re-launch of a device from the Stalin era – the 'amnesty'. In April, President Karimov had announced that anyone who admitted publicly to membership of an illegal religious group and asked for forgiveness would be pardoned – warning that guilty people who failed to give themselves up would face the severest punishment, as would their fathers.*

So many people turned themselves in – a hundred in just a few days, officials said – that special centres were opened at which the guilty could also hand over religious literature and inform on those who had 'recruited' them. And in a modern version of the methods of the 1930s, parents even appeared on television denouncing their children. Obviously these were the few, but many other mothers went down to police stations to 'confess' those of their sons who visited the mosque more than usual. In these troubled times, they felt, it was better to be safe than sorry. Arrests followed swiftly. Not all those who were arrested stayed in prison. Some richer families paid cash dollars for the return of their sons. One story doing the rounds was that a dignitary paid as much as $150,000 in return for his son, who had been picked up for possession of heroin. The extravagant *khudai*, the thanksgiving dinner laid on for the neighbourhood, must have set the family back several thousand more.

The corruption of the system, the – now immense – inequalities in wealth further hurt the dignity of the poor. The new 'business-man' might buy his child's freedom – but the great majority could not. Times had never been harder. Strict limits on currency conversion were never relaxed, despite numerous promises, making it extremely hard to trade. New businesses did not replace those that had packed up, and even more businesses, mainly Turkish, folded

---

* Another way in which Soviet and Uzbek methods dovetail is the lack of distinction between family and individual. Come 'election' time, for instance, it is normal for one family member to go to the polling station with the voting documents – that is, the passports – of the rest of the family, as a batch – so normal that many people, asked who they have voted for, are not sure.

after the Uzbek police accused their workers of being 'religious extremists' – even, at a sacking factory, taking an old fax machine from the dustbin to check whether calls had been made to 'Islamic' organisations. A teacher might take home 6–7,000 *sum* a month – at a time when a pair of socks cost 370. A *kolkhoz* worker could expect only pennies, plus a handout of wheat. The *sum*, trading at 480 to the dollar on the black market, had never been so worthless. The poor borrowed what they could to ease their condition.

'I thought Karimov was right to arrest all these troublemakers,' said a taxi driver. 'Last night, though, they picked up my neighbour's son. He's a good boy: we all know that. It makes you wonder.' Slowly, slowly, more and more ordinary people with no interest in religion found their lives touched by the purges. And a few wondered, often for the first time in their lives, whether President Karimov was doing the right thing.

Outside the capital, many more people were absolutely sure that he was not. In the Ferghana valley anger against the regime had been welling up for years; increasingly there was evident dissent in Khorezm too. In south-eastern Uzbekistan there was grief for the fate of the local boy who had become the softly-spoken 'amir' of the Glinka Street group, Bahram Abdullayev, who would shortly be put to death unless, at the last moment, the judge offered clemency.

Bahram Abdullayev's story began, in a sense, in the very foundation of the Soviet Union. The family came from the region around the river Surkhun, the Red river, which is the primary tributary of the Amu in Uzbekistan. The Surkhun region, whose main city is Termez, is one of ancient civilisation, and the Abdullayevs – who, unusually, possess a written genealogical tree – trace their lineage back to the descendents of the Caliph Ali, through the branch of Imam Husein.

Bahram's grandfather, Abdullah Khan, maintained the tradition of his line and became a noted sage, a sufi of the school of Nakhshbandi, which has its origins in Bukhara. The Surkhun region was one of those most severely hit by the wars of the 1920s, and a great part of the population crossed into Afghanistan. Abdullah Khan stayed on and was sent to a prison camp in Siberia in 1928. He was released five years later and returned to his village near Baisun, about a hundred miles north of Termez, where he lived to extreme old age, quietly at home, teaching from his private library of twenty or thirty books.

The next generations paid heavily. Abdullah Khan's children had great difficulty getting any sort of qualifications, and remained on the land. His son Abdullah Ishan – who became Bahram's father – worked on the *kolkhoz* all his life. He brought up his thirteen children, five boys and eight girls, along correct Muslim lines, encouraging them to learn their prayers and elementary Arabic from their grandfather. Several of these children were very bright indeed, and set apart by an unusual inner strength. They were proud of their inability to tell lies or tolerate injustice. In the 1970s and 1980s they failed exams after questioning the supremacy of Lenin in class. They were 'the sort that would not eat pork in the army *whatever happened*,' one contemporary put it, as soon as she set eyes on Bahram.

Two of the boys, and the girls, remained on the *kolkhoz*. The other three boys did spectacularly well, despite the incessant punishment and derision that came their way. One became an exceptional scholar of Arabic and poetry; another began a PhD at Termez Institute of Oriental Languages. When the Soviet Union began to crumble, the family did not go through the motions of rejoicing – they thanked God, in private, from the bottom of their hearts. Bahram left school as the brightest of all his brothers, a helpful, polite boy who respected his elders and took the trouble to visit his aunts regularly. His grandfather blessed him as his spiritual successor, in accordance with the sufi tradition. Bahram set his heart on becoming a doctor, and managed to pass all his exams; the medical institute in Tashkent turned him down.

Bahram turned to religion. He had a memory 'like that of al-Bukhari' says a contemporary, referring to Muhammad ibn Ismail of Bukhara, who compiled the sayings of the Prophet Muhammad in the ninth century and was famous not only for his prodigious powers of recall but for refusing to keep the company of rulers lest he say something just to please them. Bahram went briefly to live in Dushanbe, and in 1988 moved on to Andijan. There he began to study with Abduvali Mirzayev.

Bahram stayed in Andijan as a pupil of Mirzayev for three years. After this point, according to statements read at the trial, he took a job as a children's religious teacher in the tiny mountainous region of Qarachai-Cherkessia in the Caucasus. By twenty-two, he had already taken three steps that would lead him to the dock at the Tashkent Supreme Court. 'He should have been a great Qazi, the spiritual leader of his country,' said a close friend. 'It is sad that he will die at the age of twenty-nine.'

On 18 June, the Supreme Court reconvened for the last words of the accused. Each would be given two brief opportunities to take the floor and speak unscripted. The prisoners had deteriorated visibly during the week of recess. Pale, blotchy around the eyes, they stared at the floor, slumped forward in their cages. The courtroom smelt of sweat. Only two glanced upwards as the first rose to make his final speech.

'I have nothing to say,' said Abdurahmanov, handing the script to the judge.

'The prosecutor has asked for the right sentence,' said the next (Khatamshir, facing twenty years). 'I am so filled remorse that I do not know what to call myself. When people have a dangerous dog they chain it up and if it is still dangerous they shoot it. I am worse than that dog.' His tearful voice tailed off.

A bit-player, Arifkhan, was hardly recognisable as the cocksure, cheerful young man he had been the week before. His sweaty face looked narrow and dirty, there were huge red rings under his eyes, his speech had become slow and weak. 'I ask God to forgive me first, then my mother, the people, the President, my wife, my four children, the victims. If you give me a chance I can serve my people.'

There were no eleventh-hour protestations of innocence, no attempts at defence. One after another the men abased themselves, begging for a chance for atonement. One pleaded for forgiveness from his eighteen sisters, others from their parents, all from President Karimov – 'Aka' Islam,' one said, 'my elder brother'. They wept into the microphone that they passed from hand to hand.

One man, Zainuddin Askarov, one of the plotters of the Istanbul 'cell', made a stand. Head up, dry-eyed, he began in a high-pitched, almost hysterical voice. 'Look at us,' he said, through the bars of his cage, 'we are sitting like animals in the zoo. I would like to tell you that among the animals are wolves.' The court jerked awake.

Askarov began to relate how it was the vindictiveness of the system that had forced him into the position he was in now. His elder brother, he said, had been one of the 'Islamic' activists who came to the fore in 1992 and had got four years in jail, because he had 'put a prostitute backwards on a donkey and walked it around Namangan to show the people'. 'We waited for him. His time was up on 17 March 1997.' Askarov began to shout and wave his finger at the court. 'At the last minute they discovered a gram of narcotics on his bed. He never even smoked a cigarette. So he got another year and a half. We waited again. Then two days before the release date they found two bullets in his isolation cell. How could this have been? He is still in prison.'

It was Askarov who had revealed the 'sleeping-gas plot'. Even if his testimony was not to be taken seriously, he was now shouting aloud the silent story of thousands of people all over the country. 'I realised that if the wind can move a camel it can blow away a sheep completely. They could put me away for twenty years. So I did not go home, I stayed in Turkey . . . I tell you frankly, even nursery-school children in this country know anything can happen to a man in prison.'

The 'amir' of Glinka Street, Bahram Abdullayev, had looked at the floor throughout the session, neat and composed. He rose, last but one in the line, for his final words. 'Let God bless the families of the dead,' he said, expressing his condolences in a quiet voice. He then re-stated what his purpose had been: to spread religious knowledge in Uzbekistan, and then arrange military training. 'We would have moved,' he said, 'only when the time was right' – that is, when the Taleban and Ahmad Shah Mas'ud had 'resolved their differences' in Afghanistan and an Islamic-style government sat in Dushanbe. Unfortunately, he said, other members of the group had behaved as 'dogs off the lead' and gone ahead with the unsanctioned bombings.

Abdullayev apologised again. 'If I had any opportunity to make amends, I would.'

The court reassembled for the verdict on 28 June, a broiling hot day. The accused, most less tired-looking than before, sat with their wrists cuffed behind their backs. 'They like sitting like that,' said the police officer in charge.

At nine o'clock the court rose. The judge read the summary of events, then the names of the accused: each one guilty. He handed down lighter than expected sentences in many cases. The hapless baker who 'made *pilau*' for his old friend got ten years instead of four-teen. Askarov got eleven, not eighteen. Four of those who expected the death sentence had it commuted. Bahram Abdullayev was not one of them.

'The court is closed,' said the judge.

Bahram, pale and taut, leant forward, smiling slightly, to talk to his guards, in the manner of a man shaking hands as he says good-bye.

Outside the courthouse, the families waited to hear the verdicts. Bahram Abdullayev's elderly father stood silently in a blue and white turban. Someone rushed out and blurted the news at him without warning. Abdullayev's mother collapsed on the ground. Relatives pulled her up and tried to pour water into her mouth. The policemen formed a cordon and stood face to face with a row of crying mothers. Bahram Abdullayev's father spoke with dignity. 'I thank God that he gave me my son,' he said.

That evening, news passed around Tashkent that something unprecedented had happened in the Naserbek district on the edge of town, a poor area where gardens become smallholdings and the city starts to dissolve into the countryside. Two weeks before, while the trial was still going on, a forty-two-year-old man of Naserbek named Farhad Usmanov, a father of six known for his piety, had been arrested on the grounds that he belonged to Hezb-e Tahrir. The police returned the cut and bruised body for burial in the last days of June, saying Usmanov had died in his cell of a heart attack. In keeping with Muslim tradition, the family arranged the funeral quickly. Police cordoned off the area to bar the way to any outside mourners who might think of attending, and stood at the gate of the cemetery with a video camera so that anyone who did come would know that they were on record.

There had followed a scene the like of which had never been seen in Tashkent. Three or four thousand men from all over the city walked past the police lines, past the cameras, and filed into the small graveyard set between an apple orchard and a wheat field. 'I knew him only slightly, but it was too much to murder a man in that way,' said one young mourner, the son of an important *apparatchik* whose family had flourished under Karimov. 'I did not care if they took my name and saw my face.'

*

Bahram Abdullayev was put to death on 14 December 1999 – probably shot by firing squad. His family, who never saw him again, only found this out by petitioning the authorities – relatives are not generally notified of executions. The body is never returned. Eerily, statements said to have been written by Abdullayev were given in evidence in at least one of the hundreds of trials that followed Glinka Street.

13

What tomorrow brings

'And though there were a man free from preoccupations, who
could devote his whole life to study and research and his whole
attention to the recording of events, yet he could not in a long
period of time acquit himself of the account of one single
district . . .'

DUSHANBE GOT READY to celebrate the tenth year of Tajik independence from the Soviet Union. All over the city, painters
restored the sugared-almond stucco, the elegant white pilasters and
cornices dimmed by time and neglect. Even the people who thought
the whole affair a waste of good money were pleased to see the city
spring back to life, looking like its old self again. City gardeners
replanted the flower beds with arrangements so delicate that each
colour seemed to dissolve into the next, and the evening air was
scented with gilly flowers.

Tajikistan had changed a good deal after the peace treaty of 1997,
not at once, but gradually. By 2001 there were very few armed men
on the streets. People in the city centre began to visit their friends
after dusk and to take their children out for *shashlik*. A Dushanbe
singer cut one of the first compact discs in *mawara-an-nahr*. The
lyrical style of Daler Nazarov, the popular musician of the Pamir,
inspired a new generation, and Dushanbe – the only Persian-speaking capital in which pop music was legal – produced an astonishing
number of new bands.

The political situation became steadier. Imamali Rahmanov remained as President: 'You can learn how to do anything, one just
needs practice,' he is said to have said. Akbar Turajanzada came home

after Said Abdullah Nuri returned, to be part of the collaborative government that held together despite frequent alarms and flurries. The Russian troops of the 201st Division and the border guards remained in place.

In the new century, far more Tajiks went to Russia than had ever done so in the days of the Soviet Union. About a quarter of a million Tajiks were there during the course of 2001 – that is, about a quarter of the working male population – an astonishingly high proportion. The rich or fortunate managed to get proper documents, rent apartments and live as registered Russians. The poor – the great majority – went as illegal labourers, making the eight-day journey by way of Astrakhan, packed into down-at-heel trains, dogged by bandits and policemen on the make. Alighting at Paveletsky station in Moscow, they set out into the vast city few had ever set eyes on.

Many made for the Tajik settlement at Cherkisovsky bazaar, where they found work as sellers and porters, especially in the growing Chinese quarter where traders from Kashgar and Urumchi sell every sort of commodity – a sight a Muscovite of the Soviet time could scarcely have imagined. But there were many people in 2001 for whom 'the Soviet Union' was just something their parents talked about – one Tajik barrow-boy at Cherkisovsky was only two when it collapsed. To him, Lenin was no more meaningful than the amirs of Bukhara.

Cherkisovsky was only the jumping-off point for many Tajik men (and sometimes women) who often continued their long journeys into Siberia where there were jobs to be had on building sites for a hundred dollars or so a month, and work making onion sacks for forty. These were good wages for a poor Tajik, and many reckoned to take home as much as three hundred dollars in a season – enough to keep the family through another winter.

Hindustani's stepson Ubaidullah still lives in Dushanbe in the house the family found in 1947 after Hindustani was released from Kemerovo labour camp. The flower garden is as well kept as ever and Ubaidullah still grows his favourite amaryllises. A calf, a kitten and a tame ptarmigan live beneath the vines, adding to the general liveliness of this warm household of three generations. The family survived the death of Ubaidullah's son Abdullah only to lose Nurullah, who went to work in a bazaar in Moscow but was murdered there in 1999. Ubaidullah does not go now to the old country – the Ferghana

valley. He is elderly, the journey is long and expensive; and besides, Dushanbe has been his home for more than half a century.

Muhammadjan Shukurov still lives at the other end of the city, which became his home when he was fourteen, in the dreadful days of 1930. He is fairly sure he won't return to Bukhara now. The city his father knew is less recognisable than ever – though the Mir-e Arab stands, and the old bazaar. In the remains of the Ark are still some mementoes of Alim Khan, the last amir – a Russian biscuit-tin embossed with pineapples, another rosy with cherries, a brass tele-scope, a block of black tea, and a few foot-wide Tsarist banknotes. Poked into a cupboard at one side of the exhibition room is a gramo-phone with a fluted trumpet. A record by Levi Babakhanov, the Bukharan Jewish singer, still lies on the turntable – unplayed since the time when the hand of history swung around so violently and precip-itated the Bukharans into the Soviet Union.

Ninety years on, neither Tajiks, nor Uzbeks, nor Afghans, nor any of the peoples of Central Asia can look into the future and see what lies beyond tomorrow. There is barely a family who can say with confidence 'When my son is older he'll go to such and such a school', or even 'Next year, we'll paint the apartment'. Prediction is a luxury – perhaps the most wonderful luxury – one that even New Rich Central Asians cannot afford. And on Tajik independence day, 9 September 2001, the hand of history swung again.

On the far side of the river Amu, in the village of Khuja Bahahuddin, almost at the Tajik border, Ahmad Shah Mas'ud agreed to give an interview to two persistent North African journalists. Khuja Bahahuddin was a base of the Northern Alliance (a name that stuck, though its leaders preferred the more inclusive 'United Front') in the small corner of Afghanistan that was still outside Taleban hands, and it was not uncommon for Mas'ud to give inter-views. He had become, as in the Soviet time, a famous figure abroad: as the last commander standing against the Taleban, and as a man of compelling presence who had come through more than twenty years of warfare. As the journalists set up their equipment the camera or tripod, packed with explosives, detonated. Mas'ud and his transla-tor were killed. Both the assassins died too – one in the attack, the other shot by a bodyguard.

Ahmad Shah Mas'ud was buried among his people as simply as he had lived, on a mountain top near his home village of Jangalak in the Panjshir valley, one of the few parts of Afghanistan never consistently occupied in all the Soviet Army's attempts. 'Despite everything that has happened between us Afghans,' said a friend, 'they had to use foreigners to kill him. They could not find an Afghan to do the job.'

Two days after the assassination of Mas'ud, men hijacked four passenger aeroplanes in the United States and flew two into the World Trade Centre and one into the Pentagon. The fourth crash-landed. Television-watching parts of the world sat transfixed by the image of the first and then the second tower coming down like card houses, as though the real world had become a feature film. President George W. Bush laid the blame at the door of Usama bin Laden, the Arab fighter who had lived in Afghanistan since the 1980s and was currently a guest of the Taleban.* The Taleban, he said, 'must act and act immediately' to give bin Laden up. He invited the world to take sides: 'You are either with us or with the terrorists', he said. Suddenly Afghanistan was on the front pages of the world's newspapers.

For years, most foreigners had paid scant attention to the Afghans. Tens of thousands of Afghan men, women and children who had spent everything they had to make difficult and perilous journeys across the world to escape fighting, and in some cases political persecution, found themselves turned away from or even imprisoned in camps in the countries where they had hoped to find safety.

Hundreds of thousands more who had nothing left to sell decamped to the edges of their country, mainly to Pakistan and Iran. Many of these were trying to walk away from two years of ruinous drought, simply to find food. (A group of ten thousand moved to the flood-plain of the river Amu in the no-man's-land between Afghanistan and Tajikistan; their grandfathers were originally from Kulab, Hisar and, in one case, Dushanbe – two generations later, they were on the move yet again.)

---

* Usama bin Laden was not an especially well-known figure in Central Asia at that time – far less famous than he was in the United States. Fifteen out of twenty people shown his photograph in the street in Dushanbe did not recognise it. One identified it as the face of 'a man who owned a lot of restaurants', another as 'a rich man'. All, however, recognised Amad Shah Mas'ud.

The one image from Afghanistan that had caught the public imagination in the recent past was the blowing-up of the giant pre-Islamic Buddha statues at Bamian in central Afghanistan in early 2001. The Taleban, whose work it was, thereby appeared to be beyond understanding. Their public statements did not help comprehension. With parts of the country collapsing from hunger or violence, on 18 July 2001 Mulla Umar issued a decree banning the import of billiard tables, lobsters, nail polish, tie-pins and wigs.

Yet after 11 September, Washington abruptly made Afghanistan its business. The country became headline news on the American networks not only as the home of Usama bin Laden and the Taleban – whom Bush vowed to depose as 'protectors' of 'our enemy' – but also as the home of the Northern Alliance, who now had some sort of common purpose with the United States. It was widely perceived both inside the Alliance and out that this had been foreseen by the perpetrators of the air crashes, hence the assassination of Mas'ud immediately beforehand. The new military leader of the Alliance was General Fahim, a former *mujahed* who had led the move into Kabul of 1992. General Dustam had already returned from Turkey in time to muster his Uzbeks, and vowed to reclaim his old stronghold of Mazar-e Sharif. And so, with the fervent but not very clear objective of 'stamping out terrorism', the US administration marched into the web of subtle interests that had been a generation in the weaving.

Washington made an early ally of Pakistan, Afghanistan's neighbour to the east – there having been too much hostility for too long between Washington and Teheran for the Americans to look, openly at least, to Iran. President Musharraf of Pakistan promised his country's support.

At the same time, the US hastened to make friends with Russia, as the former colonial power to the north of Afghanistan and the current military power in Tajikistan, the only country bordering Northern Alliance territory and therefore of much strategic importance. President Putin pledged his support for the Americans, and said that Russia had 'no objection' to the US using air bases in Central Asia (a speech that caused many Central Asians to make wry jokes about 'ten years of independence').

All eyes then fell on Uzbekistan, the former Soviet Republic through which another army had invaded Afghanistan in 1979 – the country that 'might come in useful one day', as an American had said in 1997. 'Of course, 11 September is a gift for Karimov!' said a diplomat later in 2001. 'Now he can say, "I was right all along – look how terrible these terrorists are." He can arrest anyone he likes, and the Americans won't say a word! They'll help keep the Russians off his back too – they'll support him to the end if he gives them what they want.' On 27 September, President Karimov offered the use of air and ground space to the US, should the need arise. There were rumours that foreigners had been seen inspecting the old Soviet air bases at Termez and Khanabad. Washington put the IMU on its list of 'terrorist groups'.

The Taleban had restricted entry to Afghanistan, so journalists poured in to neighbouring Pakistan (as they had during the Soviet war) in time for the US attack on Afghanistan that seemed imminent. And they swarmed – for the first time – into a stunned Uzbekistan and Tajikistan where some people, especially those in remoter places, were still unaware of what had happened in New York. One group of Tajik elders only heard the news two weeks after the attacks, when they came down from the mountains to buy wheat in town.

A thousand, then two thousand journalists were accredited in Dushanbe. 'Dushanbe?' shouted a reporter. 'A week ago I'd never heard of the place – now our whole operation's there.' Every hotel room was taken, every price went through the roof in this suddenly famous town. Sum, the department store on Rudaki, sold microphones. Sleeping-bags, flown in from Dubai, fetched $200 each. Street boys tried their luck selling 'Taleban telephone numbers' to the gullible. Tajiks made tea and pies to sell to the hundreds of journalists queuing outside the Alliance-controlled Afghan embassy for tickets across the river Amu.

'Please God, may the soldiers leave Afghanistan alone,' said an elderly rope-maker in Barakat bazaar, speaking for many, perhaps most, ordinary people. 'Perhaps they do not understand what war does. It does not end with the fighting; it brings ignorant children and dead farm animals and soured land that cannot grow food. It brings years of poverty and hunger. And it does not happen in isolation: one country's war is the whole region's war – when fire comes, the wet stick burns with the dry.' 'Solve Afghanistan's problems by sending in weapons?' said a twenty-year-old woman selling eggs. 'I don't think so.'

On 7 October 2001, United States aircraft dropped the first bombs on Kabul, in Qandahar in southern Afghanistan, and on Jalalabad in the east. And so the American war began. Over the succeeding nights all three cities were hit again and again. Later came Mazar-e Sharif. 'We are taking out their air defences! We are destroying their airforce!' said Bush – but there was nothing to show what the bombers had hit, nor what the 'airforce' was supposed to have consisted of. On 7 October came the first unequivocal evidence of a building destroyed: an ICRC* warehouse in Kabul. The stocks of emergency flour inside burnt merrily.

'This is not a war against the Afghan people,' said Bush. To prove it, his aircraft dropped plastic packets of food – peanut butter, soya protein, vegetables and jam – as well as bombs. The refugees along the Tajik border carefully sewed the bags together to make tents. Lit from inside by small fires, they glowed yellow after dark. The Americans deployed a new weapon over Afghanistan: the AC-130, a low-flying plane mounted with machine-guns. A spokesman for Usama bin Laden delivered a statement calling on 'all Muslims' to join a '*jihad*' against the United States – like Bush, telling the world to take sides.

There was much to remind former Soviet citizens of the war of twenty years earlier, from the 'friendly ground troops' in Afghanistan to the style of the propaganda. 'We have dropped 575,000 food packets', said a Pentagon briefing in late October. Bush called upon the 'children of America' to give their pocket-money to the 'children of Afghanistan'. 'Our kids have dug deep into their piggy-banks,' announced a CNN presenter, 'and come up with half a million dollars!'

With winter fast approaching, however, the waiting game ended abruptly. The US finally bombed Taleban positions in earnest, starting with those outside Mazar-e Sharif. On Friday, 9 November, General Dustam recaptured the city he had left in 1997. Just before dawn, three days later, Northern Alliance forces drove through the Shamali plains

---

* International Committee of the Red Cross.

and through the city boundary into Kabul. Crowds came out to cheer them as they moved into the centre of the city.

The Taleban had disappeared from Kabul overnight. With them fled the young men of the IMU. In the mess of the house they had scrambled to leave, among abandoned boots and tubes of toothpaste, were handfuls of yellowed, cheap paper written on in Cyrillic. 'Let us pray beautifully! We wish the blessing of God on all Muslims . . .' read one scrap, signed 'Mujahed' Abdu Khalil. 'Here are the names of my school friends', began another. There followed a list of twenty-four names. 'How I miss Uzbekistan!' it ends. A third shows a childlike drawing of a two-storey house with curtains in the windows, a pot of flowers on the table, an electric light blazing – a dream of home as far from real life in Namangan or Khorezm as the new Uzbekistan they had hoped for, a land in which the poor found respect and did not fear the knock on the door. It is likely that many IMU '*mujahedin*' were killed, probably in Mazar-e Sharif, where they also had a house, and perhaps at Qunduz, the old points of arrival in Afghanistan. There has been not a word from the Uzbek wives and children – perhaps several hundred – who had crossed the Amu with their men.

In Kabul, in Herat and elsewhere girls went back to school and little boys took off their heavy turbans. Television resumed broadcasting, people played music in the streets. Property prices went up. Crowds queued to see the first post-Taleban play, performed in the ruins of the old National Theatre in Kabul. Down in Qandahar, Mulla Umar's large deserted house was opened to public view. Those who expected opulence and heaps of booty were disappointed by the ordinariness of the place, the only furniture a bed and a baby's cradle. Mulla Umar had vanished as abruptly as he had surfaced. A new era had dawned.

On the other side of the Amu, in Aini Square in Dushanbe, the snow fell around the massive Soviet-era bronzes depicting the story of Central Asia as once it was told – the boy yanking the chains of slavery from a vast block of sandstone, the woman unveiled, the soldier with his starred cap-badge shooting the cowering *basmachi*. People on their way home, holding their shopping and their children's hands, walked past without a glance, chatting as they went.

Sources and further reading

All epigraph quotations come from *Genghis Khan: The History of the World Conqueror* by Ata-Malik Juvaini, translated and edited by J. A. Boyle (Manchester University Press, 1958; new edition, Manchester University Press and UNESCO Publishing, Paris, 1997).

All other quoted material comes from interviews by the author between 1994 and 2001, except where stated in the text or below.

The setting: The shrine of al-Hakim of Termez

Termezi's brief autobiography (possibly the first in Arabic) and some of his discourses on sainthood have been translated into English by Bernd Radke and John O'Kane in their *The Concept of Sainthood in Early Islamic Mysticism* (Curzon Press, Surrey, 1996).

The definitive scholarly work on the geography and early history of Central Asia, including much on Termez, is W. Barthold's *Turkestan down to the Mogul Invasion*, first translated by the author into English with the assistance of H. A. R. Gibb (Luzac & Co., London, 1928) and reprinted several times by the E. J. W. Gibb memorial trust.

Lieutenant Olufsen of the Danish army travelled through the Pamir and visited Samarkand, Bukhara and Merv (Mary) in 1896–7, returning for a second trip in 1898–9. Both Danish expeditions made detailed ethnographic, botanical and archaeological studies recorded in *Through the Unknown Pamirs* (William Heinemann, London, 1904; reprinted by Greenwood, 1969) and The *Emir of Bokhara and His Country* (William Heinemann, 1911).

Naser Khusrau's *Safarnama* (Travel Journal) has been translated several times into English, most recently by W. M. Thackston in his

Naser-e Khosraw's Book of Travels (Persian Heritage Association, Bibliotheca Persica, New York, 1986). There are also translations of his verse, including *Make a Shield from Wisdom: Selected Verses from Nasir-i Khusraw's Divan*, translated and introduced by Annemarie Schimmel (Kegan Paul International Ltd for the Institute of Ismali Studies, London, 1993) and *Nasir-i Khusraw: Forty Poems from the Divin*, translated and introduced by Peter Lamborn Wilson and Gholam-Reza Aavani (Imperial Academy of Iranian Philosophy, Teheran, 1977).

Biruni's famous study of India is available in English as *Alberuni's India*, translated and edited by Edward C. Sachau (Trübner, London, 2 vols, 1888), reprinted variously, including an abridged version edited by Ainslie T. Embree (W. W. Norton & Company, New York, 1971).

There are two modern English translations of Babur's diaries, *The Baburnama*: Annette S. Beveridge, translator and editor, *The Memoirs of Babur* (Luzac and Co., London, 1912; and numerous reprints, including Low Price Publications, Delhi, 1989); and Wheeler M. Thackston, *Baburnama: Memoirs of Babur, Prince and Emperor* (Oxford University Press, 1996).

The definitive account of Tashkent in imperial times is Eugene Schuyler, *Turkistan: Notes of a Journey in Russian Turkistan, Kokand, Bukhara and Kuldja* (Scribner & Armstrong, New York, 1876).

The quotation on page 19 comes from Count K. K. Pahlen, *Mission to Turkestan* (Oxford University Press, 1964).

William Eleroy Curtis visited Bukhara as a reporter for the Chicago *Record-Herald* in 1908 and 1911. His observations are collated in *Turkestan: The Heart of Asia* (Hodder and Stoughton, London, 1911).

Chapter 1: Witnesses and actors

Muhammadjan Shakuri and Rustam Shukurov's translation of Sadr-e Zia's diaries is due for publication in 2003.

The most helpful and bias-free scholarly work on this period is Adeeb Khalid, *The Politics of Muslim Cultural Reform: Jadidism in Central Asia* (University of California Press, 1998; reprinted Oxford University Press, 2000).

Chapter 2: *Journeys in the dark – the migration across the Amu*

Kamol Abdullaev, the authority on the Central Asian migration to Afghanistan, has two forthcoming books in English – *Central Asian Emigration* 1918–1932: *Exiles of Bolshevism* (Curzon Press, Surrey, 2001) and, with Shahram Akbarzadeh, *A Historical Dictionary of Tajikistan* (Scarecrow Press, London, 2002).

The figures for individual regions come from Tsentralny Gosudarstvenny Arkhi Sovetskoy Armiy, quoted by Kamol Abdullaev in his paper 'Central Asian Émigrés in Afghanistan: First Wave, 1920–1931', in *Central Asia Monitor*, No. 4, 1994. The quotation from the correspondence between Alim Khan and the British Consul-General in Kashgar is from the India Office Records and Library, London, cited by Kamol Abdullaev.

The best-known account of Ibrahim Bek's life is given by Zeki Velidi Togun in *Turkili ve Yakin Tarihi* (Istanbul, 1942–7). The version here draws on this and on the research of Kamol Abdullaev and Namaz Hatamov, and on first-hand accounts of families whose relatives were *basmachi* fighters. I also draw on the work of Professor Reisner, as recounted by Yuri Gankovsky in 'Ibrahim Beg Lakai' in *Journal of South Asian and Middle Eastern Studies*, vol. XVI, No. 4, Summer 1993.

The leaflets said to emanate from Alim Khan appear in various sources, including Joshua Kunitz, *Dawn over Samarkand* (Lawrence & Wishart, New York, 1936).

The estimates of amounts banked by the Bukharan treasury come from F.M. Bailey, *Mission to Tashkent* (Jonathan Cape, London, 1946, reprinted with additional photographs and an introduction by Peter Hopkirk, The Folio Society, London, 1999).

The account of the basket of silverware deposited in Lloyd's Bank by Stephen Fox comes from correspondence between the bank and Fox, in the India Office Records and Library, and private papers.

The eyewitness to Alim Khan's death was Mukarama, daughter of Azam Khuja, a courtier in Alim Khan's retinue. She gave her account to the author in 2001.

Chapter 3: *The world turned upside-down*

Qader Baba spoke to Adiba Atayeva of the BBC at Qaramazeh near Urgench in January 2000. He was then about 98.

A fascinating first-hand account in English of the early 1930s in Moscow and Leningrad is Julian and Margaret Bullard (eds), *Inside Stalin's Russia: The Diaries of Reader Bullard* 1930–1934 (Day Books, Oxfordshire, 2000).

The figures for numbers dead in the famine of 1932/3 are from Robert Conquest, *The Harvest of Sorrow* (Oxford University Press, 1986).

Chapter 4: A town called Monday

There are no accounts in English of Central Asia during the Second World War. Rahman Safarov has compiled numerous works in Russian and Tajik. An excellent overview of the wider USSR is Richard Overy, *Russia's War* (TV Books Inc., USA, 1997; first UK edition Allen Lane, The Penguin Press, 1998).

The account of the Polish migration is compiled from many first-hand stories. Original research, including the counting of Polish graves in Iran, is being conducted by Stanislav Viganovski of the Polish Embassy, Teheran.

Chapter 5: 'A Paradise on earth'

An official account, including many interesting photographs, of the building of modern Dushanbe is Pavel Luknitsky, *Soviet Tajikistan* (Foreign Languages Publishing House, Moscow, 1954).

Chapter 6: 'Why were we there?' – Afghanistan

The account of the early part of the Soviet invasion, as seen from the Afghan side, comes largely from Zaher Tanin, a journalist then in Kabul and now with the BBC in London.

The list of Soviet projects undertaken in Afghanistan comes from 'Events in Kabul' by Abdullah Jan Khalil, in *Central Asia Journal* (University of Peshawar, Summer 1981).

The figures for amounts spent on the war come from Barnett Rubin, *The Fragmentation of Afghanistan* (Yale University Press, 1995).

Many of the blunders committed by the Soviet army come from Artyom Borovik, *The Hidden War* (International Relations Publishing House, Moscow, 1990; The Atlantic Month Press, USA, 1990; Faber and Faber, London, 1991). Extracts from this ground-breaking personal account of the war first appeared in *Ogonyk* magazine, Moscow.

For more on the role of Central Asian troops in the 40th Army, see Geoffrey Jukes, 'The Soviet Armed Forces and Afghanistan' in *The Soviet Withdrawal from Afghanistan*, edited by Amir Saikal and William Maley (Cambridge University Press, 1989).

Brigadier Muhamad Yousaf was chief of Afghan operations for the Pakistani Directorate of Inter-Services Intelligence between 1983 and 1987. His account of *mujahedin* operations in Soviet Central Asia comes from his book *The Bear Trap: Afghanistan's Untold Story* (Mark Cooper. 1992).

For a modern history of Afghanistan in English, with much on the relationship with imperial Russia and the USSR, see Vartan Gregorian's *The Emergence of Modern Afghanistan: Politics of Reform and Modernisation, 1880–1946* (Stanford University Press, 1969).

Chapter 7: 'What is to become of us?'

Statistics on household amenities in Tajikistan from *Vesnik Statistiky* (1987) and on population growth from *Naseleniye SSR Finansy i Statistiky* (1987), both quoted in Michael Bradshaw (ed.), *The Soviet Union: A New Regional Geography* (Belhaven Press, London, 1991).

Qahar Mahkamov's account of the August 1991 *putsch* against Gorbachev was published in the newspaper *Kommunist Tajikistana*, 30 August 1991.

Chapter 8: Kartoshka, kartushka – *war in Tajikistan*

The description of Shahidan Square in the spring of 1991 comes from a BBC World Service talk by Jane Kokan, issued on 25 April 1991.

President Karimov's characterisation of Tajikistan as a 'time bomb' was made in an interview with Marc Brunereau. Marc was the first foreign correspondent to set himself up in Central Asia after independence. He married and settled in Tashkent, where he died of a heart attack at the age of 40 in 2001.

Chapter 9: On both sides of the Amu

The case of Shaikh Kamal of Kulab is cited in 'Human Rights in Tajikistan: In the Wake of the Civil War', a report by Human Rights Watch (New York, 1993).

The figure quoted for the number of refugees at Bagh-e Sherkat camp comes from the camp commanders. The visit I made there was in early 1996 and the figures, interviews and general description relate to that time.

Chapter 10: A year in Tashkent

President Karimov's remarks on 'so-called dictators' appear in an interview with John Kohan, *Time*, November 1993.

Note on spellings

I have kept to the simplest, most international spellings throughout – 'Abdullah', for example, not 'Abdulloh' as it is often transcribed in Tajik and Uzbek names. In the few cases where an anglicised form has passed into English – 'Samarkand', 'bazaar' – these have been used for simplicity. In Russian-influenced names I have included a 'y' where it seemed useful for easy pronunciation (e.g., 'Abdullayev'), and elided words where that is usual (e.g., 'Abduquddus', not 'Abdul Quddus').

Acknowledgements

My greatest thanks go to the hundreds of people whose boundless generosity have made it such a privilege and a pleasure to live and work in Central Asia. Many cannot be named. Of those who can, I am grateful first of all to Muhammadjan Shakuri for the days he gave up to relate his unique account of the Bukharan and Soviet periods and for permission to quote extensively from his father's diaries, translated by him and his son Rustam, to whom many thanks are also due. The diaries are due to be published in 2003. The Muhammadov family went to great lengths to tell me the story of Muhammadjan Rustamov, called 'Hindustani'.

Numerous families in Peshawar, Islamabad and Karachi in Pakistan and Gorgan in Iran gave their accounts of the exodus from Central Asia in the 1920s and 1930s. Thanks go especially to Hajji Parman of Aqcha, to the Tajiks of Suhrab Godh and to Akber Ozgen, grandson of Mir Bahadir Khan. Nabijan Baqi in Tashkent and Kamol Abdullaev gave much scholarly advice on Ibrahim Bek and the migration in general. Timur Kocaoğlu put the record straight on the life of his father, Usman Khuja, the first President of the Bukharan People's Republic.

I am grateful to Rustam Qabil for the illuminating tales of his grandmother, Ikrama of Shahr-e Sabz, and to Adiba Atayeva for her interview with Qader Baba of Khorezm. Henrika Levchenko and others in Teheran told their stories of the Polish migration through Uzbekistan. Thanks are due to Kris Mineyko for the memoirs of Anna Mineyko and to Chris Gladun for permission to use the correspondence of his grandfather, Jan Sulkowski. Rahman Safarov filled in several gaps through his account of Tajiks during the Second World War and showed me the letters of Rahmatullah Azimov of

Kulab. Baimirza Hayit and his wife Eva, through Hamid Ismailov, supplied the untold tale of the Turkestan Legion.

Thanks to Ella Ivanova for her memories of exile in Siberia and life in Dushanbe in the 1950s, to Khairullah Ubaidullayev for his tales of Khujand in the 1970s and 1980s, and to the many people on each side who gave their accounts of the Soviet war in Afghanistan. Yuri Kushko has been a wonderful companion on countless expeditions in Tajikistan. I am grateful to Jane Kokan for permission to use her eye-witness account of the demonstrations in Dushanbe of 1991 and to the BBC World Service for Phil Goodwin's dispatch from Mazar-e Sharif in 1997. Many thanks are due to Wahid Bahman, Farid Hamid, Zaher Tanin and many others for their help, their stories and their knowledge of Afghanistan, past and present. Acacia Shields, who has sat through more trials than any other foreigner in Uzbekistan, kindly went through Chapter 12 with an eagle eye. Serajiddin Tolibov supplied the details about the IMU house in Kabul.

Behrouz Afagh was the most consistent supporter of this book from start to finish. Dodhudo Tuchiev was the ideal accomplice during dozens of interviews. Paul Bergne gave much help and advice on Arabic and other matters. Richard Wayman was more than generous with his photographs and time. Jenny Norton checked the Russian, translated the Soviet army ballad for Afghanistan and found the old editions of the *Turkestan Gazette*. Mark O'Brien explained economics several times over. Richard Harris read the first chapters and gave advice on India. Ivan Noble read most of the book early on. My colleagues at the BBC World Service were accommodating and encouraging despite my long absences. Liz Robinson worked on the typescript beyond the call of duty.

Thanks are due to UNHCR for permission to reproduce photographs by H. Hudson and P. Labreveux. The leaflet reprinted on pages 56–7 appears with the permission of Lawrence & Wishart.

Everyone who worked in or passed through 48 Ulitsa Ivleva added to the atmosphere that made it a journalists' household unlike any other. My thanks are also due to them all.

Index

Index

Assa (film), 136
Atatürk, Mustafa Kemal, 44, 57, 61, 73
atheism: Soviet promotion, 112
Auvaj village, 109, 176, 178–80
'Avicenna' (Abu Ali ibn Sina), 16
Awhadi, Habibullah, 73, 75–6
Azerbaijan, 141
Azimov, Rahmatullah, 86
Azimova, Aziza, 103

Babakhanov, Levi, 267
Babakhanov, Ziahuddin, 92
Babakhanov dynasty, 210
Babur, Nasrullah, 229
Babur, Zahiruddin Muhammad, 15–16
Baburnama, 16
Badakhshan (Pamir mountains), 4, 108, 123
Bagh-e Sherkat, Qunduz, 194–5, 239
Baghlan province, 90, 123
Bagram airbase, 228
Bahadir, Mir, Khan, 52–3, 61
Bailey, Colonel, 60
Baljuan, 160
Balkh, 17, 18, 126
Balkh Air, 225, 234
Bamian: Buddha statues, 269
Bandar-e Pahlavi (Iran), 85
Bandar-e Turkmen (Iran), 51
Bartang region, 108
basmachi, 54–9, 79–80, 111, 128, 193; amnesty for, 91
Batken (Kirgizstan), 258
Begin, Menachem, 85–6
beks, 21
Beloye Solntse Pustini (film), 128
Bhutto, Benazir, 229
Bi-del (poet), 34, 114, 146
Birlik (Unity) party, 149, 199
Biruni (Abu Rayhan Muhammad ibn Ahmad), 14
Bolsheviks, 111, 124; attack Bukhara, 37–41; attack Dushanbe, 78; in Kokand, 52
Bombay, 46–7
Borovik, Artem, 135
Brezhnev, Leonid, 102, 115, 117, 145, 153
Britain: Alim Khan and, 40–1, 59; and mujahedin, 124
British American Tobacco, 201
Brzezinski, Zbigniew, 121
Bukhara, 20–3; scholarship in, 16–17; language, 17; trade, 22; emirate, 21, 27, 42; Muzaffar Amir, 21; Abdulahad Amir, 22, 29, 30; Ark, 21, 30, 32, 35–6, 39, 40, 139, 267; Khush Beki, 21, 22; life in, 22–3, 27–30; social reform, pressure (1909), 22–3, 29–31; unrest

(1917), 35–8; Mir-e Arab madrasa, 25, 27, 29, 42, 144, 267; Qaziat, 29–30, 31, 143; ravshangaran, 29, 31, 35; Bolsheviks attack, 37–41; People's Republic (1920), 40, 42, 55, 61, 70; as provincial city, 43; exports, 51, 60; 'Second Revolution', 65; famine (1932–3), 70; post-Second World War, 92–3; Persian culture, 139
Bukhara-e Sharif newspaper, 31
Burhanuddin, Mulla, 29, 36
Bush, George W., President, 11; and Afghanistan, 268, 269, 271

calendar: change of, 72
Caliphate: restoration, 256
Campbellpur, near Attock, 62
Cancer Ward (Solzhenitsyn), 101
Carter, Jimmy, President, 121
Castro, Fidel, 127
Catherine the Great, Empress, 99
Ceausescu, Nikolae, 127
Central Asia: borders, 42–4, 79; famine (1932–3), 69–72; Soviet intellectual life in, 100–1, 187–8; relationship with Moscow, 104–5; see also individual countries
Chahar Bagh village, 25, 26, 33, 46, 64, 114
Chahar Tut village, 149
Chapayev: deaths (1992–3), 183
Chaqai, Mustafa, Bek, 52, 89
Chechens: in Central Asia, 98
Chechnya: Russian war in, 226
Chel-u Chahar Chashma, 112
Chernenko, Konstantin, 117
Chernayev, Major-General Mikhail, 18, 201
children: Afghan, transported to Soviet Union, 126; as cotton workers, 110; in Tajikistan, 7, 9, 101–3, 186–7
China: migration into, 49, 53; Tajikistan border, 191
Chingis Khan, 9, 16
Chirvak dam, 255
Christopher, Warren, 218
Chubek village, 4, 41, 57, 58
CIA: and mujahedin, 121, 122, 124, 128
cinema, 100–1, 102, 126, 128
CIS, see Commonwealth of Independent States
civil war, Tajik (1992–3): deaths, 178–80, 183, 184; Gharmis, 165–6, 167, 168, 170, 172, 175–6, 178–9, 180; Kirgiz, 177, 178; Kulabis, 166–7, 177; refugees, 175, 183–4, 191–2, 195–6; Uzbekistan, involvement, 170–1, 176, 177, 180, 197; Uzbeks, 167–8, 170–1, 172; weapons, procurement, 170–1, 172; see also Dushanbe; Hisar; Qurghan Tappa; Vakhsh

282

Index

Index

Index

Manbai, Davlat, 55
Manghit, 13
Maqsudi, Mansur, 201
Maqsum, Fazel, 55, 59
Marx, Karl, 44, 133
Mashhad, Iran, 115, 236
Mas'ud, Ahmad Shah: *mujahedin* leader, 125,
    158–9; takes Kabul, 158–9, 208; in Panjshir
    valley, 223, 227; in Northern Alliance,
    226–7, 231; in Jabal us-Siraj, 227–8; and
    Tajik cease-fire, 230; assassination, 267–78,
    279
mathematics, 14–15
Matkarimov, Ramazanbek, 202, 211
mawara-an-nahr, 2–3
Mazar-e Sharif, 17–18; shrine, 18, 33; émigrés
    in, 47, 53; Dustam in, 171, 207, 224–5, 228,
    231–3; military display (1997), 231–3;
    Uzbekistan supplies, 208; Malik at, 233–4;
    Taleban take, and lose (May 1997), 234–6;
    Taleban take (1998), 250–1; Dustam
    recaptures (2001), 269, 271; US attack
    (2001), 18, 271
Mecca, 47, 61
Medina, 61
Merrem, Gerd, 241
Mesketian Turks, 98
Message of the Migrant (magazine), 193–4
migration: compulsory, 99, 107–10, 167, 183–4,
    195
Mikoyan, Anastas, 105
Minbar-e Islam newspaper, 143
Mineyko, Anna, 83–4
Minsk (Belorussia), 80, 88
Mirzayev, Abdughani, 81
Mirzayev, Abduquddus, 219, 220
Mirzayev, Abduvali: friendship with Nuri, 115,
    204; reclaims Andijan mosque, 149;
    followers, 206, 250, 253, 260–1;
    disappearance, 202–4, 208–9, 210–11, 216,
    219, 238, 243, 250, 254
Moghul empire, 16
Molotov–Ribbentrop pact (1939), 83
Moscow, 89; Cherkisovsky bazaar, 266; Chinese
    trading in, 266; German march on, 81;
    glasnost (1980s), 136; relationship with
    Central Asia (1960s–70s), 104–5; Tajik peace
    talks (1994), 196
Mubarak, Hosni, 145
mu-e safids, 9
Muhammadov, Abdullah, 185, 266
Muhammadov, Nurullah, 150, 266
Muhammadov, Ubaidullah, 25; childhood, 74;
    in Dushanbe, 92, 95, 149–50; horticulture
    business, 95–6, 150, 185; on Hajj, 150; and

civil war (1992–3), 185; and Russians, 188;
    old age, 149–50, 266–7
Muhammad Sharif, in Hairatan, 122, 124
Muhammad Sharif, in Peshawar, 62–3
Mujaddedi, Sebghatullah, 159
mujahedin, 141; early, 118; development, 124;
    support groups, 124–5; international
    support, 121, 122–3, 129; propaganda
    against, 128, 130; Uzbek soldiers and, 132;
    Tajik soldiers in, 132, 133; in Kabul (1992),
    158–9, 231; Dustam and, 208
Mukhtar, Hajji Abdullah, Mufti, 210–11
mullas: under Soviet rule, 51, 64, 73, 92,
    114
Mullayanov, Colonel Ramil, 166–7
Muslim Brothers, Society, 145
Muslims: conscription (1916), 33, 52; correct
    practice, 112, 113, 114; in Soviet Union,
    51–2, 64, 92, 110, 111–13, 114
Mutahari, Mortezar, 194
Muzaffar, Amir of Bukhara, 21

Nabiev, Rahman, President: elected (1991),
    153, 154; and 'Gharmi' protest (1992), 157,
    158, 160–2; proclaims State of Emergency,
    162–3; and National Reconciliation
    Government, 164; and civil war, 168–9;
    resigns, 169–70
Najibullah, Muhammad, President, 135, 158,
    208; murder, 221–2, 223
Nakshbandi sufis, 144, 259
Namangan, Ferghana, 13, 15, 216, 248; 'Glinka
    St' trial, 243–4, 245, 249, 253, 262
'Namangani' (Jumabai Khujayev), 248
National Reconciliation Government,
    Tajikistan, 164–5, 174, 177, 180
nauruz (New Year's Day), 182–3, 184
Navjavanov, Mamadayaz, 154
Nazarov, Abedkhan, 211, 214–17; loses job,
    214, 215, 238; at human rights conference,
    219, 220–1; in exile, 257
Nazarov, Daler, 265
New Economic Policy (NEP), 65, 69
Newmont mining company, 201
newspapers, 31, 78, 139–40
New York: attacks (11 September 2001), 5, 268;
    World Trade Centre explosion (1993), 199
Nezamov, Mirza Khuja, 212
Nicholas II, Tsar, 32, 35
NKVD, 96
Northern Alliance, or United Front, 267;
    formation, 227; advance towards Kabul
    (1996), 226–7, 227–8, 231; Iran and, 229;
    Russia and, 229; US and, 269; capture
    Kabul (2001), 272